James Cotter Morison

The Service of Man

An Essay towards the Religion of the Future

James Cotter Morison

The Service of Man
An Essay towards the Religion of the Future

ISBN/EAN: 9783337130510

Printed in Europe, USA, Canada, Australia, Japan

Cover: Foto ©ninafisch / pixelio.de

More available books at **www.hansebooks.com**

THE SERVICE OF MAN.

AN ESSAY

TOWARDS

THE RELIGION OF THE FUTURE.

BY

JAMES COTTER MORISON.

THIRD EDITION.

LONDON

KEGAN PAUL, TRENCH & CO., 1, PATERNOSTER SQUARE

1888

PREFACE.

I HAVE not been able, in consequence of illness, to finish this work according to its original plan. As I may not be in a position to carry it to its proper conclusion, I should like, as briefly as possible, to mention what I wished to add to that already written.

After the last chapter in the volume, my intention had been to discuss one or two urgent social and economical questions which are daily growing in importance, even amounting to peril if satisfactory answers to them cannot be obtained.

It is generally admitted by serious and sober observers, that a large social transformation is at once desirable and inevitable. The present conditions can, one would think, give satisfaction to no one. The enormous increase of wealth consequent on the application of the steam-engine to industry, has to a very small extent been followed by a corresponding spread of general well-being such as was at one time not unreasonably expected. Even before the commencement of the present depression of trade, there were many unpleasant features in the manufacturing system of Western Europe. But profits were high, and, till within a recent period, seemed likely to increase. The workmen, by judicious and resolute strikes, were able to demand and obtain better wages ; and, although even in the most flourishing centres of industry, much pauperism and misery among the unskilled workers were generally present, so long as the revenue, in Mr. Gladstone's phrase, "went up by leaps and bounds," these minor social evils were not likely to attract notice. But, as everybody now knows only too well, a great change has come over the world in the last ten years. Profits in nearly all trades are diminishing, and will probably diminish still more. Hitherto, capitalists have been the chief sufferers ; but it cannot be long before the workmen will have their turn of loss in the form of decreased wages. At the present rate of decline, a point will, before long, be reached, when the employer will get little or no return for his capital invested in manufactures, and when the workman will be able to get no adequate wage for the labour he gives.

I do not pretend to say that if I had been able to treat this question with the fulness I desired, I should have been able to throw light on a subject which has puzzled more competent persons than myself. In truth, I fear I should be considered a Job's comforter at the best. My view is that the present industrial system is less capable of mending than ending, and that it is, in fact, doomed to a not remote extinction. And this, not because it is offensive to persons of fine taste, and destroys rural beauty (the artistic view); nor because it makes a few capitalists very rich, and leaves many workmen very poor (the current Socialist view); but because it cannot continue on its own lines ; that with more than a fair field and plenty of favour, it is yet breaking down from inherent vices for which there is no remedy.

The industrial system had its origin in the latter half of the last century, when Watt and Arkwright brought the power of steam to bear on the production of commodities. With her easily accessible coal and iron, England had an immense start of the continental countries ; and for a long time was the mart of the world. So long as other countries were content to buy our commodities instead of producing them themselves, the arrangement was highly satisfactory—to Englishmen ; and it lasted long enough for many of them to believe that it was a law of Nature that Britons should make and sell goods, and foreigners should buy them. But in time the foreigner took heart, and thought he also would like to make and sell commodities. The result has been, that most of our old customers have become our rivals ; and they compete with us not only in their own markets, which they artfully shield by protective tariffs, but in the barbarous markets of the world in China, East Africa, and elsewhere.

But the competing foreigner has come late into the field ; and trade and commerce offer no longer the same returns which they did when England, with her many advantages, set out on her industrial career. Competition is now everywhere of the keenest, and cheapness of production the primary object. The result is a race in which no competitor can absolutely win, but one in which all must, in process of time, become exhausted. For there is no fixed goal to be reached ; the goal flies before the runners, and the first in the race cannot avoid ultimate collapse. In each country manufacturers compete among themselves, while they compete also with their foreign rivals. Constantly improved machinery enables a larger out-put at less cost to be thrown upon the market, with the obvious effect, now distressing everybody,· of a well-nigh universal glut, and a growing cheapness never before witnessed. In the mean time, profits on capital and wages of labour are tending to the vanishing point ; and the only question is, how long it will be before that point is reached.

It is obvious that the conditions of trade and commerce are nearly wholly changed within the last fifty years. A small and industrious population like the English, commanding an extensive sea-board, good harbours, and a large commercial marine, surrounded moreover, by neighbours chiefly agricultural, could obtain a world-wide trade which moved the wonder and envy of contemporaries. But it was a *beau idéal* of commercial success which cannot be repeated by imitators, nor even kept up by its original inventors. Our Manchesters and Liverpools were once without rivals in the world. Now they have to contend with an ever-increasing competition, which has already told on their prosperity, and must, in the near future, tell still more. Add to this, that the vastly improved means of transport are now more and more bringing commercial competitors into one great race-course. The English farmer is exposed to competition from America, Russia, and India; and crushed by importations of corn from those countries which, owing to soil, climate, or greater cheapness of labour, have a greater advantage over England in the cheap production of cereals. Any industry may be killed, as it were by enchantment, in an old country, by the discovery of new means of cheaper production on the other side of the globe. The instability of industries is frightful. The commercial atmosphere is more uncertain and capricious than the physical atmosphere, though that is generally taken as a symbol of uncertainty. It is as if our weather were sensitive to, and influenced by, the cyclones of the Indian Ocean; or the *terra firma* of our quiet island were shattered responsively by earthquakes in Japan and South Carolina. It is little to say that such facts were not dreamed of in the olden time. They would not have been deemed possible in the recent days of Cobden and Peel.

Some persons in England, and many abroad, believe that these evils are traceable to Free Trade, and recommend Protection or Fair Trade as a remedy. It were much to be wished that so simple a cure were possible; for the threatened evils are so great,

that it is not a time to be punctilious on economic or
any theories.   The difficulty is to show how the
exclusion of foreign goods here would tend to force
the purchase of our goods by foreigners; for *that* is
what a revival of trade means. We may keep out
the foreigner as much as we like, but would he much
care?   Could any form of retaliatory tariff enable us
to dispense with corn, cotton, wool, wine, tobacco,
silk, etc., purchased from abroad or from our own
colonies?   We want to sell: refusing to buy is no
remedy if our old customers are churlish, or, for
reasons of their own, indifferent to our wares.   On
the other hand, the evidence is very far from being
in favour of Protection, even in the countries which
still maintain it.

One could wish, indeed, that it was less clear than
it is; that the evils under which modern industry is
suffering were of so slight a nature as a reform of
tariffs or any fiscal or economic change could remove.
We could bear our woes with a more patient mind if
all depended on the " bugbear " of Free Trade being
promptly exploded. We have no such consolation.
The root of the mischief lies deeper: in the exor-
bitant over-production made possible by the marvel-
lous improvement of machinery, and in the increased
facility thereby of dispensing with manual labour.

Great efforts are made to show that a general glut
of commodities is not a source of evil, and that the
appreciation of gold has been the cause of the extraordinary fall in prices. To those who hold this view,
I would put the question why ivory and whalebone

have not fallen in price, but, on the contrary, have steadily risen in price during the last decade? The plain answer, surely, is, that the enhanced price of these commodities is owing to the fact that elephants and whales not being capable of manufacture, nor, till yet, of artificial cultivation, the demand for ivory and whalebone has exceeded the natural supply, and the price of those articles has consequently gone up some 50 per cent. Oysters offer an even more instructive example. Every man of middle age can remember when oysters were sold in the shops at sixpence and eightpence a dozen, and how they rose a few years ago to prohibitory prices of three, four, and even four and sixpence a dozen. The greatly diminished demand which followed in consequence, coupled with the attention devoted to oyster-culture, have at last caused a turn in the market, and now oysters are cheaper than they have been for years. These instances cannot be explained away. The old economic doctrine, that when demand exceeds supply prices will rise, and when supply exceeds demand prices will fall, is one which is assailed in vain. If cotton yarns, pig-iron, silver, and many other commodities are cheaper than ever they were, it is because there is so much more of them than ever there was. Some points even in political economy are ascertained and beyond dispute.

If it be asked what inference I draw from such facts, the answer is that it is a melancholy one. I believe we are approaching to a great catastrophe in our industrial system, which will be a calamity without precedent since the Black Death of the fourteenth century.

The praises of the steam-engine are on every tongue, and its merits are obvious enough to a superficial glance. Whether it will turn out a benefactor in the long run remains to be seen. It, clearly enough, greatly increased wealth, but it did nothing for its moralization or more beneficial distribution. It also vastly increased population, which is a more questionable boon; or, to speak plainly, a curse. But we have it, and certainly shall not lay it aside till we are compelled. Now, the proper and direct effect of all machinery is to diminish largely the cost and the amount of manual labour required in the production of commodities. In the first instance, this result was so masked by the rapid growth of English trade, that an increased demand for labour, in form of "hands" serving steam-engines, was brought about. The folly and wickedness of workmen who smashed steam-engines was pointed out with much unction in the early part of this century. Thousands of hands, it was asserted, and quite truly, were employed in the cotton trade, where only hundreds were employed before. But a great change has come over the world with the vastly improved machinery of later years. It no longer admits of doubt that machinery is a rival, and tending to become a triumphant rival, of labour. Machinery is no longer the servant of man, but man has become the servant of the machine. The ideal of manufacture now, would be production without "hands;" except, perhaps, a stoker and an engineer. Every day new contrivances are discovered by which human labour can be dispensed with. Were trade expanding, instead of contracting, there might be a compensation in the need of more workers to serve the greater number of machines. But in our present condition the result is doubly injurious to the working classes. Production of commodities by means of improved machinery is made cheaper, and an already glutted market still more flooded at prices barely remunerative, at the very time that the merit of the improved machinery chiefly consists in doing with less manual labour.*

* See two admirable articles in the *Contemporary Review* of August and September of this year (1887), on the "Great Depression of Trade," by the Hon. David A. Wells. I much regret that these remarkable essays did not appear till several months after this preface was published; they would have afforded me an immense number of facts and arguments with which to strengthen my thesis. I quote one passage from Mr. Wells' first article.

"The Report of the United States' Commissioner of Labour for 1886 furnishes the following additional illustrations :—

"In the manufacture of agricultural implements specific evidence is submitted showing that six hundred men now do the work that fifteen or twenty years ago would have required 2,145 men : a displacement of 1545.

"The manufacture of boots and shoes offers some very wonderful facts in this connection. In one large and long-established manufactory, the proprietors testify that it would require five hundred persons working by hand processes to make as many women's boots and shoes as one hundred persons now make with the aid of machinery : a displacement of 80 per cent.

"Another firm, engaged in the manufacture of children's shoes, states that the introduction of new machinery within the last thirty years has displaced about six times the amount of hand labour required, and that the cost of the product has been reduced one-half.

It is difficult to see from what quarter an improvement of this condition of things can be expected. Is not that condition more likely to get worse? The race for cheap production is so severe, that each trade and nation in turn is forced to strain every nerve in order to keep abreast of its rivals. The well-known tendency of profits to a minimum is exemplified as it never was before. The cost of production, and the selling price of the manufactured article, must before long coincide. And then what will become of the interest of the capitalist and the wages of the artisan?

If the mass of even civilized mankind were not, as Carlyle says, mostly fools, great relief could no doubt be rapidly attained by saving the immense sums now squandered on the armaments unparalleled

"On another grade of goods the facts collected by the agents of the Bureau show that one man can now do the work which twenty years ago required ten men.

"In the manufacture of flour there has been a displacement of nearly three-fourths of the manual labour necessary to produce the same product. In the manufacture of furniture from one-half to three-fourths only of the old number of persons is now required. In the manufacture of wall paper the best evidence puts the displacement in the proportion of one hundred to one.

"In the manufacture of metals and metallic goods long-established firms testify that machinery has decreased manual labour $33\frac{1}{2}$ per cent."

Perhaps the most surprising instance of all is this, that "*one skilled workman*, paid at the rate of two and a half to three dollars a day, and working according to ante-machine methods in use a few years ago, could make up *three dozen pairs* of sleeve buttons per day. Now *one boy*, paid five dollars per week, and working on the most modern machinery, can make up *nine thousand pairs in a day*." (The italics are mine.)—See *Contemporary Review* for August, 1887, pp. 287, 288.

in human annals. And the removal of all fear of war would be even a greater gain than the suppression of war-budgets. But men must pay for their follies and passions ; and they do pay, heavily enough. The cost of indulgence in international jealousies and hatreds, even between European countries at the present day, would be difficult to exaggerate ; and even one of the supposed choice products of civilization, a free and popular press, has become a large source of evil. It is hardly saying too much that the main occupation of most of the newspapers of Europe is to inflame international animosities. Over and over again, war has been barely averted between nations whose populations had every interest, and probably every desire, to keep the peace, but which had been worked up to a pitch of fury against each other by the incendiary fustian served up to them by their daily newspapers. We narrowly escaped war with France, when diplomatic complications ensued after the Orsini conspiracy : and how nearly we grazed a fratricidal war with our American kinsfolk, after the affair of the Trent, dwells in all memories. Whatever difficulty trained diplomatists may have had to settle either of these disagreements, there can be no question that they were greatly aggravated by the incessant pouring of oil on the flame of international discord by the newspapers of all the countries concerned. The greatest misfortune which Europe has experienced in modern times—the war between France and Prussia—was largely, if not wholly, brought about by the reckless mendacity and venom of the Parisian press ; which, untaught by experience, seems again disposed to repeat its unpatriotic blunders. Not that I think the French press more evil-minded than the press of other countries ; it is only more clever, sparkling, and stimulating, and therefore more dangerous, than its rivals in other lands.

But valuable as would be a general disarmament and cessation of wars and rumours of wars, simply as affording a pause, a breathing-space, in the midst of our really social troubles, these palliatives would not produce a solution of those troubles ; they would only postpone them for a season, priceless as that postponement would be. If the war waged by cannon and rifles were to cease, the more bitter war of commercial rivalry would remain, probably fiercer than ever, as there would be no competing interest to engage men's minds.

One would think that it was obvious to casual observation that we are commencing to descend an incline, down which we shall move with accelerated speed, to be brought up at last in general calamity. The difficulty of taking new views of old things and conditions, can alone blind men from seeing the fate before them. The numbers of the unemployed in all large centres are growing from year to year. The palliatives of charity, public-works, state-aid in every form, are still talked of as if there were hope in them. But before the century is at an end, the illusion will have vanished. The production of wealth, as it has obtained in the past, can continue no longer. The

State will be impoverished along with individuals; and with increasing charges will have less revenues to meet them. Then we shall know what a general or universal commercial catastrophe really means, when the famishing unemployed will not be counted by thousands, but millions; when a page of the *Times* will suffice for the business advertisements of London; and when the richest will be glad to live on the little capital they have left, never thinking of interest.

No moralist or preacher ever had such occasion to point out the deceitfulness of riches, as will soon be afforded by the industrial collapse. For upwards of a century wealth has been produced with a speed and in a volume quite beyond precedent in former times. If the wealth of Nations were enough to ensure their prosperity and happiness, the countries of Western Europe should be now in a state of unprecedented bliss. It may be doubted if there was ever more misery in the midst of more wealth. Morality is avenged at last; and the great lesson being brought home, that wealth and its production are not the first nor even the second chief interests of a State; that the commonwealth demands something else and more from its citizens than a unique pre-occupation to make their own fortunes.

Bad, however, as the industrial and economic situation is, there is reason to fear that it may presently be made worse by rash and ill-considered attempts to mend it. I am very far from thinking with Mr. Herbert Spencer, that "*all* Socialism involves slavery," as I believe that there is a good Socialism as well as a bad ; a Socialism of love and mutual help, and a Socialism of hatred and spoliation. One must shut one's eyes to obvious facts not to realize that, under the mask and name of Socialism, projects fraught with evil to all classes, but especially to the poor, are being pushed forward with a zeal which is certainly not according to knowledge, and which is difficult to regard as according to honesty of purpose. The condition of growing distress into which large numbers of the population will inevitably fall in a near future, must offer a correspondingly wider field for demagogic arts ; which are none the less effective because they are as old as history, and flourish naturally in all periods of social suffering. Famine, or even short rations, are not calculated to put men in a philosophic frame of mind ; and even the honest and intelligent workman who has had no breakfast, and does not know where he will get a dinner, very naturally lends a willing ear to speakers and writers who tell him that all his troubles might soon be ended if only the " selfish rich " were made to disgorge a portion of their ill-gotten wealth, procured by the sweat of *his* brow, but which unjust laws have transferred from him to them. The fact is, that one can only lament that such a short and easy solution of the social difficulty as a transfer of wealth from the rich to the poor, could not be put in practice. With all its violation of the commandment, " Thou shalt not steal," it would be a boon and a relief from the chronic care and sadness which now oppress the deserving poor and rich alike. But it is precisely at this point that such proposals break down. And a little reflection shows that the suggested remedies would promptly aggravate every existing evil, and add an endless number to those we have.

The singular thing is, that in such a commercial country as ours, it should be forgotten or overlooked that trade depends on buying and selling ; and that in every purchase and sale two parties are concerned, one of whom *cannot* be coerced. Legislation, popular agitation, and resolute combined action, brought to bear on special points, may do much, though not always so much as is often thought ; but there is one thing which they cannot do : they cannot make people buy goods which they refuse to buy. The producer, whether capitalist or workman — who, though often enemies in their private relations, are partners with regard to the public—may have any number of trials of their own ; but if they cannot succeed between them in producing goods of a quality and at a price which induce the public at home or abroad to buy, they may say and do what they like ; they will remain without customers. No man of business, from the largest merchant to the petty shopkeeper, is ignorant of this fact. Yet, it is despised or ignored, as a paradox unworthy of notice, by those who urge that work is to be provided by the State for the unemployed, whether there be a demand for it or not. What is the contention ? A number of men are out of work ; it is heartrending to think that they, their wives and children, are starving.

Therefore, the State, or the parish, or somebody, ought immediately to improvise work for them. What work? This is rarely specified with accuracy. If remunerative work—work which it would pay any individual or corporation to take in hand—is it not certain that the natural cupidity of mankind would long ago have found it out and made a profit by it? If it is not remunerative, who is to bear the loss of useless work, of work of less value when performed than its primary cost? The State or the ratepayers, will probably be the answer; with the obvious assumption that the State or local bodies can bear any strain or expense. To inquire whence the State acquires its funds, and whether in a condition of decaying prosperity those funds may be regarded as of unlimited expansion, would no doubt be considered by the theorists to whom I refer, as suggested by middle-class cupidity and meanness.

Now, the modest demand only is, " the construction of wholesome, cheerful homes for the people by the municipalities and county boards;" "feeding children gratuitously in all board schools, in order to check the physical deterioration only too noticeable among the infants of the rising generation." "The undertaking of useful works for which there was admitted need in the various districts; such as embankments, roads, etc. : the establishment of light relief works, and factory-work for women—all this to be arranged by the local bodies and the State in conjunction, the wages being determined by a board of assessors, *and the profits, if any,* divided equitably among the people employed." Further, it is of the highest importance that "the people employed" should not over-work themselves ; and this is to be prevented by law—"an eight-hours' day, limited by law, in all Government employment." And then the conclusion with great serenity is drawn, "that these measures would benefit the workers, if carried out, is very clear." *

About the benefit to the workers from this scheme there will certainly be, in some minds, grave doubt as to its being very clear. But that point may be left for future discussion. The singular characteristic to be noticed in these reformers, is their extreme modesty and timidity in "asking for more" of what they consider already as their own. If "wholesome, cheerful homes for the people," and the feeding of children in board schools are to be provided gratuitously by the public, one cannot see the logic or common sense in refusing to provide boots, stockings, corduroys, indeed, all that a working-man may require, either as necessaries or luxuries. Really, it is not worth while higgling about details when the principle is admitted ; and it would be better to say at once that it is the duty of all the well-to-do people to support all the indigent "gratuitously," and so end the matter.

There is no immediate reason to fear that the thoroughly shrewd and reflective English artisan of the better class has been seduced by the sophistries

---

* Letter in the *Times*, November 17, 1886, signed, " H. M. Hyndman."

of the officious friends who assume to plead his cause. He is pretty well acquainted with the real facts of the case ; and though quite willing, and very rightly, in a rising market, to support a well-planned strike, he looks with coldness on Utopians who are equally ignorant of capital, labour, or hard work. But the intelligent and skilled artisan is an aristocrat among the great mass of workers, whether unemployed or not. He, hardly less than the capitalist, is threatened by the multitude of the unskilled labourers surging around him ; and even by the scarcely lesser multitude of highly-skilled loafers, who have become convinced that it is more profitable to bawl out that they " have got no work to do," than to attempt to find work and do it.

For the moment there appears to be no hope of staunching a morbid, or rather, a maudlin sentimentality—for genuine benevolence is out of the question —which insists upon the immediate relief of hunger, however produced. The evil results which must follow such a policy if persevered in, have been often pointed out ; especially by Mr. Herbert Spencer in his articles, " The Man *versus* the State." " The deserving poor," Mr. Spencer remarks, " are among those who are burdened to pay the costs of caring for the undeserving poor. As under the old Poor Law, the diligent and provident labourer had to pay that the good-for-nothings might not suffer, until frequently under this extra burden he broke down and himself took refuge in the workhouse—as at present it is admitted, that the total rates levied in large towns for all public purposes have now reached such a height that 'they cannot be exceeded without inflicting great hardship on the small shopkeepers and artisans who already find it difficult enough to keep themselves free from the pauper taint;' so in all cases the policy is one which intensifies the pains of those most deserving of pity, that the pains of those least deserving of pity may be mitigated." * In other words, every effort is now made by a misdirected public sentiment to check the beneficent effect of natural selection, which promotes the survival of the hardy, the strong, and the capable, but, on the contrary, to shield the production of the "unfit," the weak, the stupid, and the worthless.

At this point we reach a full view of the great problem of population. The profound thinker and benevolent man who first propounded it, has received the usual reward of sages and prophets, for seeing further and feeling more deeply than their contemporaries. Malthus and Malthusianism have long been by-words of scorn and reproach ; and, oddly enough, two parties, usually most hostile to each other, have united in this one object of casting obloquy on him. Christian priests of all denominations, anxious to repress sexual irregularities, have counselled and promoted early marriages from purely religious motives. On the other hand, Democratic Socialists, in their war against Capital and its owners, have maintained that it was only owing to the selfish greed of the rich that the poor could not multiply to the limit of their

* "Man *versus* the State," pp. 71, 72.

physical capacity. Between the two, Christians and Socialists, Malthusianism has been met with an hostility which has few parallels in modern controversy. And even to this day one must consent to be a social pariah, to stand forth as its supporter.

At last the evils of over-population are becoming too obvious to be gainsaid. Mr. Bradlaugh, with a courage which will no doubt be acknowledged after his death and when the fight is won, has borne the penalty of appearing as a champion of common-sense and human well-being. Not only over-population generally, but the disproportionate increase of the "unfit" and unworthy, is attracting attention. The provident and the thoughtful marry late and have few children. The criminal and the reckless classes propagate *ad libitum.* An excellent review of an excellent book in the *Pall Mall Gazette* of November 9, 1886, thus refers to the subject. Speaking of Mr. Arnold White's recent work, "The Problems of a Great City," it says, "He is convinced that the way things go now, it is the feeblest, the least moral, and most worthless classes of the community which multiply the most rapidly. It is the pauper and the criminal class which supplies the human rabbits who multiply in the warrens of our great city. The educated and the well-to-do increase much less rapidly. Hence the annual increase in the population proceeds mainly from the classes which add no strength to the nation ; and those who are constantly within half-a-crown of starvation, are those who bring forth the multitude of the diseased and incapable children who bubble out of the ground for torment in this world if not in the next. . . . He stands aghast, like all Malthusians, at early and improvident marriages ; and appalled at the spectacle of the criminal and pauper class, with low cerebral development, renewing the race more rapidly than those of higher attainments. He demands that statesmen should no longer stand idly by, watching the multiplication of the unfit, and the survival of the weakest and worst of the community. He would have them interfere, by imprisoning for life all habitual criminals, not as a punishment, but in order to prevent them from multiplying their kind." Nothing can be more certain than that we shall soon have a great many more views of this sort. The human race, in old countries at least, by its reckless propagation, is getting jammed into an *impasse* from which there is no escape. If it has not wisdom enough to limit, or rather, diminish its numbers by prudence, Nature will take the matter in hand, and with her summary processes of pestilence and famine make such a sweep as will somewhat amaze the world.

" Si nolles sanus, curres hydropicus."

The criminality of producing children whom one has no reasonable probability of being able to keep, must in time be seen in its true light, as one of the most unsocial and selfish proceedings of which a man nowadays is capable. The right of A. to marry, and to leave to B. the task of keeping his children, has ceased to be a matter of grim humour.

A. and his prolific spouse must be made to realize that few evil-doers are more injurious to the world than they are. They may be models of virtue according to conventional ethics, but those ethics are out of date. The barren prostitute, on whom they probably look down with scorn, does not at any rate aid in swamping the labour-market, nor even in recruiting her own class as they do. We may hope that, in the worst of times, the honest proletary will not selfishly refuse to share his half loaf with his famishing fellow. But, for the sake of the race, we may also trust that he will peremptorily refuse to share his crust with his reckless brother's eight or ten children.

These and many kindred topics bear obviously on the Service of Man. That Service will not be made lighter or simpler in a democratic Age. The complexity of social problems is so great, they need regarding from so many points of view, their right solution is so important, their wrong solution so perilous, that they can no longer be left to any official or limited class of inquirers. They concern all citizens; and few duties in our day are so imperative as their earnest, persistent, and reflective study. They do not happily need much book-lore. Clear heads and resolute hearts, aided by eyes open to the facts around them, will for this purpose more avail than academic culture. The modern man in search of well-being has two ends to bear in mind: First, his own self-cultivation, especially of his heart, as incomparably most important both to his own happiness and that of others. Secondly, it behoves him to help his fellows to the extent of his power, by such improvements in the practice and theory of life as he can make good by sound reasons. In this direction I admit that he may encounter not prosperity, but persecution or even worse; but if he is a true man he will not mind that. Nor will the probable gloom of the coming time daunt brave hearts. There is a *mauvais pas* before us all, which we must get over as best we can. But nerve and resolution can do wonders; and men never appear and act so much to their advantage as when put undisguisedly on their mettle. Not by the promise of soft and smooth things are they attracted, but by the difficult and the dangerous. Bad as the forecast is, and great as the suffering before long may be, if only adequately realized and faced with neither panic fear nor thoughtless hope, the situation might begin to improve almost at once. If only the devastating torrent of children could be arrested for a few years it would bring untold relief.

The Service of Man is too honourable and inspiring a service to let us doubt that it will be wanting in worthy recruits.

CONTENTS.

THE SERVICE OF MAN.

CHAPTER I.

INTRODUCTORY.

A RUINED temple, with its fallen columns and broken arches, has often been taken as a suggestive example and type of the transitory nature of all human handiwork. " Here we see "—so runs the parable of the moralist—" the inevitable end of man's most ambitious efforts. Time and the elements cast down and consume his proudest fabrics. He builds high, and decorates with sculptured ornament his palaces and fanes. But his work is hardly finished before decay begins to efface its beauty, and sap its strength. Soon the building follows the builder to an equal dust, and the universal empire of Death alone survives over the tombs of departed glory and greatness."

The parable of the moralist is only too true. Decay and death are stamped not only on man and his works, but on all that surrounds him, on all that he sees and touches. Nature herself decays as surely, if not as rapidly, as the work of his hands. The everlasting hills are daily and hourly being worn away. Alps, Andes, and Himalayas, are

B

all in process of a degradation of which there is no repair. Nay, the Sun himself, the universal author and giver of life in our planet, is only a temporary blaze—a fire perhaps already more than half burnt out, hastening to its final consummation of cold and lightless ashes. And probably no other fate is in store for the countless stars which bespangle the nightly firmament. The animalcule, whose existence is measured by a summer's day, and the galaxy which illumines the heavens for millions of ages, are alike subject to the common law of all life—growth, decay, and death.

Some may think that an exception ought to be made to this statement in favour of the perennial vitality of Truth. Truth, it will be said, does not wear out, decay, and die. The Elements of Euclid are as true now as they were two thousand years ago. Truths obtained by induction and verified by experiment, or by correct deduction from true principles, do not change and pass away with the generations of men who hold them. It is therefore rash, such objectors would say, to assert that all things connected with man are destined to ultimate extinction. His reason is independent of time, and has that in it which belongs to eternity. All must see this in regard to the incontrovertible truths established by science ; many see it in tuitions of the mind, and others in doctrines of religion supposed to be divinely revealed. It is often added, that it is fortunate for man that, amid the constant change going on in the phenomenal world, a permanent reality does exist, on which he can lay hold—eternal truth.

It would be careless to overlook the importance of this counter-statement. About the permanence of truth there can be no question. Whether it be obtained by observation, generalization, or deduction, verified by experiment and proof, we may safely assert that such truth will last as long as the human mind remains constituted as it is. But does *that* entitle us to claim eternal duration for any truth? No one believes that the human race will last for ever. There is a probability amounting almost to a certainty, that neither man nor his dwelling-place will exist beyond a certain, though it may be a very large number of years. Now, when the human race shall have ceased to exist, would it be correct to say that the truths cognized by the human mind will survive it? This could only be maintained by an idealist, who should place their continued existence in some extra-mundane Eternal mind—as that of God—which may be an article of faith, but hardly of reason. Moreover, if true propositions can exist after all the minds which could affirm them have disappeared, why should they not exist *before* the phenomenal appearance of those minds? Can we consistently say that the propositions of Euclid existed in the Carboniferous era? If so, why not assert that all the truths yet to be discovered in the remote future exist at present? There is no question that things undreamt of in the philosophy and science of to-day, will be trite commonplaces two or three thousand years hence. But are they truths now or yet? Not only they are not, but the great probability is, that if they were expressed in words now, they would be denounced as wild and dangerous errors.

So that it is still legitimate to say that even truth exists for a time, while we admit that verified truth will have a duration co-equal with that of the human race.

It is to be observed, that the only truths that belong to this permanent class, are the truths of simple observation, or of rigorous scientific inference. They have always been few in number, if compared with the multitude of propositions held to be true by the mass of mankind. They are now increasing with unprecedented rapidity, owing to the great development of the scientific spirit in modern times. They obviously stand quite apart from the truths supposed to be derived from divine revelation. The latter differ from them both as to the method by which they were obtained, and especially in their durability. Lengthy as may seem the existence of the great religions of the world when measured by our small scale of chronology, yet their transitory, not to say ephemeral, character, is manifest to reflection, and even to observation. Go where we will on the earth's surface, we find traces of bygone men—of their tombs, of their ashes, their temples—which testify to the former existence of religious beliefs now extinct. These beliefs embodied the most precious and profound of all truths in the devout conviction of those who held them, but they were so far from permanent that often they move the wonder and even the laughter of after-ages. Perishable as are brick, stone, and marble, they have outlived in countless instances the faiths which once wrought them into majestic architecture in their own honour. Temples often survive their creeds by thousands of years. Wind, rain, and frost disintegrate the roof and the walls of a shrine with more or less rapidity, according to climate ; but they are not so swift or potent to destroy the material fabric, as knowledge and science are to undermine the conceptions and assumptions on which the religious beliefs were founded, and for which the sumptuous fanes were erected in a spirit of reverence and sacrifice.

Not less marked in another respect is the difference between the truths derived from religion and the truths derived from science. The truths of science are found to be in complete harmony with one another. Where this harmony is wanting, it is at once felt that error has crept in unawares. We never give a thought to the alternative hypothesis, that truths in different sciences or departments of knowledge may be inconsistent and mutually hostile, and yet remain truths. On the contrary, we find that the discovery of new truth has invariably among its results the additional effect of corroborating other and older truths, instead of conflicting with them. In the history of science it has often happened that a newly-discovered truth has proved inconsistent with prevalent opinions, which had the sanction of tradition in their favour. But the position has always been felt to be intolerable, and that one of two things must happen—either the new truth must reconcile itself with the old opinions, by the necessary modification; or the old opinions must reconcile themselves with the new truth by a similar process. In astronomy the heliocentric theory, and in biology the circulation of the blood theory, produced the latter result, and revolutionized those two sciences by expelling a number of previously unsuspected errors. In modern times, on the other hand, the plausible theory of spontaneous generation has been forced to beat a retreat through its proven inconsistency with older truths firmly established.

Now, with regard to the truths announced with the credentials of a divine revelation, we find a very different state of things. There seems to be no exception to the rule, that the older religions grow the more infirm do they become, the less hold do they keep on the minds of well-informed and thoughtful men. Their truths, once accepted without question, are gradually doubted, and in the end denied by increasing numbers. This fate happened to Greek and Roman polytheism, and according to all appearances it is now happening to Hindooism, Islam, and to both Protestant and Catholic theology. We have to consider what a very surprising fact that is, on the supposition that any one of these religions is true. All the chief dogmas of the Christian and Mahometan Creeds have been for several centuries before the world. They once were not only believed, but adored. Now the numbers of those who doubt or dispute them are increasing every day. Time has not been their friend, but their enemy. Instead of becoming more firmly rooted in men's esteem and conviction, instead of revealing unexpected connection and compatibility with other truth, instead of being supported by an ever-growing mass of evidence which would make their denial insane rather than unreasonable, they are seen more and more to lack the proofs and credentials never wanting in the case of genuine truth, from which they differ in this important respect—that, whereas scientific truth, though often disputed and opposed on its first presentation to the world, invariably ends by becoming absolutely certain and unquestioned, religious conviction begins with undoubting acceptance, and, after a shorter or longer period of supremacy, with the growth of knowledge and more severe canons of criticism, passes gradually into the category of questioned and disputed theories, ending at last in the class of rejected and exploded errors.

· That the world, in its cultivated portions, has reached one of those great turning-points in the evolution of thought which mark the close of an old epoch and the opening of a new one, will hardly be disputed by any well-informed person. The system of Christian theology and thought which arose out of the ruins of the Roman empire has been gradually undermined, and its authority so shaken that its future survival is rather an object of pious hope than of reasoned judgment. Apologists, indeed, are not wanting, they are perhaps never so numerous; but they cannot stem the torrent which is rushing away from theology in the direction of science, and that negation of theology which science implies. Regarded as a question merely of speculation, the crisis is one of the most interesting which the world has seen, only to be compared to the transition from polytheism to Christianity, in the early centuries of our era, and to the great Protestant revolt from Rome. But the speculative interest pales before the momentous practical interest of the crisis. A transfer of allegiance from one set of first principles to another, especially on subjects relating to morals and conduct, cannot be effected without considerable loss of continuity and order by the way. Many will halt between the two *régimes*, and, owning allegiance to neither, will prefer discarding all unwelcome restraint on their freedom of action. The corruption of manners under the decaying polytheism in the Roman world, the analogous corruption during the Reformation and the Renaissance, offer significant precedents. It would be rash to expect that a transition, unprecedented for its width and difficulty, from theology to positivism, from the service of God to the service of Man, could be accomplished without jeopardy. Signs are not wanting that the prevalent anarchy in thought is leading to anarchy in morals. Numbers who have put off belief in God have not put on belief in Humanity. A common and lofty standard of duty is being trampled down in the fierce battle of incompatible principles. The present indecision is becoming not only wearisome, but injurious to the best interests of man. Let Theology be restored, by all means, to her old position of queen of the sciences, if it can be done in the light of modern knowledge and common sense. If this cannot be done frankly, on the faith of witnesses who can stand cross-examination in open court, let us honestly take our side, and admit that the *Civitas Dei* is a dream of the past, and that we should strive to realize that *Regnum Hominis* which Bacon foresaw and predicted.

CHAPTER II.

THE DECAY OF BELIEF.

OPINIONS and systems of thought as well as institutions which enjoy a considerable lease of life in the world, have many of the characteristics of organisms, or at least of organs belonging to animated beings. The fact that they came into existence and survived during a longer or shorter period, proves that they discharged a function of more or less utility ; that they were in harmony with the surrounding conditions, and hence, found both exercise and nourishment for their support. If in time they gradually cease to discharge a useful function, become atrophied and disappear, their case is almost exactly parallel to the rudimentary organs found in so many animals, which, having ceased to be of use, become shrunken and meaningless, and only persist in an abortive form by virtue of the law of heredity. Such organs in the body politic resemble these analogues in the body natural, in that they often continue to exist long after their presence has ceased to subserve any useful purpose of life. The common trait of rudimentary organs belonging to either category, biological or sociological, is that they survive their use, that they are nourished and live at the expense of the organism in which they exist, and long after they have ceased to make any return for the support they obtain. In the animal world, rudimentary organs may or may not be noxious to the organism in which they inhere : in the social organism they unquestionably are so, especially by their occupying the room and preventing the development of active and efficient organs which would succeed and replace them.

That the Christian religion is rapidly approaching, if it has not already reached, this position, is a part of the thesis maintained in these pages. The decay of belief now general over Christendom, may be regarded from two points of view, and traced up to two distinct causes—one rational, the other moral. The current faith has come increasingly into conflict with science in proportion as the latter has extended in depth and area. The isolated points of collision of former days have been so multiplied, that the shock now is along the whole conterminous line between science and theology ; and it would not be easy to name a department of inquiry which has not, in some measure, contributed aid to the forces arrayed against the popular belief. More important still is the changed tone of feeling with regard to this subject. Time was, and even a recent time, when the prestige of Christianity was so great, that even its opponents were overawed by it. But now men are ready to openly avow that they find a great deal in the Christian scheme which is morally shocking ; and in the estimation of many minds nowadays, probably the moral difficulties outweigh the intellectual.

Nothing is more common than the assertion that any objections now made to Christianity are worn-out sophisms, which have been answered and disposed of over and over again by previous apologists. Sometimes we are told that the objections are as old as the time of Celsus, and were refuted by Origen ; but, generally, Bishop Butler is the favourite champion who is credited with a preordained victory over all opponents, past, present, and future. Butler was so great a man, and his work, considered as a reply to the shallow deism of his day, was in many respects so successful, that it argues a certain irreverence for his character to load him with false praise and unmerited laurels. But these claims, often made for Butler and others, have their interesting and instructive side. They show how little apt the theological mind is to see the real points at issue, and to recognize the full gravity of the present crisis. To suppose that arguments directed against such disputants as Toland, Collins, or Tindal—pertinent as they might be, and, indeed, for the most part were—are equally potent when directed against the methods and results of modern science, implies a complete misconception of the true bearings of the question under discussion. In the early eighteenth century, the light of science had hardly got beyond the first glimmerings of dawn. Mathematics and astronomy were the only sciences which had passed into the positive and final stage. Chemistry, geology, biology, historical criticism, were not yet in a position to speak with authority even on subjects in their own province, and were far from being in possession of vast stores of verified truth obtained by rigorous application of correct methods, such as now impose respect on the most ignorant and careless. The deists were, to say the least, as unscientific as the theologians. Their fancies about the "light of Nature," which was to replace the Christian religion, were as arbitrary and absurd as any mythological legend. Tindal declared the light of Nature to be "a clear and certain light which enlightened all men," and from this fact he inferred that "our duty both to God and man must, from the beginning of the world to the end, remain unalterable, be always alike plain and perspicuous ;"

a doctrine which had the serious defect of being contradicted by the total experience of the human race. Butler had no difficulty in showing that to advance such opinions, was to "talk wildly and at random." No blame attaches to the deists, able and worthy men most of them, for not transcending the knowledge of the age. They attempted prematurely to solve a problem, before the means of solution were at hand. What they would have liked to do was to give a rational explanation of Christianity as an historical phenomenon; but they had neither the historical nor the scientific knowledge requisite for such an undertaking. They consequently fell back on such vague metaphysical conceptions as the "light of Nature," and essayed to show that Christianity was not mysterious, or that it was as old as the creation—mere sophisms which they probably believed, but which were quite incapable of scientific proof.

It is not a little surprising that apologists in the present day should be able to deceive themselves as to the immeasurable distance which separates arguments of this kind from the inferences unfavourable to theology deduced from science. The object of science is not to supply hostile data for the use of agnostics against religion; though there is reason to think that many do believe that to be its chief end and aim. The object of science is knowledge, the increased number of those truths which are capable of verification and proof. If here and there its conclusions conflict with the current theology, the fact is of secondary importance, and of no permanent interest at all to science as such, which is concerned with positive, not negative, results. Every statement and proposition in the most elementary scientific primer probably conflicts with some theology or other. Yet it often seems to be assumed that the sole or the chief object of the labours of scientific men was to find means and arguments to damage the Bible. Scientific men, a most hard-worked and industrious class, have a better appreciation of the value of time, and of the wisdom of minding their own business. They, no doubt, come upon results which are fatal to the currently received opinions about the Bible. But these results interest them much less than they do those who are assured that the Bible is the Word of God. The tables have been turned since the days when Science timidly sued for leave to examine nature, and to draw a few conclusions of her own. Then Theology was queen, and made her power felt. Inquirers worked then, so to speak, with a halter about their necks, and were anxious, above all things, to appease their mighty enemy by every mark of deference and docility. Now the old sovereign has become the suppliant—a rather importunate and intrusive suppliant—but still by her demeanour, if not her words, admitting that she has been discrowned. She no longer, with haughty bearing, issues her anathemas on the progress of the human mind, but she is in great anxiety to show that, appearances notwithstanding, this progress is not incompatible with her pretensions. Geology seems to contradict Genesis in a very direct and final way. "That is all your mistake," says Theology; "Geology and Genesis are in most perfect union ; in fact, the science confirms the Scripture so wonderfully, that each reflects light on the other." The fact that the geology thus warmly accepted now, was once resisted with energy and anger as an impious and futile science, is passed over. New light as to its harmony with Scripture was not noticed, until it had attained a position of power which made it more desirable as a friend than as a foe. The fact is suggestive.

A convenient mode of showing the way in which science

has cut the ground from under the feet of theology, will be a quotation from a once famous and remarkable book, which, in its day, and for a long time after, was regarded, with justice, as a powerful piece of argument in favour of the current religion.   Dr. Samuel Clarke was a man of considerable ability, and of very great attainments ; he was also a man of high and honourable character, and his Boyle lectures, commonly known as his two Discourses "On the Being and Attributes of God," and on "The Truth and Certainty of the Christian Revelation," enjoyed an immense popularity, not only at home but abroad, all through the eighteenth century.   The book is now read only by the curious in religious archæology.   In an elaborate argument, intended to show that although the Christian doctrines "may not be discoverable by bare Reason unassisted by Revelation, yet when they are discovered by Revelation they are found most agreeable to sound, unprejudiced Reason," Clarke proceeds to prove that the account in Genesis of the formation of the earth is entirely credible, in the following passage : "That, about the space of six thousand years since, the earth was without form and void, that is, a confused chaos, out of which God formed this beautiful and useful fabrick we now inhabit, and stocked it with the seeds of all kinds of plants, and formed upon it man, and all other specimens of animals it is now furnished with—is very agreeable to right reason.   For though the precise time, indeed, when all this was done, could not now have been known exactly without Revelation ; yet, even at this day, there are remaining many considerable and very strong rational proofs which make it exceedingly probable (separate from the authority of Revelation) *that this present frame and constitution of the earth cannot have been of a very much longer date.*   The universal tradition delivered down from all the most ancient nations of the world, both learned and barbarous; the constant and agreeing doctrine of all ancient philosophers and poets concerning the earth's being formed within such a period of time out of water and chaos; the manifest absurdities and contradictions of those few accounts which pretend to a much greater antiquity; the numbers of men with which the earth is at present inhabited; the late original of learning and all useful arts and sciences; the changes that must necessarily fall out naturally in the earth in vast length of time, *as by the sinking and washing down of mountains, the consumption of water by plants*, and innumerable other such like accidents, —these, I say, and many more arguments drawn from Nature, Reason, and Observation, make that account of the earth's formation exceedingly probable in itself, which, from the revelation delivered in Scripture-history, we believe to be certain." *

This passage shows what a comparatively easy matter the defence of the Bible was in Dr. Clarke's day. He could, without fear of serious contradiction, make assumptions which no one would venture to make now. The "strong rational proofs," which show that the earth cannot be much more than six thousand years old, would be hard to find. Why the shrinking and washing down of mountains was evidence of the *recent* date of the earth is difficult to see; and the "consumption of water by plants," implying that the water of the globe was being rapidly used up and annihilated, is an interesting example of old notions on chemistry. In the earlier discourse on the existence of God, Clarke had been enthusiastic over the support given to his thesis by the discoveries of his day :—

* "Truth and Certainty of Christian Revelation," p. 187; edition 1724.

"If Galen, so many ages since, could find in the construction and constitution of the parts of the human body such undeniable marks of contrivance and design as forced him then to acknowledge and admire the wisdom of its Author, what would he have said if he had known the late discoveries in anatomy and physic, the circulation of the blood, the exact structure of the heart and brain, the uses of numberless glands and valves for the secretion and motion of the juices in the body : besides several veins and other vessels and receptacles not at all known or so much as imagined to have any existence in his days, but which now are discovered to serve the wisest and most exquisite ends imaginable ?" *

Bacon's famous maxim, that "a little philosophy inclineth men's minds to atheism ; but depth in philosophy bringeth men's minds back to religion," is now being reversed. The early glimpses of the marvels of nature afforded by modern science undoubtedly were favourable to natural theology in the first instance. Knowledge revealed so many wonders which had not been suspected by ignorance, that a general increase of awe and reverence for the Creator was the natural, though not very logical, consequence. But a deeper philosophy, or, rather, biology, has rudely disturbed the satisfaction with which "the wisest and most exquisite ends" were once regarded. It is now known that for one case of successful adaptation of means to ends in the animal world, there are hundreds of failures. If organs which serve an obvious end justify the assumption of an intelligent designer, what are we to say of organs which serve no end at all, but are quite useless and meaningless ? Such are the rudimentary organs in plants and animals, the design of which seems only to point to an unintelligent designer.

* Page 103.

"Some of the cases of rudimentary organs are extremely curious—the presence of teeth in fœtal whales which, when grown up, have not a tooth in their heads, and the presence of teeth which never cut through the gums in the upper jaws of our unborn calves. . . . Nothing can be plainer than that wings are formed for flight; yet in how many insects do we see wings so reduced in size as to be utterly incapable of flight, and not rarely lying under wing-cases, firmly soldered together." * Again, " Eyes which do not see form the most striking example of rudimentary organs. These are found in very many animals, which live in the dark, as in caves or underground. Their eyes often exist in a well-developed condition, but they are covered by membrane, so that no ray of light can enter, and they can never see. Such eyes, without the function of sight, are found in several species of moles and mice which live underground, in serpents and lizards, in amphibious animals (*Proteus, Cæcilia*), and in fishes; also in numerous invertebrate animals, which pass their lives in the dark, as do many beetles, crabs, snails, worms," etc.† Another strange instance is, " the rudiment of the tail which man possesses in his 3—5 tail vertebræ, and which, in the human embryo, stands out prominently during the first two months of its development. It afterwards becomes completely hidden. The rudimentary little tail of man is an irrefutable proof of the fact that he is descended from tailed ancestors. In woman the tail is generally by one vertebra longer than in man. There still exist rudimentary muscles in the human tail which formerly moved it." ‡

That facts of this nature, which have only been a short

* "Origin of Species," p. 450.
† Haeckel, "History of Creation," vol. i. p. 13.
‡ Ibid., vol. i. p. 289.

time before the world, should fail to convince theologians brought up in a completely different order of ideas, is in no wise surprising. The due weight of facts will no more be allowed than the due weight of arguments, by minds which habit and education, and, perhaps, even a sense of duty, have combined to bias against them. But the effect on the younger and succeeding generations is very great, and is already perceptible. When theology was attacked in front with metaphysical arguments, such as were used by the old deists, it was able to make a very stout and plausible resistance. But now its position, in military phrase, has been turned; the heights around it and behind are occupied by an artillery which render further defence impossible. Take the instance of the origin of man. The whole scheme of Christian theology is meaningless except on the assumption of the fall of man from a primitive state of innocence and virtue. Unless theologians are prepared to throw over St. Paul, they must hold that "as in Adam all die, even so in Christ shall all be made alive." Perhaps no one doctrine ever believed by man has had a more terrible history than that of "original or birth-sin," which, as the Ninth Article says, is "the fault and corruption of the nature of every man, that naturally is ingendered of the offspring of Adam; whereby man is very far gone from original righteousness, and is of his own nature inclined to evil, so that the flesh lusteth always contrary to the spirit; and therefore in every person born into this world, it deserveth God's wrath and damnation." But if ever a thesis was demonstrated, it is that man has not fallen, but risen, and that from the lowest level of animal existence. No court of justice ever witnessed a more complete discomfiture of an unfounded claim to a noble title and estate, than the defeat of this theological claim for man, that he was made in the image of God, placed in Paradise in a state of purity, ,from which he fell through disobedience. The result is serious. The New Testament endorses the fall in the most emphatic way; the Incarnation itself had no other object than that of neutralizing its effects. Yet it is proved to be a mere fiction of a primitive cosmogony.

The general rejection of miracles is another system of the decay of belief. The once active controversy as to the possibility of miracles has become nearly extinct, because one of the parties to it has been growing steadily in numbers and authority, while the other party has declined. The refuters of Hume address constantly decreasing audiences, and the belief in miracles will shortly (like the belief in witchcraft in the seventeenth century) die a natural death among the educated classes. The notion that the testimony of men, however worthy and sincere, can suffice to establish a miraculous event, is no longer felt to be serious. The testimony of *credible* witnesses is valueless, unless they be *competent* witnesses as well—competent to observe with patience, accuracy, and coolness, the alleged facts. Were such observers present at the working of the miracles in Palestine which Paley patronizes? The argument against miracles has gained immensely in force since Hume's day through the growth of the historic method, and the larger conceptions of human evolution which have led to the incipient science of sociology. Hume's principle was tersely and fairly enough stated by Paley thus:—"That it is contrary to experience that testimony should be true, but not contrary to experience that testimony should be false;" a true statement, but not beyond the reach of plausible objection, as Paley showed. The moment we introduce the historic element, the question seems transferred to a higher court. Primitive, early, and unscientific man, is at all times and everywhere prone to see miracle in everything that appears odd or strange to his limited experience. Ignorant of nature's laws, he finds no difficulty in assuming their violation ; he lives in an atmosphere of fiction, fable, and myth, and much prefers a miraculous explanation of an event to a rational or real one. The belief in miracles is universal in wholly unscientific times. With the growth of culture it diminishes; with the extension of science it disappears. Miracles are never supposed to occur except where and when an antecedent belief in them exists. In other words, the belief in miracles depends not upon objective facts, but on the subjective conditions of the witnesses' minds.

Paley tried to parry the obvious objection that the best way to silence the gainsayers of miracles would be to repeat them. " To expect, concerning a miracle, that it should succeed upon repetition, is to expect that which would make it cease to be a miracle ; which is contrary to its nature as such, and would totally destroy the use and purpose for which it was wrought ; " * a remark less acute than Paley's remarks usually are. Assuming that a miracle reveals the presence of a supernatural power, why should its repetition destroy its miraculous character ; above all, why should it destroy its use ? If miracles are intended to convert the stiff-necked and hard of heart, what more likely way of bringing them to submission than the repetition of miracles ? And according to Scripture, this was precisely the way in which Pharaoh, King of Egypt, was humbled. He resisted the miracles wrought by Moses and Aaron with stubbornness all through the first nine plagues ; but the universal slaying of the first-born broke even his spirit. Such must always be the effect of repeated miracles ; and there can be no doubt that even at this day, in the midst

* " Paley's Evidences : Preparatory Considerations."

of all this science and scepticism, if miracles were again wrought in a public place and manner, so as to remove the suspicion of trickery and legerdemain, the effect of them would be·greater than ever it was. Suppose a prophet of God were to appear among us, and announce that he had a revelation to make. According to Paley, his only way of making it would be by miracle ; he therefore would perform miracles. As all difficulties vanish before Almighty power, one miracle would be the same as another to him ; and let us suppose him to walk on the water, down the centre of the Thames, from Putney to Mortlake. May we not be sure that one such achievement would produce a sensation perfectly overwhelming, not only in London, but to the furthest limits of the civilized world? If he rapidly followed up this miracle by others—fed with a few loaves the crowds on Hampstead Heath on a Bank Holiday, or those on Epsom Downs on the Derby day; gave sight to a man notoriously blind from his birth, or raised from the dead a putrescent corpse which had lain four days in the grave—can we remotely conceive a limit to the excitement which would ensue? Would not such a reaction against current scientific notions set in, as would sweep everything before it? Supposing always that the miracles were *bonâ fide* miracles, such as are assumed to have been wrought in Judæa some eighteen hundred years ago, we may even be sure that many, if not all, of the chief men of science would be among the most impressed, if not the most excited, and be prompt to own that they had made a great mistake in asserting the invariability of nature's laws. A complete recast of the philosophy of the inductive sciences would be one of the least results of a manifestation of genuine miracles. As for its effect on the cause of religion, there can be little room for doubt. The passionate yet hopeless yearning, which now fills so many minds, to retain a rational belief in the supernatural, would be replaced by a serene joy over the triumph of faith. It may suit Paley to say that repetition of miracles would destroy their use, but he must be a lukewarm theologian who does not at times wish from the depth of his heart that an authentic miracle could be produced. Yet it is at this momentous crisis in the religious affairs of the world, when the enemy is carrying one position after another, and has all but penetrated to the citadel of belief, that no miracles occur—that no miracles are claimed, except, indeed, of the compromising species made at Lourdes, and now and then of a fasting girl exhibited in Belgium and in Wales. When no one doubted the possibility or the frequency of miracles they abounded, we are told; that is, when by reason of their number and the ready credit accorded to them, their effect was the least startling, then they were lavished on a believing world. Now, when they are denied and insulted as the figments of a barbarous age, when the faith they might support is in such jeopardy as it never was before, when a tithe of the wonders wasted in the deserts of Sinai and the "parts beyond Jordan" would shake the nations with astonishment and surprise—when, in short, the least expenditure of miracle would produce the maximum of result—then miracles mysteriously cease. This fact, which is utterly beyond contest, has borne fruit, and will yet bear more.

Instead of a short chapter, a long volume would be needed to set forth in detail even a *spicilegium* of the rationalistic arguments which have operated to produce a decay of belief. Any one interested in the subject will easily find them in the appropriate quarters—in the attacks on, and still better, in the defences of, the Bible. The width of the breach between reason and faith, between theology and science, is hardly denied ; and the noteworthy fact is, that only one of the parties hopes for, or believes in, an ultimate reconciliation. Reason and science have made up their minds on the subject, and would gladly leave it alone, and attend to their own affairs. It is theology that cannot resign herself to a permanent quarrel, and is always pursuing science with a mixture of entreaty and reproach, and begging the latter to hear her cause over again, and not to say with cruel harshness that the separation is for good and all. We may, therefore, leave this side of our subject with a concluding observation.

On no point were apologists more confident than on the impossibility of explaining the uprise of Christianity otherwise than by a supernatural principle. In the words of Archbishop Whately, " No complete and consistent account has ever been given of the manner in which the Christian religion, supposing it a human contrivance, could have arisen and prevailed as it did. The religion exists ; that is, the phenomenon ; those who will not allow it to have come from God are bound to solve the phenomenon on some other hypothesis less open to objection ; they are not indeed called on to prove that it actually did arise in this or that way, but to suggest (consistently with acknowledged facts) some probable way in which it may have arisen, reconcilable with all the circumstances of the case. That infidels have never done this, though they have had nearly two thousand years to try, amounts to a confession that no such hypothesis can be devised, which will not be open to greater objections than lie against Christianity." * The passage is interesting on other grounds than the particular one with which we are concerned, and leaves us the alternative of a low opinion either of Whately's candour or of his perspicacity. The

* " Logic," bk. iii. § 17.

suggestion that infidels had or could have been "trying" for nearly two thousand years to concoct an hypothesis adverse to Christianity, could only be based on a strange ignorance of the state of the human mind during at least three-fourths of that period, or on the safety of such an innuendo in the dark ages when the "Logic" was published (1829). But this need not detain us. The important point to observe is how completely Whately's assertion that a rational explanation of the origin of Christianity has never been given has, by the biblical and historical studies of the last half century, been overthrown. Strauss, F. Ch. Baur, Keim, and Hausrath, to name only the chief writers, have made the early history of Christianity at least as intelligible as other scholars have made the early history of Rome. To the unhistoric minds of the eighteenth century, the uprise of a religion in Palestine in the first century, claiming supernatural authority, seemed as extraordinary and unaccountable as a similar phenomenon would have been in Paris or London. The religious passions, especially among uncivilized races, were at once disliked and misunderstood. Even Robertson the historian could only see in the Crusades "a singular monument of human folly." There was supposed to be no alternative between a truly divine relation and an artful fraud designed by priests for their own benefit. Whately's phrase, "supposing Christianity a human contrivance," points to this crude notion. With enlarged conceptions of the variety of man's nature, and historical development, the spontaneous appearance of such a religion as Christianity is now seen to be quite natural and regular in such an age as the first century. The mythopœic faculty of the human mind at certain stages is capable of more wonderful achievements than any exhibited in the New Testament, and is at this day in full operation in British

India, weaving legends and creating gods with unchecked luxuriance. Meanwhile the historical character of the Gospels, and the Acts of the Apostles, and the genuineness of several epistles ascribed to St. Paul, have been gravely impugned, and, in the opinion of many, seriously damaged; an opinion not shaken by the counter-efforts of the Christian apologists. Again, the fortress of theology has been surrounded and commanded by the forces at the disposal of knowledge.

But mere rationalism, however cogent to some minds, often remains powerless on others, and those frequently possessing the best qualities of intellect and character. The deepest change which this age has seen in reference to men's attitude towards the current theology, has taken place, not in the region of the understanding, but in that of the heart. It is not so much that the Bible, with its miracles and legends, is felt to be untrue and incredible by the trained reason; a great number of theological dogmas are felt to be morally repulsive and horrible, by the more humane conscience of modern times. This change of sentiment is so great and far-reaching, that there is no wonder that its import is imperfectly seized, or even wholly missed by those whom the accidents of education and surroundings have preserved from its influence. It is a change not less momentous than that which placed the Christian converts of the Roman period in a position of passionate hostility to the immoralities and indecencies of decaying polytheism. Even divines are becoming aware that the eternity of hell-torments is a doctrine of waning efficacy, on which it is easy to insist too much. Some are discovering that it lacks Scriptural authority, and beseech us not to believe that anything so dreadful is delivered in the Word of God. The minimising of irksome tenets is a frequent resource and an unfailing symptom of decaying faiths. Julian and his pagan sophists essayed to spiritualize offensive Greek myths. There is no ground for doubting the *bonâ fides* of such attempts, but they rarely succeed. The obvious question, " If your new interpretation is the right one, why was it not discovered before? why did what you admit to be dreadful error receive apparently for a long time Divine sanction?" cannot be answered; and the question is followed by another : " If your predecessors taught error in the dogmas you discard, what guarantee have you to offer that those dogmas which you still maintain may not some day be discovered to be equally untenable? How can you be sure that your successors, when hard pressed by the science of their day, will not, like yourselves, find good reasons for throwing them over?" The eternity of hell torments is a doctrine discarded by a number of divines, who yet cling to the doctrines of the Incarnation and the Atonement. There is nothing to assure us that, in a hundred years' time, these also will not be discovered to be unscriptural.

The Christian theology, in its main features, was evolved during the most calamitous period which the human race has lived through in historic times. The decline and fall of the Roman empire still remains the greatest catastrophe on record; the slow death protracted over five centuries of the ancient world. Every evil afflicted men in that terrible time; arbitrary power, the most remorseless and cruel; a grinding fiscality, which at last exterminated wealth; pestilences, which became endemic and depopulated whole provinces; and, to crown all, a series of invasions by barbarous hordes, who passed over the countries like a consuming fire. It was in this age that the foundations of Christian theology were laid—the theology of the Councils and the Fathers. The conception of God, of His relation to, and dealings with, the world, was evolved in a society which groaned under unexampled oppression, misery, and affliction. Needless to say, it was an age of great and almost morbid cruelty: the games of the circus were a constant discipline of the inhuman passions. After the empire had vanished, for long centuries there was no great improvement. The barbarism of the Frankish period may be seen at full length in the pages of Gregory of Tours. The Carling empire was an oppressive tyranny; the Feudal Age, one of lawless rapine on the part of the strong, and cowering anguish on the part of the weak. It was in this evil time that the Christian Theology was evolved, commencing with the great doctrines defined by the Fathers, and afterwards reduced to a logical system by the scholastics, especially by St. Thomas, the Angel of the schools.

With such visible rulers of the world before them, it is no wonder that men formed very dark and cruel notions of the invisible ruler, who disposed of all things. Cruelty, injustice, arbitrary power, were too familiar to be shocking, too constant to be supposed accidental or transitory. The real world before their eyes was taken as a dim pattern and foreshadowing of the ideal world beyond the grave. God was an Almighty Emperor, a transcendental Diocletian or Constantine, doing as he list with his own. His edicts ran through all space and time, his punishments were eternal, and whatever he did his justice must not be questioned. And thus those words came to be written, " Therefore hath he mercy on whom he will have mercy, and whom he will he hardeneth. Thou wilt say then unto me, Why doth he yet find fault? For who hath resisted his will? Nay but, O man, who art thou that repliest against God? Shall the thing formed say to him that formed it, Why hast thou

made me thus?   Hath not the potter power over the clay,
of the same lump to make one vessel unto honour, and
another unto dishonour?"* which, probably, have added
more to human misery than any other utterances made by
man.   St. Paul's teaching fell on a fertile soil.   For some
fifteen hundred years the human conscience was not shocked
by it.   Since the rise of the Arminian theology there has
been a gradual and growing revulsion of feeling, and now
it is said plainly that the "potter has no right to be angry
with his pots.   If he wanted them different he should have
made them different."   The pretensions of " an omnipotent
devil desiring to be complimented " as all-merciful, when
he is exerting the most fiendish cruelty, are no longer
admitted in abashed silence.   But if the great difficulty of
hell and eternal punishments were happily surmounted,
there remain, in the whole Christian scheme of redemption,
moral iniquities and obliquities which no good man of the
present day, whatever his religion or theology, would willingly
be guilty of himself.   The notion that God wanted to be
propitiated by the death of the innocent Christ, is a
thoroughly base and barbarous one ;   natural enough in
rude ages, when costly sacrifice was a recognized mode of
appeasing angry deities, but repellent now.   Hardly the
most depraved man, in his right mind, would accept the
vicarious punishment of one who had not offended him, in
lieu of one who had.   A high-minded man would endure
almost anything rather than countenance such an enormity.
The idea is barbarous, well worthy of Chinese conceptions
of justice, content if the executioner gets a subject to
operate on, but indifferent whether it be the culprit or not.
Yet this cruel and barbarous notion is the centre of the
Christian religion ; at least, it has not yet been discovered

* Romans ix. 18–21.

to be unscriptural, I believe. Again, Satan may well give latitudinarian theologians trouble in this world as in the next. When they have explained away his *eternal* function of tormenting souls in hell, they will have to extenuate his strange temporal avocations on earth, and to explain how they can be permitted by a merciful God. A fallen angel of vast skill, subtlety, and guile, is allowed to tempt men and women, even young children, to commit sin, to allure them away from Christ, to jeopardize their hopes of Paradise. And God, who permits this, is supposed to hate sin. If he had wished sin to abound, what could he have done more than to allow the arch-fiend, aided by legions of minor devils, to go about like a roaring lion seeking whom he may devour, with constant access to men, nay, to their most inward minds, whispering evil thoughts, stimulating criminal passions, and, however often driven away by holy prayer, ever renewing his assaults on poor souls, up to the last moment of mortal agony, when he oftener succeeds than fails in carrying them off to his place of torment. Christ's petition, " Lead us not into temptation, but deliver us from the evil one," has never been heard, or it has not been granted. We are always being led into temptation ; we are never delivered from the evil one on this side of the gates of death. A supernatural being who wrecked man's felicity in Paradise, and brought sin and death into the world, is appointed to the office of tempting men at all times, in all places, throughout life ; he is able to enter into the minds of his victims and pervert their souls, in society and in solitude, in sleep, and even in prayer, capable of assuming all disguises, even to appearing as an angel of light. A human seducer, however artful and vile, is restricted as to times and opportunities in corrupting the innocent. Satan has constant and invisible access. Now, a parent or guardian

who allowed children under his charge to associate with
bad characters, would be justly condemned as wanting in
a sense of duty and humanity. But God permits something
infinitely worse, by the whole difference between an immortal evil spirit and the most profligate of earthly tempters.
Let any human father try and imagine the anguish with
which he would see his innocent, inexperienced daughter
walking arm-in-arm with an accomplished and fascinating
seducer. Would not his instantaneous step be to put an
end to such corrupting intercourse? Would not public
opinion largely condone violent measures on his part, if it
should appear that the designs of the villain had been
crowned with a calamitous success? Yet the heavenly
father is supposed to see this and far worse every hour and
minute of the day; to see the young, the weak, the unpro-
tected, assailed by a supernatural tempter, his own creature,
his rebel angel, wholly evil and malignant; and to see him
succeed in his attempt to ruin souls. And then the be-
trayed, poor human victim, not the fiend, is punished. The
fiend, indeed, is punished, but not for these acts against
humanity. The righteous God promptly avenged insubordination and disrespect to himself. But ever since man's
creation Satan has had compensations. His dominion is
ever extending (as all orthodox theologians admit that the
number of the damned far exceeds that of the saved), and
he is well entitled to boast in the words of the poet—

> "To reign is worth ambition though in Hell;
>   Better to reign in Hell than serve in Heaven."

The old answer to such considerations was that they were
horribly profane, and "must be put down with a strong
hand." They impiously meddled with "mysteries" which
man in his fallen state could not fathom, but must reve-

rently adore. To which it is now replied, that there is no mystery at all in the matter. Barbarous and cruel ages have ever generated barbarous and cruel religions. Nay, obscene and revolting rites and practices, which cannot be named, have been and still are sanctioned by religion. These were outgrown by the progressive nations of the West when Christian monotheism prevailed. And now Christian monotheism is sharing the fate of its predecessors ; it is being superseded by the growing conscience of mankind.

But the fact is that these somewhat old-fashioned controversies about the credibility of miracles, the evidences of Christianity, the authenticity of portions of Scripture, and similar topics, are now dwarfed and overshadowed by a far mightier question which has come to the front with great rapidity in this age. The being and attributes of a God have been a subject of esoteric discussion in the schools of philosophers for centuries, but only recently have been seen to pass from the closet to the market-place, and to become one of the deepest questions of the day. No more surprising change of fundamental conceptions will be recorded by the future historians of philosophy, than that which has supervened in the last twenty-five or thirty years in reference to the idea of God. Up to a recent time the sturdiest sceptics as to the truth of revelation were mostly deists or pantheists, and often repudiated atheism with warmth. The wittiest scoffer who ever attacked Christianity, Voltaire, was a firm deist, and declared that if God did not exist he would have to be invented. The extreme school of Diderot and D'Holbach, even in the sceptical eighteenth century, failed of a wide acceptance. Now the conception of God is freely treated by many of the leaders of philosophical and scientific opinion as a transitory phase of thought which the growth of knowledge has finally terminated. The natural history and evolution of the idea of God is traced in calm outline from its cradle to its grave—from its nascent form in Animism to its metaphysical presentation as an inscrutable First Cause, the absolute, unconditioned, and unrelated to the phenomenal world. The idea of God has been "defecated to a pure transparency," as one eminent writer phrases it; it has been "deanthropomorphised," to use the language of another. A new and widely-current word has been invented to designate the large class of persons (mostly persons of exceptional knowledge and ability) who refuse to entertain any more the idea of a single divine Being, maker of all things in heaven and earth. Agnostics are to be met with on every side; the place of honour is given to their articles in the most popular monthly reviews; and, just as in the fourth century the mysteries of the Trinity and the Incarnation were discussed in the streets of Constantinople by shopkeepers and their customers, so now, at dinner parties and gatherings of both sexes, the existence of God emerges from time to time as a topic of conversation, ending often in negative conclusions. Every middle-aged man can remember a time when such a transformation of sentiments and opinions would have appeared beyond the pale of possibility.

As in the case of the Christian theology, the difficulties are twofold, intellectual and moral, which have extinguished in many minds the traditional belief in a Supreme Being. So long as men were able and content to believe in an anthropomorphic deity—an infinitely glorified and exalted man—then difficulties were not perceived; a feeling also of religious awe daunted the mind from looking up and scrutinizing even its own conceptions with a steady gaze.

But the growth of knowledge and a higher morality have made the conception of an anthropomorphic God less and less endurable, even to professed theologians, who have been as ready as philosophers to dehumanize the deity. But the difficulty is that, in proportion as the conception of God is stripped of its human attributes and removed away into the absolute, in the same proportion does the conception cease to offer an object capable of exciting human sympathy, and, what is not less important, does it cease to be conceivable. "Similarly, with the logical incongruities, more and more conspicuous to growing intelligence. Passing over the familiar difficulties—that sundry of the implied divine traits are in contradiction with the divine attributes otherwise ascribed; that a god who repents of what he has done must be lacking either in power or foresight; that his anger presupposes an occurrence that has been contrary to his intention, and so indicates defect of means—we come to the greater difficulty: that such emotions, like all emotions, can exist only in a consciousness which is limited. Every emotion has its antecedent ideas, and antecedent ideas are habitually supposed to occur in God. He is represented as seeing and hearing this or the other, and as being emotionally affected thereby. That is, the conception of a divinity possessing these traits of character necessarily continues anthropomorphic, not only in the sense that the emotions ascribed are like those of human beings, but also in the sense that they form parts of a consciousness which, like the human consciousness, is formed of successive states. And such a conception of the divine consciousness is irreconcilable with the unchangeableness otherwise alleged, and with the omniscience otherwise alleged. For a consciousness, constituted of ideas and feelings caused by objects and

D

occurrences, cannot be simultaneously occupied with all objects and all occurrences throughout the universe. To believe in a divine consciousness, men must refrain from thinking what is meant by consciousness—must stop short with verbal propositions; and propositions which they are debarred from rendering into thought, will more and more fail to satisfy them. Of course like difficulties present themselves when the will of God is spoken of. So long as we refrain from giving a definite meaning to the word 'will,' we may say that it is possessed by the Cause of all things, as readily as we may say that love of approbation is possessed by a circle; but when, from the words, we pass to the thoughts they stand for, we find that we can no more unite in consciousness the terms of the one proposition than we can those of the other. Whoever conceives of any other will than his own, must do so in terms of his own will, which is the sole will directly known to him, all other wills being only inferred. But will, as such, is conscious, if it presupposes a motive, a prompting desire of some kind; absolute indifference excludes the conception of will. Moreover, will, as implying a prompting desire, connotes some end contemplated as one to be achieved, and ceases with the achievement of it; some other will referring to some other end taking its place. That is to say, will, like emotion, necessarily supposes a series of states of consciousness. The conception of a divine will, derived from the human will, involves, like it, localization in space and time; the willing of each end excluding from consciousness, for an interval, the willing of other ends, and therefore being inconsistent with that omnipresent activity which simultaneously works out an infinity of ends. It is the same with the ascription of intelligence. Not to dwell on the seriality and limitation implied as before, we may note that intelligence, as alone conceivable by us, presupposes existence independent of it and objective to it. It is carried on in terms of changes primarily wrought by alien activities—the impressions generated by things beyond consciousness and the ideas derived from such impressions. To speak of an intelligence which exists in the absence of all such alien activities, is to use a meaningless word. If to the corollary that the First Cause, considered as intelligent, must be continually affected by independent objective activities, it is replied that these have become such by act of creation, and were previously included in the First Cause; then the reply is, that, in such case, the First Cause could, before their creation, have had nothing to generate in it such changes as those constituting what we call intelligence, and must therefore have been unintelligent at the time when intelligence was most called for. Hence it is clear that the intelligence ascribed answers in no respect to that which we know by the name. It is intelligence out of which all the characters constituting it have vanished." *

On the <u>moral</u> side it is found impossible to reconcile the attributes of mercy and benevolence in the Creator with the condition of the animal world, which presents an almost continued scene of carnage and cruelty, and has done so from its commencement. Not only are the stronger carnivora fashioned and armed for the purpose of hunting and killing their prey—a gazelle or antelope, in a state of nature, is compelled to fly three times daily for its life—but innumerable parasites exist in the bodies and at the expense of animals generally much their superiors. " Of the animal kingdom as a whole, more than half the species are parasites." If each individual species, as Agassiz said,

* Herbert Spencer, *Nineteenth Century Review*, 1885.

is an " embodied creative thought of God," his benevolence must be acknowledged to be of a singular character.

The best apologists admit that a mere metaphysical deity, an absolute First Cause defecated to a pure transparency, is not enough. What they wish to restore is a belief in the God to whom they learned to pray by their mother's knee. And they are abundantly justified from their point of view in such a wish. The only God whom Western Europeans, with a Christian ancestry of a thousand years behind them, can worship, is the God of Abraham, Isaac, and Jacob; or, rather, of St. Paul, St. Augustine, St. Bernard, and of the innumerable " blessed saints," canonized or not, who peopled the Ages of Faith. No one wants, no one cares for, an abstract God, an Unknowable, an Absolute, with whom we stand in no human or intelligible. relation. What pious hearts wish to feel and believe is the existence, "behind the veil" of the visible world, of an invisible Personality, friendly to. man, at once a brother and God. The unequalled potency of Christianity as a religion of the heart, has ever consisted in the admirable conception of the Man God, Jesus Christ. Even a power hostile to man, if conceived as embodied in <u>a person,</u> has been felt preferable to vague, passionless, unintelligent force; because a hostile person could be propitiated, could be appealed to, could be brought over to mercy and good-will by prayer and sacrifice. That is to say, that an anthropomorphic God is the only God whom men can worship, and also the God whom modern thought finds it increasingly difficult to believe in.

CHAPTER III.

WHY MEN HESITATE.

THE series of arguments and considerations against the current theology, of which a very imperfect summary was attempted in the last chapter, might seem sufficient to bring about a rapid extinction of the vulgar belief; and possibly that extinction is not so far off as both those who wish it, and those who deprecate it, may be apt to think. Still, whatever may be the case in France and Germany, Christianity, if moribund, is by no means dead, in this country at least: the land which has done most to work out the philosophy of evolution, is perhaps still the most Christian in faith and practice remaining in the world. The question arises, why has rationalism, after such brilliant victories, not triumphed completely? Why is the British Sunday without a parallel in Europe? Why on that day are museums and theatres still closed, and the churches and chapels full? The obvious answer that we are the most conservative of races is not satisfactory. We can overturn quickly enough institutions with which we are really discontented. The inference is, that the mass of Englishmen, in spite of the wide prevalence of agnostic views, are not yet satisfied in their hearts that an improved substitute for Christianity can be found. Intellectually, their allegiance to it has been much shaken, but their feelings have not been changed in a similar degree. This may be explained in two ways. First, a certain slow-footed sureness in the national character, which refuses to move with haste in matters of paramount importance. Among the peoples who embraced the Reformation, the English were the most tardy in their open and general revolt from Rome. Secondly, in no country has Christianity of late years been less offensive to any class of dissidents. Unlimited religious liberty has permitted every shade of religious or irreligious sentiment to assert itself after its own heart, in its own fashion. Even the established church, once so insolent and oppressive, has, on the whole, shown a wise spirit of compromise and toleration, and is, perhaps, less hated now than at any past period of its history. A touch of genuine persecution would long ago have caused an explosion, which would not only have annihilated the establishment, but have reacted injuriously on the other sects.

In the absence of the stimulus given by persecution even to unpopular opinions, agnosticism has had to make its way on its own merits, so to speak, on a fair field, and certainly with no favour. Among certain groups, with whom intellectual cultivation is the main business of life, it has had a great success, far greater than could have been expected in only a recent past; but it has not extended and penetrated through the great mass of the middle and upper classes. And the obvious reason is, that agnosticism, so far, has not only not had feeling with it, but it has had feeling against it. A belief in the unknowable kindles no enthusiasm. Science wins a verdict in its favour before any competent intellectual tribunal; but numbers of men, and the vast majority of women, ignore the finding of the jury of experts. They cling passionately to the belief in the supernatural; they listen even with patience and flattering hope to the deeply suspicious and suspected professors of spiritualism and thought-reading, athirst for a hint, a suggestion, an evanescent fact, which would lighten the gloom of the grave. Above all, they will believe, in spite of science and the laws of their consciousness, in a good God, who loves them and cares for them and their little wants and trials, and will, if they only please him, take them at last to his bosom, and "wipe the tears for ever from their eyes."

> " À l'enfant il faut sa mère,
> À l'âme il faut son Dieu."

In this respect, at least, Carlyle was a true son of his age, and expressed one of its deepest heart-pangs in that bitter cry of the Everlasting No :—" To me the Universe was all void of Life, of Purpose, of Volition, even of Hostility : it was one huge, dead, immeasurable Steam-engine, rolling on, in its dead indifference, to grind me limb from limb. O the vast, gloomy, solitary Golgotha, and Mill of Death ! Why was the Living banished thither companionless, conscious ? Why, if there is no Devil; nay, unless the Devil is your God ? " That is the true voice of a Christian man who has lost his faith. Some thousand or fifteen hundred years of Christian training has given this passionate turn to the feelings, this infinite craving for sympathy with the Invisible Lord; who must exist, men fondly say, because to doubt him is to despair. Again Carlyle is representative : " Fore-shadows, call them rather fore-splendours— of that Truth, and Beginning of Truths, fell mysteriously over my soul. Sweeter than Day-spring to the Shipwrecked in Nova Zembla; ah ! like the mother's voice to her little child that strays bewildered, weeping, in unknown tumults ; like soft streamings of celestial music to my too exasperated heart, came that Evangel. The Universe is not dead and demoniacal, a charnel-house with spectres; but godlike, and my Father's!"

How little the celestial music soothed the exasperated heart of the care-laden man, his tragic biography is a melancholy witness.

Though perhaps the chief, the yearning for divine sympathy is not the only ground of men's hesitation to follow the guidance of intellect in this matter. The idea still prevails that Christianity is, after all, the best support of morality extant. What system of ethics, it is asked, can compare with the Sermon on the Mount? There are even some who hold that paradise and hell can ill be spared; the one as incentive to good, the other as a deterrent from evil. How can you expect, it is inquired, self-sacrifice, devotion to duty, if man is to die the death of a dog, and to look for no hereafter? It is assumed as obvious to common sense that in that case we shall eat and drink, for to-morrow we die. Self-indulgence the most gross, crime the most unscrupulous, are taken for granted to be the natural and spontaneous predispositions of man, if he did not dread having to pay dear for them in the next world. Wickedness and sin are what he naturally likes, virtue and righteousness what he naturally detests. The pleasures of lying, robbery, impurity, and murder are beyond dispute; they would fill the cup of enjoyment to the brim, could one only get it without fear of after-consequences in the lake of brimstone. Who can be so ignorant of human nature, nay, of his own heart, as to doubt of these all too fascinating temptations and attractions? As it is, even with the fires of Tophet flaming in the distance, men cannot resist their allurements, or prefer

> " The lilies and languors of virtue
> To the roses and raptures of vice."

Therefore, it is only too certain that a general abrogation of Christianity would be at once followed by a reign of universal licence; and, by the lower order of apologists, it is not seldom broadly hinted that *that* is the desired result. Take away the mingled fear and hope of a future state of rewards and punishments, and what possible check can be imagined to the universal indulgence of unbridled desires?

Without staying to point out that reasoners of this class, whatever their other merits, cannot be complimented on their estimate of human nature, and that they, at least, can with little grace reproach any opponents with degrading man, we have to remark that the conclusions of the reason, so far as they are adverse to Christianity, are here met, not with arguments, but with threats, with appeals to the passions of a very powerful kind; and that it can excite no surprise that, on the whole, passion has the advantage in the conflict. We shall try to examine these points with some care, and inquire (1) if religion has really been in the past the solace and consolation it is asserted; (2) whether Christianity is such a stay and support to morality as it is said to be; and (3) whether a general outbreak of crime and debauchery may be expected as a natural result of the disappearance of the established theology?

CHAPTER IV.

THE ALLEGED CONSOLATIONS OF THE CHRISTIAN RELIGION.

IT is worthy of remark that, in proportion as Christianity has met with intellectual opposition, a progressive tendency has been shown by divines to veil the harsher and more inhuman features of their creed. The older race of theologians, with no fear of criticism before their eyes, spoke out freely; they preached high doctrine, and found an austere pleasure in dwelling on the awful judgments of God. The small number of the saved, the multitude of the damned, the narrowness of the way which leads to life, the breadth of that which leads to destruction, were topics on which they loved to dwell and the congregation to ponder. To a large extent this tone has been dropped, and replaced by one to which it is the direct contrary. Preachers prefer to dwell on the cheerful and bright side of religion—on its glorious promises, on the delights of the Heavenly Jerusalem. They certainly speak with much less unction of the "wrath to come;" and if they say nothing to impair the belief in God's justice, which leads him to punish sin with endless torments, they enlarge more on his "mercy," and "the things he hath prepared for them that love him." In some cases, religion is chiefly recommended as offering a graceful and pleasing appendix to life, as depriving death of its sting and the grave of its victory, and opening a prospect up to the sunlit heavens, amid clouds and glory and the most sublime scenery that can be imagined.

This change of tone which, as a broad matter of fact, cannot, I apprehend, be denied, has followed on as a wide result of the great humanitarian movement which began towards the middle of the last century. When legislation and manners were equally marked by cruelty; when criminals were tortured to death, and prisoners kept in noisome dungeons reeking with jail fever and swarming with vermin; when popular sports largely consisted in inflicting pain on men and animals—it is no wonder that gloomy and inhuman views of religion passed without challenge, or even with favour. The alteration of feeling, together with its cause, were quaintly expressed by an American divine, who had been reproached by an English visitor for too slight an insistance on the eternal damnation of the wicked : "Our people would not stand it, sir," was the reply. But the point which more immediately concerns us is whether the old religion of terror, or its modified and softened modern version, was, or is such a source of solace and inward joy as is commonly assumed. Any one who has had the privilege of knowing intimately one of those rare and beautiful souls in whom a single-hearted piety seems spontaneous, would be slow to deny that such solace may exist. The meek and chastened spirits do occasionally know that peace of God which passeth all understanding. But it is equally certain that that peace is subject to painful interruptions, and that in almost exact proportion with the growth of a tender and watchful conscience does the liability to such eclipses increase. It is the presumptuous, not the truly devout, who dwell always in a complacent conviction of their acceptance and favour with God. All spiritual doctors abound in warnings against the two opposite dangers, on the one hand, of over-confidence, self-righteousness, Pharisaism; on the other, of despair and hopeless despondency of ever pleasing God. The proud content of the Pharisee can never be put to the credit of religion, as it is the temper which is most of all condemned by true piety. "Humility, and modesty of judgment and of hope, are very good instruments to procure mercy and a fair reception at the day of our death; but presumption or bold opinion serves no end of God or man, and is always imprudent, even fatal, and of all things in the world is its own greatest enemy; for the more any man presumes the greater reason he has to fear." * Any solace, therefore, of this kind, derived from religion, must be repudiated and struck off the account as illegitimate and in a manner fraudulent—a deadly spiritual sin seizing the reward of perfected saintliness. It is the anxious and careworn penitent whom we have to consider, those who, when they have done all that they can, still regard themselves as unprofitable servants. Theologians prescribe elaborate remedies against despair as a "temptation and a horrid sin;" but it is a sin to which the humble, the meek, and the truly devout are exposed, and not the wicked and worldly. How often it has been pushed to the destruction of reason, resulting in religious madness, the statistics of insanity are there to show. Even when it stops short of this fearful consummation, and appears in the milder form of desponding anxiety, and fear lest the sinner has lost favour in the sight of God, those moments of coldness and tediousness of spirit form a heavy deduction from the hours of peace and happiness enjoyed between, as every book of devotion, from the Psalms downward, abundantly shows. "My God, my God, look upon me; why hast thou forsaken me: and art so far from my health, and from the

* "Holy Dying," ch. v. s. 6.

words of my complaint ?   O my God, I cry in the day-time, but thou hearest not : and in the night-season also I take no rest."

Thomas à Kempis denies that the truly contrite sinner has any ground even to hope for consolation. " Lord, I am not worthy of thy consolation, nor of any spiritual visita tion ; and therefore thou dealest justly with me when thou leavest me poor and desolate. For if I could shed tears as the sea, yet should I not be worthy of thy consolation. Wherefore I am worthy only to be scourged and punished, because I have grievously and often offended thee, and in many things greatly sinned ; so, then, on a true account, I have not deserved even the smallest consolation." *

Cardinal Wiseman, in his preface to the English transla- tion of the works of St. John of the Cross, has the following remarkable passage : " It may be considered a rule in this highest spiritual life that, before it is attained, there must be a period of severe probation, lasting often many years, and separating it from the previous state, which may have been one of most exalted virtue. Probably, many whom the Catholic Church honours as saints have never received this singular gift. But in reading the biography of such as have been favoured with it, we shall invariably find that the possession of it has been preceded, not only by a voluntary course of mortification of sense, fervent devotion, constant meditation, and separation from the world ; but also by a trying course of dryness, weariness of spirit, insipidity of devotional duties, and, what is infinitely worse, dejection, despondency, temptation to give up all in disgust, and almost despair. During this tremendous probation, the soul is dark, parched, and wayless, as earth without water, as one staggering across a desert, or, to rise to a nobler

* " Imitation," iii. 52.

illustration, like Him remotely who lay on the ground on Olivet, loathing the cup which He had longed for, beyond the sweet chalice which He had drunk with His apostles just before." A prince of the Church may, no doubt, be trusted to speak correctly on this matter.

In order to show that these afflictions are not peculiar to Catholics, a few sentences may with advantage be quoted from that strange book of Bunyan's, "Grace Abounding to the Chief of Sinners:"—"And now was I both a burden and terror to myself; nor did I ever so know as now what it was to be weary of my life and yet afraid to die. Oh, how gladly now would I have been anybody but myself, anything but a man, and in any condition but my own; for there was nothing did pass more frequently over my mind than that it was impossible for me to be forgiven my transgression and to be saved from wrath to come. . . , I found it hard work now to pray to God, because despair was swallowing me up. I thought I was, as with a tempest, driven away from God, for always when I cried to God for mercy this would come in, ' 'Tis too late; I am lost: God has let me fall, not to my correction, but to my condemnation.' About this time I did light on that dreadful story of that miserable mortal, Francis Spira—a book that was to my troubled spirit as salt when rubbed into a fresh wound. Every sentence in that book, every groan of that man, with all the rest of his actions in his griefs; as his tears, his prayers, his gnashing of teeth, his wringing of hands, his twisting and languishing and pining away under that mighty hand of God that was upon him, were as knives and daggers in my soul. Especially that sentence of his was frightful to me: ' Man knows the beginning of sin, but who bounds the issues thereof?' Then would the former sentence as the conclusion of all fall like an hot thunderbolt against my conscience; for you know how that afterwards, when he would have inherited the blessing, he was rejected, for he found no place of repentance, though he sought it carefully with tears.

"Then should I be struck into a very great trembling, insomuch that at sometimes I could for whole days together feel my very body as well as my mind to shake and totter under the sense of this dreadful judgment of God that should fall on those that have sinned that most fearful and unpardonable sin. I felt also such a clogging and heat at my stomach, by reason of this my terror, that I was especially at sometimes as if my breast-bone would split asunder : then I thought concerning that of Judas, who, by his falling headlong, burst asunder, and all his bowels gushed out."

If we admit that such periods of depression are at last more than compensated by the ecstasy which may follow them, yet it is obvious that the religious life, in its highest forms, is very far from uniformly leading through paths of pleasantness and peace, as is sometimes assumed. A state bordering on despair, which lasts for years, is no light matter ; and it would be no conclusive proof of a carnal mind to hesitate before encountering such anguish, even with the ultimate certainty of its transmutation into ineffable joy. But, as Cardinal Wiseman tells us, there is no certainty of such in this life : only in heaven can the Christian hope for an adequate return for his spiritual trials in this world. "If in this life only we have hope in Christ, we are of all men most miserable," said St. Paul of himself and fellow Christians ; and it follows that neither in the design nor in the result is Christianity adapted to confer the highest earthly happiness : it is not a present solace, but the promise of one hereafter. A future life, however, is one of the most enormous assumptions, without proof, ever made ; and yet, on this immense postulate, all the alleged consolations of religion of necessity hang. By considering the case of the truly religious, we have discussed the question, on the most favourable terms to Christianity, as a source of happiness. The profoundly pious are at times refreshed with the " beatific vision " in the course of their pilgrimage. But there are numbers of the half-converted, the worldly, the openly wicked, who believe enough to be full of anxiety and fear, and yet never attain to assurance of complete peace with God ; and perhaps these constitute the majority of professing Christians. If you obtain access to their inmost thoughts you will rarely find that religion has been a consolation to them, but a perpetual source of inward unrest and alarm, though they never have had the strength or the grace to turn finally to God. These pains of the spirit are by no means the only trials which the Christian has to encounter. The prevalence of heresy and schism has ever afflicted devout men in proportion to their devoutness. One of the peculiarities of this age, indeed, is the extraordinary cessation of controversy and absence of new doctrines within the Christian communion. Never, perhaps, since the Council of Jerusalem, has there been so marked an abeyance of serious theological dispute. Middle-aged and old men, who can remember the Tractarian controversy, and the Gorham controversy, when the country was filled with tumult about matters of faith, can appreciate the strange, great calm which now prevails. Whether true believers have any reason to rejoice in the change may be doubted. The differences within have been followed by far more serious hostilities from without, and it is the deadly war with the sceptic and the infidel which justly pre-occupies the earnest thoughts of Christian men. This last state, which is worse than the first, tends to make us forget how painful were the anxieties as to the threatened prevalence of "grave error," whenever serious controversies arose; what fiery pamphlets were published by deans, archdeacons, and even by bishops; what agitated letters appeared even in the secular newspapers; what meetings were convened, and what danger to Christian verity was apprehended if the faithful did not see to it. The world has rolled so far away from this state of things, that even those who witnessed it, retain but an imperfect recollection of the remote scene. Who can easily recall the excitement consequent on the publication of so anodyne a work as Professor Jowett's edition of St. Paul's Epistles? How difficult to remember the time when the illustrious Master of Balliol was a persecuted man, considered more than passing rich with forty pounds a year, for teaching Greek as it had not been taught by a Regius professor from time immemorial? But faith was still lively and vigilant, even in that recent past—a very pale reflection of its former brightness no doubt. To realize what it once was, and what mental distress it could cause, we must have recourse to reading; and, with such historical imagination as we can command, revive an extinct controversy; not one of the mightier disputes of the sixteenth century, the dust-cloud of· which reached up to the heavens and obscured the stars; but a relatively minor one, and only an episode in that, the fate of Jacqueline Pascal.

Jacqueline, the younger sister of Blaise Pascal, was remarkable for talent and beauty even in her own family, in which beauty and talent were hereditary gifts. Like Pope, she lisped in numbers, and composed verses which were not contemptible before she had learned to read. Her grace of person and manner caused her to be invited to play in a comedy before Richelieu, and though only nine years of age, she so charmed the Cardinal that he recalled her father, who had incurred his displeasure, from exile. We have letters of hers written in her twentieth year, in which she gives to her sister, Madame Périer, a lucid and intelligent account of a conference between her brother Blaise and Descartes, when they discussed the discovery of the barometer, and the phenomena of atmospheric pressure. But religion already occupied all her thoughts, and she resolved to become a nun of Port Royal, though, out of deference to her father's wish, she refrained from taking the veil until after his death. "She made all her preparations in my presence," says her sister, Madame Périer, "and fixed the fourth of January as the day for entering the convent. On the eve of that day she begged me to speak about it to my brother, to avoid taking him by surprise. . . . He was much touched, and retired very sad to his room without seeing my sister, who was in a small apartment where she was wont to pray. She did not leave it till my brother had gone, fearing that the sight of her might give him pain. I gave her the tender messages he had charged me with, after which we all went to bed. But I could not sleep. Although I approved heartily of her resolution, its magnitude so filled my mind that I lay awake all night. At seven the next morning, as I saw that Jacqueline did not rise, I thought that she also had not slept, and I found her fast asleep. The noise I made awakened her, and she asked me the time. I told her, and inquired how she felt, and if she had slept well. She replied she was well and had had a good night. Then she arose, dressed herself, and went away; doing this, as all things, with a tranquillity and composure of soul which cannot be conceived. We took no farewell of each other from fear of breaking down, and I turned away from her path when I saw her ready to go out. In this way she left the world; it was the fourth of January, of the year 1652, she being twenty-six years and three months old."

Sister Jacqueline, of Saint Euphemia Pascal, was for nine years a nun at Port Royal, and became subprioress and mistress of the Novices. In the latter character, the duty of teaching young children to read devolved upon her, and she introduced into the convent the new system of giving merely the phonetic value of the letters and not calling them by misleading names, which was the invention of her brother Blaise, and obtained afterwards great renown in the "Grammaire Générale" of Port Royal. But the pious Jansenist foundation was already doomed. The Jesuits had not yet avenged the Provincial Letters. Strong with the support of the pope and the king, they produced a formulary, the signature of which was compulsory on all ecclesiastics. It referred to the eternal question of the Five Propositions, and declared that they were in the book *Augustinus* of Bishop Jansenius, and were contrary to the faith. Much subtlety was employed to find a means of signing it in a non-natural sense, and the chiefs of the Jansenist party, to escape destruction, visibly wavered. But Jacqueline, like her brother Blaise, was made of sterner stuff, and resisted all compromise with passionate zeal. At last the great authority of Arnauld and Nicole prevailed upon their followers to accept the bitter cup prepared for them by their enemies. Pascal swooned away when this decision was taken. Jacqueline yielded at last to the pressure of her superiors, and signed the formulary, but with such grief and anguish of soul that she predicted she would die of it; as indeed she did in less than six months.

The affliction of the just and the prosperity of the wicked

has always been a serious difficulty to pious persons who combined reflection with devotion. "Wherefore do the wicked live, become old, yea, are mighty in power? Their seed is established in their sight with them, and their offspring before their eyes. Their houses are safe from fear, neither is the rod of God upon them." * And the prophet goes on to say in his anguish—"God hath delivered me to the ungodly, and turned me over into the hands of the wicked. . . . He breaketh me with breach upon breach, he runneth upon me like a giant. . . . My face is foul with weeping, and on my eyelids is the shadow of death ; not for any injustice in mine hands : also my prayer is pure." † Probably few religious persons have escaped the bitterness of feeling that they were unjustly chastened, that the rod of God was upon them and not upon the wicked. They no doubt repelled the thought with an *"Apage Satana!"* regarding it as a snare of the tempter. But because the thought was banished from the mind, was the load removed from the heart? This is a trial which theologians must admit is all their own—a clear addition to the weary weight "of all this unintelligible world." Agnostics at least, when smitten by the sharp arrows of fate, by disease, poverty, bereavement, do not complicate their misery by anxious misgivings and painful wonder why they are thus treated by the God of their salvation. The pitiless, brazen heavens overarch them and believers alike ; they bear their trials, or their hearts break, according to their strength. But one pang is spared them, the mystery of God's wrath that he should visit them so sorely. The exceeding bitter cry of the dying Jesus, "My God, my God, why hast thou forsaken me?" never comes to their lips, for it never rises in their hearts. "Jesus, when he had cried again with a loud voice, yielded up the

* Job xxi. 7–9.   † Job xvi. 11, 14–17.

ghost." A fitting yet terrible end of the Passion ; for what more awful thought could come to a devout believer in God than that he was forsaken of God ? It may well have been *this*, even more than the nails through his feet and hands, and the spear in his side, which broke the heart of the Son of man, and made Him yield up the ghost. Christ's followers have discovered consolations and *viatica* in the hour of death which were denied Him. But the most truly humble and devout at times find their chief anguish there where they have most looked for relief. A more pious, God-fearing woman than the charming French poetess, Madame Desbordes Valmore, could not easily be found. But her life was one long scene of bitter trial, poverty and bereavement. At last the cup runs over, and this plaintive cry escapes her : " Yes, Camille, it is very poignant ; here I am alone, without brother or sisters, alone and severed from all the dear souls I have so loved, without the consolation of surviving them and being able to accomplish their desire, which was ever to do some good. . . . What can one say in the presence of these decrees of Providence ? If one has deserved them, the case is more sad. I often search my heart and try to find out what may have caused me to be so heavily smitten by our dear Creator; for it is impossible for his justice to punish thus without a cause, and that thought very often suffices to overwhelm me." *

The above extracts will probably be considered sufficient to show that it is by no means so plain as it is often assumed to be, that the loss of the Christian religion would deprive men of an immense consolation and an abiding source of inward happiness amid the trials of life. There is a serious set-off on the other side, and this was admitted

* Sainte-Beuve, " Nouveaux Lundis," vol. xii.

with no difficulty in the days when the faith was menaced by no danger. "Do not seek," says Jeremy Taylor, "for deliciousness and sensible sweetness in the actions of religion, but only regard the duty and the conscience of it. For although, in the beginning of religion most frequently, and at other times irregularly, God complies with our infirmity, and encourages our duty with little overflowings of spiritual joy and sensible pleasure and delicacies in prayer, so as we seem to feel some little nearer of heaven, and great refreshment from the spirit of consolation ; yet this is not always safe for us to have, neither safe for us to expect and look for ; and when we do, it is apt to make us cool in our inquiries and waitings upon Christ when we want them ; it is running after him, not for the miracles, but for the loaves ; not for the wonderful things of God and the desire of pleasing him, but for the pleasure of pleasing ourselves." * Nowadays, the effort made is in the opposite direction, and to dwell on the "sensible pleasures" and "delicacies in prayer," in order to enhance the contrast between the bright glory and prospects afforded by the religious life, and the gloomy and hopeless future which are supposed to afflict the infidel. The object now is to make religion attractive, and it has been pursued with very marked success. Let any one compare the taste and beauty of a choral service in a modern church or cathedral, with the harsh and grating ugliness which made "going to church" in the days of our youth an ascetic exercise. The coarse, untutored voice of the village shoemaker or tailor, who acted as clerk ; the hideous boxes called pews ; the dolorous and droning music ; the whole framed in a choice specimen of Georgian architecture, barbaric with white-wash and clumsy ornament, will still return to the

* "Holy Living," cap. iv. § 7.

memory in a dreamy mood. These things have gone, and are replaced by what is very often a real artistic success; good music and singing, the dim religious light of stained windows, flowers, mosaics, or paintings, in churches often not untouched by the spirit of mediæval beauty. This great reform in the ordering of divine service has passed beyond the limits of the Establishment, and penetrated even among the dissenters, whose chapels no longer display the resolute deformity of a past age. The outward change has been preceded and accompanied by a deeper inward change; the doctrine of terror has been laid aside, and replaced by a doctrine of mildness and hope, so much so that few realize the gloomy horrors of the old creed. The younger generation has hardly an idea of the dismal spiritual pit in which their fathers lived. In the eighteenth century the case was still worse. The chill shade of religious dread spread beyond the circle of the professedly devout, and darkened life and literature. Only profane revellers passed out of it, and their example was not edifying. In what a cavern of black thoughts did Samuel Johnson pass his life, and what a fearful " Horror of the Last " gat hold of him in his latter days. Edward Young, who inveighed against wealth and honours in order to obtain them, adjusted with skill and care the strains of his venal muse to the popular taste, and sang that

> " A God all mercy is a God unjust."

Few books in the last century were more popular with serious persons than the " Meditations " of James Hervey, which ran through numerous editions when it first appeared, and was still a favourite with pious folk in the earlier portion of the present century. Such pompous and tawdry fustian one would hope could hardly have been accepted for eloquence, had it not been supposed to convey vital religious truth. As a poetaster of the day expressed it :—

> " In these loved scenes what rapturous graces shine,
>   Live in each leaf, and breathe in every line ;
>   What sacred beauties beam throughout the whole,
>   To charm the sense and steal upon the soul."

Soul and sense are charmed in this wise :—

" The wicked seem to lie here, like malefactors in a deep and strong dungeon; reserved against the day of trial. ' *Their departure* was without peace.' Clouds of horror sat lowering upon their closing eyelids; most sadly foreboding the blackness of darkness for ever. When the last sickness seized their frame, and the inevitable change advanced ; when they saw the fatal arrow fitting to the strings; saw the deadly archer, aiming at their life; and felt the envenomed shaft fastened in their vitals—good God! what fearfulness came upon them! What horrible dread overwhelmed them! How did they stand shuddering upon the tremendous precipice, excessively afraid to die, yet utterly unable to live.—O! what pale reviews, what startling prospects, conspire to augment their sorrows! They look backward; and behold! a most melancholy scene! Sins unrepented of, mercy slighted, and the day of grace ending. They look forward, and nothing presents itself but the righteous Judge, the dreadful tribunal, and a most solemn reckoning. They roll around their affrighted eyes on attending friends, and, if accomplices in debauchery, it sharpens their anguish to consider this further aggravation of their guilt, That they have not sinned alone, but drawn others into the snare. If religious acquaintance, it strikes a fresh gash into their hearts, to think of never seeing them any more, but only at an unapproachable distance, separated by the unpassable gulph." *

Will any one presume to say that for one death-bed which has been smoothed by religion, a thousand have not been turned into beds of torture by such teaching as this !

But we must go back to the palmy days of Calvinism, to Scotland in the seventeenth century, to realize fully the revolting devil-worship which once passed under the name of Christianity, and, what is more, really was Christianity, gospel-truth, supported by texts, at every point taken from scripture. No class of literature lies buried deeper in oblivion than old-fashioned theological literature. Its brilliant but transitory life is followed by a perennial death, from which there is no resurrection. Dead divinity is the deadest thing that ever lived. Only now and then a literary historian recalls one of these vanished spectres ; the mass of believers are content to ignore their spiritual ancestry. Take the case of the Rev. Thomas Boston, a minister of the Church of Scotland, who lived in the latter end of the seventeenth and beginning of the eighteenth century. Boston was one of the most shining lights of the Scottish Church, and his most famous book, " Human Nature in its Fourfold State," was for a long period almost placed on a level with Holy Scripture. It is certainly a very wonderful book, written with great power, and eloquence of a kind which might well impose upon readers who accepted the writer's premises. It seems written in a white heat of sustained passion, in which the devil-worshipper (for Boston is nothing else), persuaded that he had conciliated his devil for his own purposes, deals damnation on all poor wretches not so favoured, with an exultant and fiery

* "Meditations among the Tombs," vol. i. p. 94.

joy which is really astounding to witness. The man would have delighted, one would say, to be a stoker in the infernal regions. Out of a volume of five hundred pages I select a page or two which are nothing but average specimens of a tone of thought which I apprehend would be generally repudiated by theologians nowadays; so far have we declined from Christian verity.*

" Consider what a God he is with whom thou hast to do, and whose wrath thou art liable unto. He is the God of infinite knowledge and wisdom ; so that none of thy sins, however secret, can be hid from him. He infallibly finds out all means, whereby wrath may be executed, towards the satisfying of justice. He is of infinite power, and so can do what he will against the sinner. How heavy must the strokes of wrath be, which are laid on by an omnipotent hand ! Infinite power can make the sinner prisoner, even when he is in his greatest rage against Heaven. It can bring again the several parcels of dust out of the grave, put them together again, re-unite the soul and body, summon them before the tribunal, hurry them away to the pit, and hold them up with the one hand, through eternity, while they are lashed with the other. He is infinitely just, and therefore must punish ; it were acting contrary to his nature to suffer the sinner to escape wrath. Hence the execution of his wrath is pleasing to him ; for though the Lord hath no delight in the death of a sinner, as it is the destruction of his own creature, yet he delights in it, as it is the execution of justice. ' Upon the wicked he shall rain snares, fire and brimstone, and an horrible tempest.' Mark the reason : ' For the righteous Lord loveth righteousness ' (Ps. xi. 6, 7) ; ' I will cause my fury to rest upon them, and I will

* Boston's book first appeared in 1720. It has been republished by the Religious Tract Society.

be comforted' (Ezek. v. 13); 'I also will laugh at your calamity' (Prov. i. 26).　Finally, he lives for ever, to pursue the quarrel.　Let us therefore conclude, 'It is a fearful thing to fall into the hands of the living God.'"*

Again, in another place of the same chapter, Boston says "There is wrath upon his soul.　He can have no communion with God; he is 'foolish, and shall not stand in God's sight' (Ps. v. 5). . . . There is war between Heaven and them (natural men), and so all commerce is cut off. . . . God casts a portion of worldly goods to them, more or less as a bone is thrown to a dog; but, alas! his wrath against them appears, in that they get no grace. . . . They lie open to fearful additional plagues on their souls, even in this life.　Sometimes they meet with deadening strokes, silent blows from the hand of an angry God; arrows of wrath, that enter into their souls without noise.　'Make the heart of this people fat, and make their ears heavy, and shut their eyes, lest they see with their eyes' (Isa. vi. 10).　God strives with them for a while, and convictions enter their consciences; but they rebel against the light; and, by a secret judgment, they receive a blow on the head; so that from that time they do, as it were, live and rot above ground.　Their hearts are deadened, their affections withered, their consciences stupefied, and their whole souls blasted; 'cast forth as a branch and withered' (John xv. 6).　They are plagued with judicial blindness.　They shut their eyes against the light; and they are given over to the devil, the god of this world, to be blinded more (2 Cor. iv. 4).　Yea, 'God sends them strong delusions, that they should believe a lie' (2 Thess. ii. 11).　Even conscience, like a false light on the shore, leads them upon rocks, by which they are broken in pieces.

* T. Boston, "Human Nature in its Fourfold State.　The Misery of Man's Natural State," Motive 4.

They harden themselves against God, and he leaves them to Satan and their own hearts, whereby they are hardened more and more. They are often 'given up unto vile affections' (Rom. i. 26). . . . Sometimes they meet with sharp fiery strokes, whereby their souls become like mount Sinai, where nothing is seen but fire and smoke, nothing heard but the thunder of God's wrath, and the voice of the trumpet of a broken law, waxing louder and louder, which makes them, like Pashur (Jer. xx. 4), 'a terror to themselves.' God takes the filthy garments of their sins, which they were wont to sleep in securely, overlays them with brimstone, and sets them on fire about their ears, so they have a hell within them."

It may be doubted if, among all the aberrations of the human mind, anything so horrible as this was ever attained elsewhere; and this was the creed of the poor Scots for more than two hundred years. In reading the works of such a man as Boston, one is tempted to admit one of his favourite dogmas, that the heart of man· is deceitful above all things and desperately wicked. He evidently gloats and revels in the ideas of wrath, brimstone, fiery strokes, stunning blows, and all the apparatus of his infernal torture-chamber. There is a sort of concupiscence of lust in his passion for cruelty; it tickles his prurient appetite, and reaches to a depravity almost insane. If he stood alone, the case would be merely one of pathology; but he was a representative man, and spoke in the names of millions in this country and abroad. The power of the human mind to throw up and nourish poisonous growths of this kind is a very sad and regrettable one. It has stained with blood many pages of history, and is not, one is sorry to say, an abomination confined to Christians. The inhuman fanatics of the French Revolution, Marat, Hébert, Fouquier-Tinville and Robespierre, are inferior specimens of the same breed. But their lust of cruelty, hideous as it was, had not the infinite scope and transcendental character of Boston's; yet the Reign of Terror in France, which lasted but a few months, is still pointed to by Christians as a supreme instance of the wickedness into which unbelievers inevitably fall. The reign of terror in Scotland, which lasted two centuries, is quietly dropped out of memory, or certainly is never consigned to the everlasting infamy which is supposed to have overtaken the atheists. On the whole this is an advantage, and the less we deal in retrospective anathema the better; but then all parties should benefit by the amnesty. Even Carlyle, who ever remained a sort of distorted Calvinist, could see that nothing was gained by " shrieking." over the horrors of the French Revolution; and agnostics would do well to abstain from hard words about Calvinists. Determinists and evolutionists must hold that all phenomena of the human mind, whether welcome or otherwise, had a very good reason for their existence, in that they were caused like any other phenomena. Calvinistic or Terrorist principles cannot be too forcibly condemned, discouraged, or counteracted. Like frightful forms of disease they show what terrible evils human nature is exposed to. But we do not properly blame disease, if we are wise; we strive to combat it and prevent its recurring again. The poor victims of disease, whether mental or physical, rather deserve our pity than our scorn. They contracted it because they were exposed to its noxious germs. The antecedent evolution of Scotland and France had produced the moral miasma and the minds ready to receive it, which led to the breaking out of those two dreadful pestilences, Scotch Calvinism and French Terrorism. While they prevailed in their greatest virulence, the minds of men were deformed and made hideous, as their bodies might be by small-pox or elephantiasis.

In this slight retrospect over the darker side of theology, I should misrepresent my meaning if I seemed to blame the men who held opinions, according to my view, very pernicious. Our war should be not with men but with dogmas, principles. The dogmas, under the conditions, were inevitable, just as the Plague of London, under the then conditions of over-crowding and neglect of cleanliness, was inevitable. But we cannot blame the men who suffered from the Plague; we cannot even blame their ignorance of the laws of health, because they could not then have known better. We now do know better, and we keep down the Plague. In the same way, Calvinism was a creed held by men who could not know better. The antecedent history of Scottish thought had led to a superstitious adoration of a fragment of old oriental literature, the Bible, which was supposed to contain the authentic will and testament of the Creator of the universe. This supposed divine word had been, so it was thought, somewhat kept in the background and slighted by the powerful Catholic Church, which had reigned supreme for centuries, and pressed on men's minds with no light yoke. Every word of this old oriental book, very interesting and valuable in its own way, as a specimen and picture of primitive culture, was imagined to be in the handwriting of the Most High. Every bloody deed recorded, every fantastic and horrible thought enunciated, such as must appear in such a document or collection of documents compiled in such an age, was regarded as approved and authenticated by Almighty Wisdom. When these and similar facts are considered, it does not seem inexplicable that the Scotch and other Calvinists thought and acted as they did. They came to horrible results and conclusions, but these were logical conclusions from the premises. Similarly Rousseau and Robespierre were the most logical of men. The fault lies in the premises, in the one case, that the Bible is the word of God ; in the other, that the *Contrat Social* is the utterance of pure reason.

CHAPTER V.

ON CHRISTIANITY AS A GUIDE TO CONDUCT.

THE next point to be considered is whether the Christian religion is really so strong and efficient a support of morality as it is common to suppose. An affirmative answer is generally taken for granted, as if the case were too obvious to admit of doubt or even of argument. The purity and elevation of the ethics of the gospel are indeed often asserted to be a sufficient proof of its divine origin. Those theologians who wince somewhat under the scientific argument against miracles, recover all their self-possession when they dwell on the ethical side of their creed. If the casting out of devils from demoniacs is admitted to present difficulties, on the ground that it was and still is a common Eastern superstition to regard lunatics as possessed by evil spirits, a superstition which the evangelists shared with their countrymen and contemporaries, it is maintained that the Sermon on the Mount is its own evidence of divine inspiration. "Never man spake like this man." The spiritual depth and sublimity of Christ's teaching must, it is argued, be superhuman, from the fact that to this day it has never been surpassed or approached, and never will be in the most remote future. It is agreed that all the great changes and improvements that have been made in public and private morals, between pagan and modern times, must

be set down to the vivifying effects of Christianity, which
has raised woman, struck the fetters from the limbs of the
slave, moralized war, conquest and commerce, in short,
done every good thing that has been done in the last sixteen
or eighteen centuries. This is that moral evidence for
Christianity which is far more convincing than the evidence
derived from works of power. Not that the latter is to be
slighted or ignored; but one speaks to the heart, and must
abide valid and persuasive through all time; the other
addresses the head, and perhaps may not always be equally
cogent.

Now it will not be necessary for the purpose of this
inquiry to dispute the claims thus advanced. Many of
them indeed are obviously without foundation, as the raising
of the status of women, and the liberation of the slave.
But, for the sake of argument, and to avoid complicated
side issues, let them be granted; and even then we maintain that it can be *proved* that Christianity is not favourable
to morality in the way and degree commonly supposed.
And by morality is meant right conduct here on earth;
those outward acts and inward sentiments, which, by the
suppression of the selfish passions, conduce most to the
public and private well-being of the race.

Paley, with that clear, but at times somewhat cynical,
common sense which marked his acute intellect, is willing
to admit that " the teaching of morality was not the primary
design" of the gospeL "If I were to describe," he goes
on to say, "in a very few words, the scope of Christianity,
as a *revelation*, I should say, that it was to influence the
conduct of human life, by establishing the proof of a future
state of reward and punishment,—' to bring life and immortality to light.' The direct object, therefore, of the design
is, to supply motives, and not rules; sanctions, and not

precepts. And these were what mankind stood most in need of. The members of civilized society can, in all ordinary cases, judge tolerably well how they ought to act: but without a future state, or, which is the same thing, without credited evidence of that state, they want a *motive* to their duty; they want, at least, strength of motive, sufficient to bear up against the force of passion, and the temptation of present advantage. Their rules want authority. The most important service that can be rendered to human life, and that, consequently, which, one might expect before-hand would be the great end and office of a revelation from God, is to convey to the world authorized assurances of the reality of a future existence. And although doing this, or by the ministry of the same person by whom this is done, moral precepts or examples, or illustrations of moral precepts, may be occasionally given, and be highly valuable, yet still they do not form the original purpose of the mission." * In other words, the purpose of the mission was to make men fit for a future state of reward, and to supply sanctions which would deter them from conduct which would make them fit for a future state of punishment. Salvation in the next world is the object of the scheme, not morality in this; and although the two objects may occasionally coincide, it is only a casual coincidence. Such difference of ends must lead to a difference of means. The road which is intended to lead to happiness in heaven, must diverge from the road which is intended to lead to happiness limited to this earth. And if anybody says that he does not see the necessity of such divergence, that happiness in heaven may well be only a prolongation of happiness on earth, he may be asked to reflect on the inevitable dwarfing and subordination of this life, a transi-

* " Evidences of Christianity," Part ii. cap. 2.

tory space of a few years, to a prospect of eternal life in heaven. Clearly, if this life is only a short, probationary trial-scene, preparatory to entrance upon eternity ; if, moreover, conduct here is supposed to influence or decide our status there, happiness in this life is not a thing to be considered by prudent and thoughtful persons ; and the conduct which conduces to happiness, either in ourselves or others, here, is evidently a trivial matter compared to the conduct which conduces to happiness hereafter. An eternal future must, in minds capable of even remotely realizing such an idea, overwhelm and crush into insignificance a minute, temporal present. Even a long temporal future suffices to do this. The inconveniences, for instance, of a sea-voyage which is going to land us in an abiding home in the Colonies or India, are born with comparative equanimity or indifference, on the ground that they will soon be over, that it does not very much matter, as the real object is not to live happily at sea, but to prepare for happiness and prosperity in the distant land for which we are bound. A colonist does not prepare the outfit of a seaman, does not look upon the ship which carries him as his permanent dwelling-place. He no doubt secures what comfort he can at sea ; but, if he is a wise man, his meditations are directed to his future life on land beyond the ocean. It would be very questionable prudence in him to learn seamanship or navigation, to study charts, and make himself master of the position of shoals and rocks. He would say that such matters concerned persons who intended to pass their working lives on the sea, whereas he had wholly different objects in view ; the soil, the climate, and the crops proper to the country he intended to inhabit, were the things that concerned him. The parallel only fails in the inadequacy of the analogy between the longest life in a colony, and eternal life in heaven. If life is only a short voyage, destined to terminate in paradise or hell, what thoughtful person could care how he passed it? If, moreover, he were told on good authority, or such as he considered transcendently good, as being divine, that happiness during this life's voyage was more than likely to risk eternal happiness hereafter, his indifference to happiness here, would probably become enmity to it. He would lend but a careless ear to those who urged him to study the conditions and follow the conduct, often painful and irksome, which conduced most to earthly happiness. He would say, as good Christians have always said, "That is not the one thing needful. What do I care for happiness in this vale of tears? My thoughts are naturally engrossed with the means of securing eternal happiness in the world which is to come." And the reply would be dictated by prudence and common sense. How it happens that, as a matter of fact, so few persons, who yet believe, or say they do, in the future state of reward and punishment referred to by Paley, by the admission of all preachers, take this serious view of their position and duties, is a matter of interesting inquiry, but one which does not concern us at this moment.

If these arguments are sound, and I scarcely apprehend that they will be disputed, it follows that on *à priori* grounds we should be justified in concluding that morality would be waived as an end, in comparison with salvation, among the most devout Christians. And this is what we find does happen. It happens also in all churches and sects, showing that it is not an accidental but an essential characteristic of the Christian scheme. But this is a very inadequate statement of the case as it really stands. It is not going too far to say, that the doctrine of all Christians in the final result is antinomian and positively immoral.

They do not only not support and strengthen morality as they claim to do; they deliberately reject and scorn it. They place on a level the most virtuous and the most flagitious conduct, carried on throughout a long lifetime; and this certainly must be held to be putting as great an affront on morality as it is possible to inflict.

As these assertions may be regarded as savouring of paradox, I proceed not to give more or less plausible reasons for accepting them as true, but to *prove* them, and that by the most authoritative utterances of representative Christian doctors.

It is admitted by all Christians that man is saved only through the merits and passion of Christ. But difficulties arise concerning the true doctrine of justification. The Protestants, speaking generally, hold that a man is justified by *faith alone.* The Catholics hold that co-operation with grace is needed on the part of man, to ensure salvation. It will not be necessary to enter the labyrinth of subtle disputations which have surrounded this question from the days of the Reformation. To the impartial spectator it would appear that the Catholic view is the more rational, and the Protestant the more scriptural. But this domestic quarrel among theologians does not concern us at this moment, inasmuch as all Christian doctors agree that true repentance and turning to God, however these may be brought about, are rewarded by salvation. Past sins, nay, a whole life of sin, if repented of before death, are a far less obstacle to entrance into paradise, than the most exemplary and virtuous life, if unaccompanied by true faith in Christ. And this, surely, is to discountenance morality in the most direct way, making it the "filthy rags" of which the Calvinists have so much to say. That this is the genuine doctrine of all Christians I proceed to show by a few quotations. The Established Church may well come first with the eighteenth article of her creed. " They also are to be had accursed that presume to say, That every man shall be saved by the Law or Sect which he professeth, so that he be diligent to frame his life according to that Law, and the light of Nature. For holy Scripture doth set out unto us only the Name of Jesus Christ, whereby men must be saved."

True faith and repentance at the last moment, even *in articulo mortis,* are sufficient to blot out a life of sin. " There never was a doubt in the Church," says Dr. Pusey, " that all who die in a state of grace, although one minute before they were not in a state of grace, are saved. . . . We know not what God may do in one agony of loving penitence for one who accepts his last grace in that almost sacrament of death." *   Thus penitence is everything and morality nothing.   Years of sin which may, which are sure to have caused widespread moral evils, to have been a source of corruption and leading astray to the weak and ignorant, are all obliterated by one moment of loving penitence; that is, they are obliterated as regards their effects on the sinner's status in the next world.   He is washed in the blood of the Lamb, and goes to glory.   But the partners and companions of his sins, whom he probably seduced, the women he ruined, the youths his example depraved, they survive and will be punished, unless indeed they follow his example to the letter, and close a life of wickedness by an act of timely repentance; and in that case, like him, they will be as well off as if they had led the most virtuous of lives.   Can any one presume to say that such doctrine encourages morality?   What could discourage it more ?

* " What is of Faith as to Everlasting Punishment," p. 115.

The Article just quoted, and the words of Dr. Pusey, may be allowed to stand warrant for the English Church in this particular. Now, let us turn to the Catholic Church. And we will take as her representative an illustrious Saint and Doctor, whose works have received the approbation of his superiors, St. Alphonso de' Liguori. In the first chapter of a book called "The Glories of Mary," it is written : "We read in the life of Sister Catherine, of St. Augustine, that in the place where she resided, there was a woman, of the name of Mary, who in her youth was a sinner, and in her old age continued so obstinate in wickedness, that she was driven out of the city, and reduced to live in a secluded cave; there she died, half consumed by disease, and without the sacraments, and was consequently interred in a field like a beast. Sister Catherine, who always recommended the souls of those who departed from this world, with great fervour, to God, on hearing the unfortunate end of this poor old woman, never thought of praying for her, and she looked upon her, as did every one else, as irrevocably lost. One day, four years afterwards, a suffering soul appeared to her, and exclaimed, 'How unfortunate is my lot, sister Catherine ! Thou recommendest the souls of all those that die, to God; on my soul alone thou hast not compassion ?' 'And who art thou ?' asked the servant of God. 'I am,' she replied, 'that poor Mary, who died in the cave.' 'And art thou saved ?' said Catherine. 'Yes,' she answered, 'by the mercy of the Blessed Virgin Mary.' 'And how ?' 'When I saw myself at the point of death, loaded with sins, and abandoned by all, I had recourse to the Mother of God, saying, "Lady, thou art the refuge of abandoned creatures : behold me at this moment, abandoned by all; thou art my only hope; thou alone canst help me; have pity on me." The Blessed

Virgin obtained me the grace to make an act of contrition. I died, and am saved; and besides this, she, my Queen, obtained that my purgatory should be shortened, by enduring, in intensity, that which otherwise would have lasted for many years. I now only want a few masses to be entirely delivered; I beg thee to get them said, and on my part, I promise always to pray for thee to God and to Mary.' Sister Catherine immediately had the masses said; and after a few days that soul again appeared to her, shining like the sun, and said, 'I thank thee, Catherine: behold, I go to Paradise, to sing the mercies of my God, and to pray for thee.'" *

Nothing can be more plain. A life from youth to old age continued in "obstinate wickedness," is cancelled by an act of contrition, and, after a short purgatorial purification, the sinner appears "shining like the sun." Could a life of blameless self-denial and virtue have led to a better result? The book I quote is full of such stories. Here is another :—

"Belluacensis relates, that in an English city, about the year 1430, there was a young nobleman, called Ernest, who, having distributed the whole of his patrimony to the poor, became a monk, and in the monastery to which he retired led so perfect a life, that he was highly esteemed by his superiors, and this esteem was greatly increased by their knowledge of his tender devotion to the most Blessed Virgin. It happened that the city was attacked by the plague, and the inhabitants had recourse to the monastery, in order that the religious might help them by their prayers. The abbot commanded Ernest to go and pray before the

* "The Glories of Mary," translated from the Italian of St. Alphonso de' Liguori, founder of the Congregation of the Most Holy Redeemer. By a father of the same congregation. Page 19. London, 1852.

altar of Mary, forbidding him to leave it until he should have received an answer from our Blessed Lady. The young man, after remaining three days in prayer, received an answer from Mary to the effect, that certain prayers were to be said : this was done, and the plague ceased. After a time Ernest cooled in his devotion towards Mary : the devil attacked him with many temptations, and particularly with those against purity, and also to leave his monastery. From not having recommended himself to Mary, he unfortunately yielded to the temptation, and resolved to escape by climbing over a wall. Passing before an image of Mary which was in the corridor, the Mother of God addressed him, saying, ‘My son, why dost thou leave me ?’ Ernest, thunderstruck and repentant, sunk to the ground, and replied, ‘But, Lady, dost thou not see that I can no longer resist ; why dost thou not assist me ?’ ‘And why hast thou not invoked me ?’ said our Blessed Lady. ‘ If thou hadst recommended thyself to me, thou wouldst not have fallen so low ; but from henceforth do so and fear nothing.’ Ernest returned to his cell, his temptations recommenced, again he neglected to recommend himself to Mary, and at last fled from his monastery. He then gave himself up to a most wicked life, fell from one sin into another, and at length became an assassin ; for, having hired an inn, during the night he used to murder the poor travellers who slept there. Amongst others, he one night killed the cousin of the governor of the place. For this crime he was tried and sentenced to death. It so happened that before he was made a prisoner, and whilst evidence was being collected, a young nobleman arrived at the inn. The wicked Ernest, as usual, determined to murder him, and entered the room at night for this purpose ; but lo ! instead of finding the young man, he beheld a crucifix on the bed, all covered with wounds. The image cast a look of compassion on him, and exclaimed, 'Ungrateful wretch! is it not enough that I have died once for thee? Wilt thou again take my life? Be it so. Raise thy hand, strike!' Filled with confusion, poor Ernest began to weep, and sobbing, said, 'Behold me, Lord; since thou shewest me such mercy, I will return to thee.' Immediately he left the inn, to return to his monastery, there to do penance for his crimes; but on the road he was taken by the ministers of justice, was led before the judge, and acknowledged all the murders he had committed. He was sentenced to be hung, without having the time given him to go to confession. He recommended himself to Mary, and was thrown from the ladder; but the Blessed Virgin preserved his life, and she herself loosened the rope, and then addressed him, saying, 'Go, return to thy monastery, do penance, and when thou seest a paper in my hands, announcing the pardon of thy sins, prepare for death.' Ernest returned, related all to his abbot, and did great penance. After many years, he saw the paper in the hands of Mary, which announced his pardon; he immediately prepared for death, and in a most holy manner breathed forth his souL" *

It is quite clear that an ardent zeal to save souls is compatible with great indifference as to bodies. One would like to know what became of the poor travellers whom the ruffian Ernest murdered in their sleep. Was time granted them to make an act of contrition? But it is absurd to take such a narrative *au serieux.* What is serious is the unmistakable character of the teaching implied. And can anything be imagined more cynically immoral? Here is a man represented as falling into the most abominable anti-social crime which it is possible to commit. The wretch

* "The Glories of Mary," p. 48.

deserved a hundred deaths for his dastardly midnight murders; conduct more injurious than his to society simply cannot be conceived. Yet he is not only saved from the gallows by the Mother of God herself, but his life is prolonged in order that he may have time to repent and to get his precious soul taken to heaven, a place which, by the way, if it contain many such characters as he, would offer very unpleasant company to moral men.

And let no one reject with impatience the above specimens of Christian teaching on the ground that they are not Christian at all, but abject popish superstitions and inventions. Our next witness to prove that in this matter all Christians agree in vilipending a moral life and conduct, and placing it below a life of crime, provided the latter be terminated by an act of repentance and turning to God in time to cheat the devil, shall be the Rev. C. H. Spurgeon, who will not be suspected of any leaning to Romish error. This is what he says :—

"Regeneration is an instantaneous work, and justification an instantaneous gift. Man fell in a moment. . . . Shall the devil destroy us in a moment, and Jesus be unable to save us in a moment?"* Again, "My dear hearer, whoever thou mayst be, whatever thy past life may have been, if thou wilt trust Christ, thou shalt be saved from all thy sin in a moment; the whole of thy past life shall be blotted out; there shall not remain in God's book so much as a single charge against thy soul, for Christ, who died for thee, shall take thy guilt away, and leave thee without a blot before the face of God." Again, "Ah! my friend, let me assure you . . . that there is hope for the vilest through the precious blood of Jesus. No man can

* "Jesus at Bethesda;" a sermon delivered by C. H. Spurgeon, April 7, 1867.

have gone too far for the long arm of Christ to reach him. Christ delights to save the biggest sinners. . . . O ye despairing sinners, there is no·room for despair this side the gates of hell. If you have gone through the foulest kennels of iniquity, no stain can stand out against the power of the cleansing blood. . . . You great sinners shall have no back seats in heaven ! There shall be no outer court for you. You great sinners shall have as much love as the best, as much joy as the brightest of saints. You shall be near to Christ ; you shall sit with him upon his throne ; you shall wear the crown ; your fingers shall touch the golden harps ; you shall rejoice with the joy which is unspeakable and full of glory. . . . Thirty years of sin shall be forgiven, and it shall not take thirty minutes to do it in. Fifty, sixty, seventy years of iniquity shall all disappear as the morning's hoar-frost disappears before the sun." *

Two things are to be remarked in connection with these quotations : first, that we have here a singular agreement on one particular point, among divines who usually are in complete antagonism. Dr. Pusey, St. Alfonso de' Liguori, and Mr. Spurgeon, may be regarded as representatives of opinions as widely divergent as could well be found among men calling themselves Christians. Yet they agree in the opinion, that no amount or duration of sin can be accounted as a bar to salvation, provided a suitable act of repentance or contrition has been performed on " this side of the gates of hell." They differ at once, if you ask for details as to how the act of contrition or repentance is to be carried out. Mr. Spurgeon bids the sinner turn to Jesus. St. Alfonso tells him to have recourse to the Mother of God ; the mere words of which precept the great Baptist minister would

---

* " A Sermon to Open Neglecters and Nominal Followers of Religion ;" March 24, 1867.

probably regard as savouring of blasphemy. But the result is the same. A long life devoted to sin can be blotted out in a moment by a change in the sinner's mind. Secondly, this result has exclusive reference to the next world. By the hypothesis in each case, the life in this world is supposed to be as good as over; and it has been a life of iniquity, says Mr. Spurgeon, of obstinacy in wickedness, says St. Alfonso. But paradise is attained, nevertheless. Now, can this doctrine be regarded as one leading to morality in this world? Must it not, rather, have a directly opposite effect? As many as believe it, and how many millions have, are invited, nay, entreated to believe also that it makes absolutely no difference as to their future welfare whether they lead virtuous lives here below, or the most profligate; provided they repent a moment before death. Preachers may insist as they will on the dangers of deferring repentance to the last, on the awful results which will follow if the sinner is suddenly cut off, without having had time to make his peace with God. One part of their teaching destroys the effect of the other part. They admit, they proclaim that repentance, however late, will take the sinner to heaven. Human nature being as it is, we cannot wonder that the result in this world is varied, and on the whole very unsatisfactory. The minute minority of naturally pious and tender minds embrace the cross with passion and ardent love, not unmixed with holy fear; they realize fully that they stand in jeopardy every hour; they work out their salvation in fear and trembling, and not unfrequently are exposed to a strain too severe for their faculties, and they become, like Pascal, morbidly anxious about their future state, or, like Cowper, they pass the limits of sanity, and fall for a longer or shorter time into utter despair. But these are the small minority of *âmes d'élite.* The bulk of mankind are commonplace all round, in their virtues and vices equally; and they languidly believe and languidly practice their belief; but so imperfectly and perfunctorily, that it is the universal complaint and lamentation of preachers of all denominations, that the world lieth in wickedness and is dead in its sins. Nothing could be more frank and candid than Mr. Spurgeon's language to his congregation on this head: "You sin, and yet you come to a place of worship, and tremble under the word; you transgress, and you weep and transgress again. . . . You are as religious as the seats you sit upon, but no more; and you are as likely to get to heaven as those seats are, but not one whit more, for you are dead in sin, and death cannot enter heaven." * Bourdaloue, the greatest preacher in the classic age of French pulpit eloquence, said: "Nous sommes Chrétiens, et nous vivons en païens; nous avons une foi de spéculation, et dans la pratique toute notre conduite n'est qu'infidélité. Nous croyons d'une façon, et nous agissons de l'autre. . . . Avoir la foi, et vivre en infidèles, voilà ce qui fait le prodige. . . . Ah! Chrétiens, faisons cesser ce prodige, accordons nous avec nous-mêmes; accordons nos mœurs avec notre foi; autrement que n'avons-nous pas à craindre de cette foi profanée, de cette foi scandalisée, de cette foi déshonorée?" †

Again, he says: "N'entend on pas dire sans cesse que tout est renversé dans le monde, que le déréglement y est général; qu'il n'y a ni âge, ni sexe, ni état, qui en soit exempt; qu'on ne trouve presque nulle part ni religion, ni crainte de Dieu, ni probité, ni droiture, ni bonne foi, ni justice, ni charité, ni honnêteté, ni pudeur; que ce n'est partout, ou presque partout, que libertinage, que disso-

* "A Sermon to Open Neglecters," etc.
† "Sermon sur la Religion Chrétienne."

lution, que mensonges, que tromperies, qu'envie de s'aggran
dir et de dominer, qu'avarice, qu'usure, que concussions,
que médisances, qu'un monstrueux assemblage de toutes
les iniquités." *

"The title of Christian," says Wilberforce, "implies no
more than a sort of formal general assent to Christianity in
the gross, and a degree of morality in practice, little, if at
all, superior to that for which we look in a good Deist,
Mussulman, or Hindoo." †

It seems difficult to reconcile these candid admissions by
eminent authorities with the current claim made for Christianity as a supremely moralizing influence. But we can
hardly be wrong in tracing the general failure of preachers
to arouse their flocks to the fact, already dwelt on, that
they undo with one hand what they do with the other ;
that, anxious above all things to save souls in the next
world, and making that infinitely the most important object,
they one and all present the doctrine of Justification,
though varying much from one another in minor points, in
a form which necessarily depreciates the value of morality
in this world. With one voice they tell men that all they
do is evil and wicked, and that there is no health in them.
They dwell with exaggerated language on the sinfulness of
sin, and the extent and vileness of human corruption.
But, except in a few special cases of unusually sensitive
natures, they do not awaken the prick of conscience ; men
feeling in a dumb, inarticulate way, that their tone is unreal
and conventional, or even merely professional. Even when
they do alarm the conscience, they as promptly send it to
sleep again by their doctrine that a moment's repentance
can put everything straight, and that one plunge in the

---

* "Opuscules : Petit Nombre des Élus."
† "Practical View," cap. iv.

blood of the Lamb will remove all the guilty stains from a sinner's soul. Mr. Spurgeon, in the sermon from which I have already quoted some passages, avows this very openly. "It is the easiest thing," he says, "in the world to impress some of you by a sermon, but I fear me you never will go beyond transient impressions. Like the water when lashed, the wound soon heals. You know, and you know, and you know, and you feel, and feel, and feel again, and yet your sins, your self-righteousness, your carelessness and wilful wickedness cause you, after having said, ' I go, sir,' to forget the promise and lie unto God." But the eloquent preacher had apparently forgotten what he had himself said on the previous page, or at least he had not sufficiently weighed the natural effect of his words. " Thirty years of sin shall be forgiven, and it shall not take thirty minutes to do it in." It is no wonder if men and women, with hearts and minds made dull and heavy with toil and trouble, should remember more easily and pleasantly the consolation conveyed in the last remark than the objurgation of the previous one ; and should dwell more on the efficacy of repentance when once set about, than on its immediate need and urgency. Consequently, we find that it is the most scrupulous and tender consciences which have most difficulty in embracing the great Protestant dogma of justification by faith alone. " The essence of Luther's gospel is this : that a person so affected, that is, with scruples of conscience, has only one great struggle to go through in order that he may attain the indefectible promise of eternal salvation, and that the struggle is not against those sins, but against his own conscience, which would fain impede his full assurance of immediate pardon." *
The records of execution show, on the other hand, that

* Ward, " Ideal of a Christian Church :" second edition, p. 171.

malefactors of the deepest dye have often little or no difficulty in turning to Jesus when circumstances compel it.   This is acknowledged by the *Christian Observer:* *
" Thousands of deeply penitent and humble-minded persons have lived many years, and perhaps died in a state of deep depression, because they could not attain to that confident assurance that their sins were pardoned, which they were told was essential to salvation ; while murderers have gone to the gibbet, exulting in strains of rapture, as though they were being carried to the stake as faithful martyrs of Jesus Christ."

But the most momentous authority for holding a life of wickedness on earth immaterial, and no impediment to the promptest ascent into heaven, provided an act of contrition has been performed in time, has yet to be cited.   It is that of Christ himself as he hung upon the cross.   "And one of the malefactors which were hanged railed on him, saying, If thou be Christ, save thyself and us.   But the other answering rebuked him, saying, Dost not thou fear God, seeing thou art in the same condemnation ?   And we indeed justly ; for we receive the due reward of our deeds : but this man hath done nothing amiss.   And he said unto Jesus, Lord, remember me when thou comest into thy kingdom.   And Jesus said unto him, Verily I say unto thee, To day shalt thou be with me in paradise." †

This is almost exactly parallel with the case cited by St. Alphonso of the woman "who was a sinner."   Though it is not mentioned in the gospel, we may suppose and grant that the penitent thief made a due act of contrition ; that Christ was able to see to the bottom of his heart, and that he truly repented him of his sins.   Does that in the least

* Jan., 1844, p. 16.   † Luke xxiii. 39–43.

remove the slight which Christ passed upon morality by taking him to paradise in spite of his past evil life? What did his repentance do to cancel that? The evil that he had done in the world was still left working behind him; his bad example; the insecurity to person and property involved in his robber's career; the pain and suffering he had caused in any case: all his immorality, in short, was left to work on, and contributed, no doubt, its share to that frightful depravity of the Jewish nation which made them at last insupportable to the Roman world. Yet, was he punished or made to do penance, to make amends to the society he had injured? The human law did indeed give him his deserts, by hanging him as a thief and probably a murderer, and so far morality was avenged. A powerful deterrent was applied, not unlikely to prevent others from doing likewise. But Christ undid all the effect of that salutary severity in a moment, when he promised him immediate salvation, and for what? For deferential speech to himself, which the hypothesis that Christ saw to the bottom of his heart will not allow us to regard as a piece of artful time-serving, suggested as politic in his desperate circumstances; but which, without that hypothesis, would undoubtedly be open to such a suspicion. Thus preachers have the very highest authority for asserting that turning to God, even at the last moment, will save a soul in the next world, the admitted object of Christianity; and agnostics have equally a right to declare that Christianity thereby shows itself hostile to morality in this world. The penitent thief's life, we may assume, was a pernicious one as far as this world was concerned. What good could his repentance do to any denizen of this earth? If it be said that it might lead others to repent after a life of crime, the answer is, that in proportion as they resembled him they also would be qualifying for heaven, and not for well-doing in this world. Man may injure his fellows in their most vital interests ; he may rob, murder, " go through the foulest kennels of iniquity ; " there shall not remain in God's book a single charge against his soul, provided he looks to the bleeding Lamb. On the other hand, the best of good works are of no account, are worse than "filthy rags," and no doubt have the nature of sin "unless they be consummated in real vital communion with Christ." It would not be easy to conceive a doctrine more injurious to morality than this Christian scheme, on which the morality of the world, as on the surest foundation, is supposed to rest.

Indeed this inherent opposition between morality and the gospel has been held by large sections of Christians as an article of faith. " Luther," says Moehler, " not only taught that Christ had not come to impart to men a purer ethical code, but even maintained that he had come to *abolish* the moral law, to liberate true believers from its curse both for the past and for the future, and in that way to make them free. The evangelical liberty which Luther propounded, announces that even the decalogue shall not be brought into account against the believer, nor its violation be allowed to disturb the conscience of the Christian, for he is exalted above it and its contents." Moehler goes on to say that the reformers refer to Christ not as the strengthener and sanctifier, but exclusively as the forgiver of sins ; ."..they regarded the mediator only in his capacity of pardoner." The great Catholic divine is at pains to show the superior moral tone of his communion in this respect. But the extracts just cited from St. Alphonso de' Liguori prove that the Catholic Church has no advantage over the Protestant on this point. The Virgin takes the place of Christ as a free pardoner of the grossest sins, in consideration of an act of contrition and genuine repentance.

To the above considerations, it may be added that the doctrine of grace is presented in a way to become a standing rebuke and depreciator of morality. "Humility," says Canon Liddon, "is the condition and guarantee of grace ; and, as St. Augustine says, there is no reason, apart from the grace of God, why the highest saints should not be the worst of criminals." * In that statement I suppose all theologians would concur. But it is easy to see how fatal such a doctrine is to a systematic culture of morality. If, at any moment, the best men may become the worst, and *vice versâ,* as they may be touched by grace or not, it is obvious that morality is a figment of the fancy, having no substantial existence or foundation in the nature of things. The difference is not between good and bad men, whose goodness and badness depends on their moral endowment *plus* the training they receive, but between the recipients of grace and the non-recipients ; and these are interchangeable according to the good pleasure of God. We can never tell, therefore, whether the greatest sinner now, may not become the greatest saint before his end ; nor whether the best of men may not suddenly become prodigies of wickedness. This unknown factor of Grace vitiates all calculation. No doctrine more inconsistent with the facts of human nature can well be conceived, and therefore no more misleading guide of conduct could be adopted. Imagine such a theory applied to agriculture, and that there was no reason, apart from the grace of God, why the most fertile soil should not become the most barren, or the reverse. If such were the case, what inducement would a farmer have to choose good land, and cultivate it with care ? The

* "Oxford Sermons ;" VI.

worst land might serve him as well as the best, and bring him overflowing crops ; and that with no effort on his part, for "God giveth the increase." He has only to wait or pray for fertilizing grace. Or apply it to the raising of horses or cattle. The grazier or breeder cannot trust to the qualities of his stock. His thoroughbreds may suddenly become valueless animals, which no one would take at a gift ; while his neighbour, who had nothing but screws and low-breeds, has all at once a magnificent collection of superb cattle. Men differ at least as much as animals in their inherited qualities ; and to say that a man naturally courageous, high-minded, benevolent, and just, can become vile and cruel, cowardly or criminal, is not a whit less irrational than to say that a thoroughbred Arab can become a cart-horse. The faulty theory leads, as a matter of course, to disastrous practice. It is no exaggeration to say that the vigilant, painstaking cultivation of the moral side of man's nature has never been taken in hand with earnest persistence, because theology has always been celebrating the power of grace, to the depreciation of ethics. A miracle of grace, which removes the heart of stone and replaces it by a heart of flesh, might always be expected, or at least hoped for. Punctual performance of the moral law, social duty to the community and individuals, could well be postponed without harm, in view of the celestial transfiguration which converts a sinner from a bond-slave of Satan into a saint of God. If this conversion takes place in the last hour or minute of life, we have seen that by the unanimous consent of theologians of all schools, it is enough ; the object has been attained ; a soul has been saved ; the sinner's past wickedness has been blotted out, *as regards its effects upon him.* But its effects on society are not considered, and the result must be, and is, solely injurious to morality so far as it relates to conduct in this world. That depends on the performance of social duty ; salvation depends on repentance and the subjective attitude of the soul towards God. And this repentance is powerful to cancel any number of previous breaches of the moral law. In other words, morality is *not* the one thing needful. but repentance *is*.

CHAPTER VI.

MORALITY IN THE AGES OF FAITH.

In the previous chapter we saw on the best evidence, that
of eminent doctors in various denominations, that true
Christian doctrine postponed morality to repentance ; and
that salvation in the next world depended on other things
than good conduct in this. The obvious inference was,
that under such a scheme morality must necessarily be
more or less slighted and undervalued, and that the alleged
support afforded to ethics by the Christian religion must be
either denied or considerably diminished. It will be perhaps useful to confirm this abstract deduction, by examples
taken from the past of the actual working of Christian
doctrine. If only a tithe of the compliments which it is
usual to pay that doctrine be true, it is clear that the more we
retrograde into the ages where it held undisputed sway over
men's minds, the more moral we ought to find the public
and private life of the world. Wickedness and crime are
assumed to be the natural result of neglected religion. No
other cause is usually thought of in explaining the atrocities
of the French Revolution. Here we see, it is remarked,
the proper effect of atheism, and forsaking of the divine
light of the gospel. Again, the corruption and immorality
of the lower Roman Empire show what becomes of man
when left to himself. The line of argument is too familiar
to need further repetition of it. Now, we may profitably

consult history as to the truth of these assumptions. Do we find, as a matter of fact, that the Ages of Faith were distinguished by a high morality? Were they superior in this respect to the present age, which is nearly on all hands acknowledged not to be an age of Faith? The answer must be in the negative. Taking them broadly, the Ages of Faith were emphatically ages of crime, of gross and scandalous wickedness, of cruelty, and, in a word, of immorality. And it is noteworthy that in proportion as we recede backward from the present age, and return into the Ages of Faith, we find that the crime and the sin become denser and blacker. The temperature of faith rises steadily as we penetrate into the past, almost with the regularity which marks the rise of the physical temperature of the air as we descend into a deep mine; but a neglect and defiance of morality are found to ascend in a corresponding ratio. This, it must be owned, is an anomalous result, if morality be indeed so dependent on Christianity as is commonly supposed. When all men believed and doubted not, we should have found, according to the Christian hypothesis, a godly world; devout people living always with the great Day of Judgment before their eyes, crushing down the lusts of the flesh, in view of the tremendous penalties prepared for those who indulged them. But we find nothing of the kind. On the contrary, we find a state of things to which our imaginations are scarcely able to do justice in these comparatively tame and moral days. A progressive improvement has taken place in men's conduct, both public and private, but it has coincided not with an increase, but with a decay, of faith. This, beyond any question, is the most moral age which the world has seen; and it is as certainly the least believing age since Christianity became the religion of the West. The inference is plain, that Christianity has not been so favourable to morality as is usually assumed.

Let us turn back, and take a brief excursion through the ages behind us.

The present century need not detain us long. Most persons would admit that the state of morals when George the Fourth was king left much to be desired. The scandals of the court were bad enough; but no court, however bad, can compromise a nation. The mass of the population was coarse, insolent, and cruel, and permitted things which would not be tolerated for a moment now. That there were exceptions, not only of individuals, but of whole though small classes, no one would deny. The Clapham Sect was a conspicuous example in a corrupt world; and many of the dissenters were truly pious, God-fearing people, who had turned away from the prevailing grossness. But these were only fractions of the nation. The general tone was low, violent, and brutal. The drinking, gambling, prize-fighting, cock-fighting, bull-baiting England of the Regency, is hardly to be realized in these decorous days; though old men "still creep among us," who can partly resuscitate it for us, if carefully questioned. Let one of those venerable seniors be induced to describe the condition of London in his youth, and no hearer will have any doubt as to the extraordinary change for the better which has taken place in the last two generations.

From this century we pass into history; and as the object is to ascertain the *moral tone* of previous ages, let us quote the following passages from a writer, who was selected by common acclamation as "the great moralist," and was one of the most brave, noble, and conscientious men who have ever lived, Samuel Johnson.

" He talked of the heinousness of the crime of adultery,

by which the peace of families was destroyed. He said, 'Confusion of progeny constitutes the essence of the crime; and, therefore, a woman who breaks her marriage vows is much more criminal than a man who does it. A man, to be sure, is criminal in the sight of God; but he does not do his wife a very material injury, if he does not insult her; if, for instance, from mere wantonness of appetite, he steals privately to her chambermaid. Sir, a wife ought not greatly to resent this. I would not receive home a daughter who had run away from her husband on that account.'"* This was Johnson's settled opinion, as, eleven years after, we find Boswell recording another conversation, in which the same thought recurs. "I mentioned to him a dispute between a friend of mine and his lady, concerning conjugal infidelity, which my friend had maintained was by no means so bad in the husband as in the wife. JOHNSON. Your friend was in the right, Sir. Between a man and his Maker it is a different question: but between a man and his wife, a husband's infidelity is nothing. They are connected by children, by fortune, by serious considerations of community. Wise married women don't trouble themselves about infidelity in their husbands." †

Now, this is a very good instance of the improvement which has taken place in the course of the last hundred years. That very offence for which Johnson said he would not receive his daughter home, if it were committed by a husband, is now so universally admitted to be an injury of the most serious kind, that the statutory law of the land does precisely what Johnson said he would not do, give protection to the injured wife.

As we go further back in the century, we make a visible approach to the state of nature. Cowardly murders and

* Croker's "Boswell," chap 21.   † *Ibid.*, chap. 69.

brutal outrages are perpetrated almost with impunity and very little loss of credit by people of the highest rank. The exploits of the Mohocks must have rendered the streets of London in the reign of Queen Anne considerably more dangerous and disgusting than any Californian diggings frequented by the rabble and outlaws of Europe and America in the early days of the gold discoveries. A contemporary says, "There are a certain set of persons, amongst whom there are some of too great a character to be named in these barbarous and ridiculous encounters, did they not expose themselves by such mean and ridiculous exploits;" and their portrait is thus drawn by the *Spectator :*—"A set of men who have erected themselves into a nocturnal fraternity, under the title of The Mohock Club, a name borrowed, it seems, from a sort of cannibals in India, who subsist by plundering and devouring all the nations about them. The president is styled Emperor of the Mohocks, and his arms are a Turkish crescent. Agreeable to their name, the avowed design of their institution is mischief, and upon this foundation all their rules and orders are founded. An outrageous ambition of doing all possible hurt to their fellow-creatures is the great cement of their assembly, and the only qualification required in the members. In order to exert this principle in its full strength and perfection, they take care to drink themselves to a pitch that is beyond the possibility of attending to any motive of reason and humanity, then make a general sally, and attack all that are so unfortunate as to walk the streets through which they patrol. Some are knocked down, others stabbed, others cut and carbonadoed. . . . The particular talents by which these misanthropes are distinguished from one another, consist in various kinds of barbarities which they execute upon their prisoners. Some are celebrated for a happy dexterity in tipping the lion upon them, which is performed by squeezing the nose flat on the face, and boring out the eyes with their fingers. Others are called the dancing-masters, and teach their scholars to cut capers by running swords through their legs. . . . A third are the tumblers, whose office is to set women on their heads, and commit certain indecencies, or rather, barbarities, on the limbs which they expose." * Slitting noses, cutting people down the back, and putting women in tubs which were rolled down Snow Hill, were among their diversions.

The manners and customs of persons of quality were those of semi-savages. Thackeray, who knew the period well, does not go too far when he says, "You could no more suffer in a British drawing-room, under the reign of Queen Victoria, a fine gentleman or a fine lady of Queen Anne's time, or hear what they heard and said, than you would receive an ancient Briton." This is the manner in which "gentlemen" quarrelled in the good old times : Sir Cholmley Dering, knight of the shire for Kent, and Mr. Thornhill fought a duel, in which the former was killed. This caused a judicial inquiry, and "the first Evidences were such as related to the quarrel begun at the Toy at Hampton Court, April 27, 1711, who deposed that an assembly of about eighteen gentlemen met there at that time, a difference happened between the deceased and the prisoner. Upon their struggling and contending with each other, the wainscot of the room broke in, and Mr. Thornhill falling down, had some teeth struck out by Sir Cholmley Dering's stamping upon him." † Naturally a duel followed. "They fought," says Swift, "at sword and pistol this morning in Tuttlefields, their pistols so near that the muzzles

---

* *Spectator*, No. 324.
† Ashton, " Social Life in the Reign of Queen Anne," ch. 38.

touched. Thornhill discharged first, and Dering, having received the shot, discharged his pistol as he was falling, so it went into the air." Thornhill was convicted for manslaughter, but he was apparently soon abroad again, as he was murdered by two men, who stabbed him on horseback, five months afterwards, at Turnham Green.

The well-known case of the murder of Will Mountford, the actor, by Lord Mohun and Captain Hill, in a ruffianly ambuscade, would seem well suited to show the profligate temper and degraded public opinion in the reign of William the Third. The incident is thus related by Thackeray :—

"My lord's friend, a Captain Hill, smitten with the charms of the beautiful Mrs. Bracegirdle, and anxious to marry her at all hazards, determined to carry her off, and for this purpose hired a hackney coach with six horses and half a dozen soldiers to aid him in the storm. The coach with a pair of horses (the four leaders being in waiting elsewhere) took its station opposite my Lord Craven's house in Drury Lane, by which door Mrs. Bracegirdle was to pass on her way from the theatre. As she passed, in company of her mamma and a friend Mr. Page, the captain seized her by the hand, the soldiers hustled Mr. Page and attacked him sword in hand, and Captain Hill and his noble friend endeavoured to force Madam Bracegirdle into the coach. Mr. Page called for help ; the population of Drury Lane rose ; it was impossible to effect the capture, and, bidding the soldiers go about their business, and the coach to drive off, Hill let go his prey sulkily, and he waited for other opportunities of revenge. The man of whom he was most jealous was Will Mountford, the comedian. Will removed, he thought Mrs. Bracegirdle might be his ; and accordingly the captain and his lordship lay that night in wait for Will, and as he was coming out of a house in Norfolk Street, while Mohun engaged him in talk, Hill, in the words of the Attorney-general, made a pass and run him clean through the body." *

Mohun was tried for the murder by his peers of the upper house, and acquitted by sixty-nine votes against four-teen. "One great nobleman," says Macaulay, "was so brutal and stupid as to say, After all, the fellow was but a player, and players are rogues." † This on the first blush seems downright atrocious. But there are slightly extenu-ating circumstances connected with the case which make it a degree less horrible. In the first place, the murder and the judgment, as Macaulay points out, were generally con-demned by public opinion. In the second place, the Lords were actuated by a violent *esprit de corps*, and defending their privileges which were being attacked by the Com-mons. That which largely neutralizes these considerations is the fact that Mohun was a popular character in London, and that the anecdotists speak very kindly of his practical jokes. In the next reign he was singled out for honourable distinction, and accompanied "Lord Macclesfield's embassy to the Elector of Hanover when Queen Anne sent the Garter to H.E. Highness."

Were the men of that generation infidels, despisers of God's Holy Word, and demoralized by a dreary disbelief in the unseen world ? On the contrary, they were fanatically religious. Their zeal about spiritual matters was fervid in the extreme. A hint that the Church was in danger filled them with gloomy passion. As soon as Sacheverell's trial began "it took up all men's thoughts, so that other business was at a stand. It was clear from the very outset of the trial, that the popular favour was wholly on the doctor's

* "Lectures on the Humourists."
† Macaulay's "History of England."

side. He lodged in the Temple, and came every day in solemn procession through the Strand to Westminster Hall. As he passed, great crowds gathered round his coach, striving to kiss his hand and shouting, 'Sacheverell and the Church for ever!' Those who would not join in the shouts were often insulted or knocked down. The ardour of the multitude was even less justifiably shown by their attacks on some meeting-houses, in which the pews were demolished and burned."* The connection between Christianity and morality does not seem very plain here.

If we now cross the Channel and examine the condition of morals under the Old Monarchy of France, we shall find that the record of Catholicism in this respect is in no wise purer than that of the rival communion. It is a common opinion that the very great licence of manners which distinguished the French upper classes in the latter part of the eighteenth century, was one of the many evil results of the prevalent infidelity propagated by Rousseau, Diderot, and Voltaire. But such an idea has no foundation. Corrupt as was the society which read the novels of Louvet and the younger Crébillon, it was in a variety of ways superior to the society to which Bossuet and Bourdaloue preached, and which flocked to hear the sacred dramas of the spotless Racine. The whole of the reign of Louis XIV. was marked by a great depravity of manners, and this depravity was found quite compatible with an ostentatious and possibly sincere attachment to religion. The king, in spite of the gross immorality of his private life, was a bigot in matters of faith, and he was not an ungraceful or inadequate representative of the people who looked up to him as to an almost supernatural being. No stress need be laid on the laxity of the gay lords and ladies who filled his brilliant

* Lord Stanhope, "Reign of Queen Anne," chap. 12.

court, although if a firm belief in Christianity were the safe-guard of pure morals, as it is supposed to be, their lives present an unaccountable anomaly; for, as Bourdaloue said to their faces, they lived like pagans though they believed like Christians. The point of interest for us is to note how largely Christianity failed to overcome the flesh and the devil, even in an age when it had entirely its own way, was zealously supported by the State, and able to wield its tremendous sanctions without pause or hesitation. And, again, what we have to take most account of, is the average tone and temper of public opinion with regard to crime and immorality. Sporadic and exceptional crime may occur in any age, and yet cast no reflection on the average standard of morals. It is otherwise when immorality is common, if not general, and when a life of great licence and scandal may be passed without attracting discredit or remark. And this rule applies especially to the conduct of ministers of religion. If the clerical order can indulge in abandoned courses without exciting reprobation, we may be sure that we do an age no injustice in pronouncing its standard of morality to be low. When the officers of an army give an example of cowardice and insubordination, we know what to expect of the rank and file.

We have many instances during the reign of Louis XIV. which show the great corruption of the clergy in that age, and the little resentment or surprise which it caused. The lives of some of the most prominent ecclesiastics were openly scandalous. The famous Cardinal de Retz led a life of which any decent layman would now be ashamed. But it may be said that de Retz was one of those political church-men who took orders merely with ambitious views to worldly advancement, and who ought not to be considered as true clerics. He also lived in times of revolution, when men's

morality is apt to break down. So we will pass him over.
These remarks do not apply to Harley de Champvallon,
archbishop of Paris. He lived in times of profound internal
peace, he never played any part in politics, and he was for
years the acknowledged leader and representative of the
French Church. He was permanent chairman of the
Assembly of the French Clergy, and a preacher of such
popularity and power that during a course of his Lenten
sermons, the church was kept open at all hours, and foot-
men, in order to retain the best places, were forced to spend
the whole night in them. Yet he was a man of profligate
private life, and not so very private, as his amours were
notorious.

> " Notre Archevêque de Paris,
> Quoiqu'il soit jeune, a des faiblesses ;
> Voyant qu'il en avait trop pris,
> Il a retranché ses maîtresses ;
> Les quatre qu'il eut autrefois
> Sont à présent réduites à trois."

Several great ladies of the Court, la Marquise de Gonville,
la Maréchale d'Aumont, Madame de Brisseu, were among
his conquests, but Madame de Bretonvilliers was his
maîtresse en titre, as la Montespan was of Louis XIV. He
was not even content with these irregularities, but carried
off by force Mademoiselle de la Varenne, a public singer,
the mistress of a gentleman named Pierrepont. The latter
avenged himself in a way characteristic of the age ; he lay
in wait with three men, seized the faithless Varenne (who
seems to have made no objection to the exchange of a poor
for a rich lover) as she was returning to the house the archbishop had given her, and had her ummercifully beaten
with rods. It was probably his only mode of retaliation.
Meddling with Monseigneur and his pleasures was attended
with danger and punished severely. Two priests who had

lampooned him were sent to the galleys, one for life. One of the archbishop's mistresses was the Countess of Northumberland, a former favourite of Charles II. The prelate used to visit her in a convent of Benedictines at Conflans. He died suddenly at a good old age in the presence of his last "amie," la Duchesse de Lesdiguières, and had his funeral oration pronounced by le père Gaillard. It appears there was some little trouble in finding a preacher, a fact creditable to the time, as far as it goes.

The convents, not without reason, had a bad reputation. Louis XIV., who was not a man to speak evil of religious orders, said of the Carmelites, "Je savais bien qu'elles étaient des friponnes, des intrigeuses, des ravaudeuses, des brodeuses, des bouquetières, mais je ne croyais pas qu'elles fussent des empoisonneuses." * "There were often," says Michelet, "twelve parlours in a convent, in which each nun, without being heard, could converse with her lover or a female intriguer yet more dangerous." † But Protestants and infidels are only too ready to believe evil of convents as if they all must necessarily be nests of iniquity, a most unjust supposition. Port Royal at this very time contained women of angelic purity. We may therefore leave them, and pass to the lower ranks of the secular clergy.

A good example of the tone of public opinion with regard to clerical irregularity will be found in the following story :—

"On the 7th of November, 1665, the curé of Saint-Babel was condemned to death for a crime he had committed three years before. He was a man of parts, intelligent in matters of business, but carried away by his passions, and not particular in setting a good example in his parish. He

---

* Madame de Sévigné, "Lettres," Oct. 15, 1677.
† "Histoire de France: Louis XIV.," note iii.

was especially ill-famed for his amours, and amusing stories were told about him, amusing if the tone had not been connected with sin and wholly unbecoming his sacred profession. He was accused in the world of having instructed his female parishioners in an entirely novel manner, and having inspired them with a love remote from the love of God. His turn for gallantry would show itself at such unseasonable moments, that on one occasion, having been sent for by a good woman in mortal sickness to hear her confession, he neglected to administer to her the Sacraments, in order to amuse himself in winning the affections of a girl to his liking, whom he found in the house; and thought no more of the salvation of the mistress, in his design against the honour of the maid. He forgot his character as a priest as soon as he had seen her personal charms, and love overcame duty. Instead of listening to the confession of the one, he employed his time in making his declaration to the other; and far from exhorting the sick person to die piously, he solicited her who was in good health to live in sin; and taking her by the hand and the chin, he said, ' What a trial it is for me to be called by a person whom age and sickness have reduced to extremity, and what a joy it would be to come and see you who have youth and beauty. I own that I do not like to hear the story of past sins which these good old women relate to us, and that the sins of youth are much more agreeable. Let madame your mistress think over the way in which she has passed her years, and let us consider how we will pass ours; let her examine and see if she has sinned, and let me know if you can love one who loves you. Do not be surprised if you see me abandon my duties in order to satisfy my inclination, and, if you love me, regard me as a man and not as a curé, and reflect that you can be at once my mistress and my parishioner, and that you will find in me a pastor and a lover equally devoted.'"

This worthy priest was not interfered with for this and similar indiscretions. He came to an untimely end by being hanged for the more serious offence of murder, into which he was tempted by a natural exasperation at having been placed in a ridiculous and painful position by one of his flock. It happened thus. At a short distance from his parish he had a grange in which he kept, not only his corn and fruit, but, when occasion required it, the young women whom he fancied. He took reasonable precautions to ensure privacy, and even diverted a road which ran past the grange, in order to escape the curiosity of passers by who might feel a wish to inquire what he was doing in his retreat. Still suspicion was excited, and a peasant, more enterprising and mischievous than the rest, artfully closed the door of the grange and fastened it on the outside, when he had good reason to think that the curé was within, as, indeed, he was, with a young woman, whom he had chosen out of his own church. The imprisoned pair were forced to wait till liberated by a chance wayfarer, and the exposure of the curé was complete. He vowed a terrible vengeance on his betrayer, and soon carried it out by having him beaten to death. The very next day he said mass for the defunct, but the friends of the latter brought the curé before a local tribunal, which acquitted him. It was only three years later, when a special commission of judges, known as Les Grands-jours d'Auvergne, were sent by Louis XIV. to suppress the unbridled crime in Auvergne, that M. Guillaume Boyer, the curé in question, came by his deserts. The Church did all it could to save him. But Colbert was at the head of affairs, and lay-justice had its way.

Now, to whom are we indebted for this interesting story?

To no other than the illustrious Fléchier, the eloquent preacher who became bishop of Nîmes. His "Mémoires sur les Grands-jours d'Auvergne," are among the choicest pieces of French prose of the early classical period, not without a flavour of "bel esprit" and "préciosité," recalling the Hôtel de Rambouillet, but still, by their finesse and style, worthy of the Great Age. But all must admit that the tone of sly humour in which the crimes of the priest are recorded is very singular, and conclusive that clerical irregularities were considered objects rather of mirth and pleasantry than of serious reprobation. Would any clergyman, especially of so high a character as Fléchier, dream of speaking of them in such a strain now?

We will now take the case of the famous Abbé de Choisy, as illustrating the kind of life a churchman might lead under Louis XIV., not only without discredit, but with general respect and esteem. The Abbé de Choisy came of a good family "of the robe," that is to say, he belonged to that rich and powerful class of hereditary civil servants who carried on the government of the old French monarchy. His position in the world is sufficiently shown by the fact that his mother, a woman distinguished by her wit and fine manners, could say to the young Louis XIV. that if he wished to become a polished man he ought to frequent her society. One may suppose she did not neglect the education of her son, and we know, indeed, that she loved him to excess. This was the result of her bringing up. After leaving the theological seminary, for he was intended for the Church from the first, Choisy immediately became an actor, or rather an actress, and for several months appeared on the stage at Bordeaux. His mother, in his childhood, had taken pleasure in dressing him as a girl, partly, perhaps, from private whim, but more probably to please the perverted tastes of Monsieur (Duke of Orleans), the king's brother, who had a passion for wearing female attire. Choisy was nothing loath, and soon surpassed his Royal Highness in his fondness for a woman's costume. In order to gratify his propensity he bought a house, as he himself tells us, in the Faubourg Saint-Marceau, in the centre of the "bourgoisie of the people," that he might " dress himself as he liked, among folks who would not complain of anything he did." He soon became noted for his elegant female attire, and though his sex was well known, no one seems to have been scandalized. So far from that, his services were requested in the parish church to present the holy bread and collect the offertory. He became one of the attractions of the church, and a source of great profit to his employers. In one day he collected two hundred and seventy-two livres. People came from other parishes when it was known he was going to collect. "I will admit," he says, "that in the evening at the salut (the benediction) I experienced a great pleasure. It was night, when the talk is free. I heard several times, in different parts of the church, people saying, ' But can it be true that that is a man ? He has good reasons for wishing to pass for a woman.' "

It may well be supposed that this comedy was continued beyond the walls of the church, for objects less innocent than making strangers stare. Choisy took a large country house near Bourges, where he passed as la Comtesse des Barres, and spent four years in a round of systematic seduction. Details cannot be given ; they are to be found in his own narrative by the curious in such moral monstrosities. Even more singular than his turpitudes is the chuckling cynicism with which he relates them. Yet he never lost caste for his rascality. Once only, apparently, was he reproved, by the Duc de Montausier, who told him he ought to be ashamed of himself for such conduct; but his clerical brethren seem to have been as accommodating as he could wish. When he went to Bourges, he imparted his secret to the curé, which, as he says, it was only fair to do. But the curé was not in the least scandalized, and came to dine and sup at the rake's house, sitting at table with the innocent little victims, mere children often, of the latter's licentiousness. But that is not all. When the Cardinal de Bouillon went to Rome to attend the Conclave for electing a new Pope, he took Choisy with him as his "conclaviste." He afterwards occupied the same post in the service of the Cardinal de Retz (a worthy pair), and took a part, if we may believe him, in the election of Odescalchi (Leo XI.). He lived till eighty, and was *doyen* of the French Academy, when he died in great honour as a man of wit and fine manners. It is needless to add that he was "converted" before the end, with what profit to the world does not appear.

Scotland and Spain share the bad pre-eminence of having been, each in their way, the most fanatical nations in Europe. It would be difficult to say in which of the two religion was made most repulsive and inhuman. In both countries nearly every object was postponed to the protection and propagation of the national faith. But Calvinism in Scotland was more blighting and deadly to all things beautiful than Catholicism in Spain. Terrible as it must have been to know that the invisible eye of the Holy Office was fixed upon your movements, and even upon your thoughts, and that at any moment you might disappear behind its dreaded walls, only to emerge in a San Benito in the ghastly procession to an Auto da Fé, yet Spanish life was not blackened and gnawed into hideousness by the Spanish Inquisition as Scottish life was by the Scottish

Inquisition. After all, there was joy, laughter, and song in Spain ; there were poetry and painting ; Cervantes, Calderon, and Murillo, bright children of the South in whom the world still finds delight. But in Scotland every green and whole-some thing was smitten as by a black frost. "To be poor, dirty, and hungry, to pass through life in misery, and to leave it with fear, to be plagued with boils and sores and diseases of every kind, to be always sighing and groaning, to have the face streaming with tears and the chest heaving with sobs ; in a word, to suffer constant affliction and to be tormented in all possible ways ; to undergo these things was deemed a proof of goodness, just as the contrary was a proof of evil. . . . It was a sin to go from one town to another on Sunday, however pressing the business might be. . . . No one on Sunday should pay attention to his health, or think of his body at all. On that day horse-exercise was sinful ; so was walking in the fields, or in the meadows, or in the streets, or enjoying the fine weather by sitting at the door of your own house. To go to sleep on Sunday before the duties of the day were over was also sinful, and deserved church censure. Bathing, being pleasant as well as whole-some, was a particularly grievous offence; and no man could be allowed to swim on Sunday. It was, in fact, doubtful whether swimming was lawful for a Christian at any time, even on week days, and it was certain that God had, on one occasion, shown his disapproval, by taking away the life of a boy while he was indulging in that carnal practice."[*] Life must have been made intolerable by a system of spies and informers who were paid for delating breaches of the Sabbath.[†] "Sometimes a brother and sister, or a man and

---

[*] Buckle, " History of Civilization in England," vol. ii. pp. 395–398. Buckle corroborates every statement by redundant evidence.

[†] Chambers's " Domestic Annals of Scotland," vol. iii. p. 344.

his wife, walking quietly together, would find themselves under the observation of the emissaries of the Kirk. In short, if fanatical belief in Christianity, coupled with the most intemperate zeal in enforcing the precepts of the Bible, could have made a people moral, the Scotch should have been a moral people towards the middle and end of the seventeenth century. Nearly a century of gospel-teaching at the highest pressure should, if Christianity be as favourable to morality as is commonly supposed, have produced very marked results, in the form of correct and orderly living.

The reality does not correspond with this pleasing inference. Indeed, to judge from the accounts left us by Spalding and other contemporaries, the country districts of Scotland presented a savage scene of lawless violence, frequently ending in murder. Gentlemen, neighbours, and often relatives, quarrel and fight and kill each other like barbarians, with or without provocation. However, homicide, which of all crimes in a peaceful state of society is the most injurious and detested, is often viewed with strange leniency in periods agitated by fervent religious and social or political revolution. In the eyes of ferocious partisans, killing is no murder, when it thins the ranks of their enemies. This was the case in Scotland at the time referred to ; it was so in France, both under the Red and White Terror ; and only recently it was the same in Ireland. We will, therefore, pass over the Scotch manslaying of the seventeenth century, and refer to that milder form of vice which has nearly usurped the name of " immorality " for its own exclusive use in familiar speech, illicit intercourse between the sexes. On no part of ethics have Christians of all denominations laid greater stress than on chastity, yet with far less result in the way of producing purity of manners than might have been expected, even among those who made a particular display of religion.

In 1640, a portion of the covenanting army was under General Monro, on its way from Banff to Aberdeen. "Then Monro and his solders," says Spalding, "marched that night (Friday) to Turriff; Saturday, they marched therefrae to Inverurie and Kintore; Sunday, they marched therefrae to Aberdeen, and by the way, at Bucksburn, they had a sermon taught by their own minister." They no doubt "hungered and thirsted by the way," and could not pass the Sabbath, though on military duty, without hearing the Word. But when they reached their quarters in Aberdeen, their behaviour left much to be desired. "Of the performances of the covenanting troops occasionally posted in Aberdeen, we hear from the commissary clerk of 'daily deboching' and 'drinking,' night walking, combating and swearing, and bringing sundry honest women-servants to great misery. Sixty-five of this honest sisterhood were delated before the church courts; twelve of them, after being paraded through the streets by the hangman, were banished from the burgh. Several were imprisoned in a loathsome vault, while others, more fortunate, found safety in flight." * What was done to the pious profligates who had brought them to this "great misery" does not appear. Later on in the century, the General Assembly felt called upon to proclaim a general fast on account of the backslidings of the people. "There hath been a great neglect," they say, "of the worship of God in public, but especially in families and in secret. The wonted care of sanctifying the Lord's Day is gone, cities full of violence, so that blood touched blood. Yea, Sodom's sins have abounded among us—pride, fulness of blood,

* Burton, "History of Scotland," vol. vi. p. 322.

idleness, vanities of apparel, and shameful sensuality." *
And there is no reason to believe that this is one of the
rhetorical exaggerations of sinfulness common to religious
persons in moods of depression. Referring to a slightly
earlier date, Mr. Chambers says, "The number of cases of
uncommon turpitude in a time of extraordinary religious
purism forces itself upon our attention. . . . Offences of a
horrible and unnatural kind continued to abound to a
degree which makes the daylight profligacy of the subsequent reign (Charles the Second's) shine white in comparison. 'More,' says Nicoll, 'within these six or seven years,
nor within these fifty years preceding and more.' Culprits
of all ages, from boys to old men, are heard of every few
months as burned upon the Castle Hill of Edinburgh.
Sometimes two together—young women who had murdered
their own infants—were frequently brought to the same
scene of punishment. John Nicoll states that on one day,
October 15, 1656, five persons, two men and three women,
were burnt on Castle Hill for offences of the several kinds
here glanced at, while two others were scourged through
the city for minor degrees of the same offences." †

The meaner vices of fraud and cheating, often supposed
to be modern inventions from which the pious old times
were free, were not uncommon in Edinburgh in the seventeenth century. "The beer, ale, and wine sold in the city
were all greatly adulterated. It was customary to mix wine
with milk, brimstone, and other ingredients. Ale was made
strong and heady with hemp seed, coriander seed, Turkish
pepper, soot, salt, and by casting strong wash under the
cauldron when the ale was brewing. Blown mutton and
corrupted veal, fusty bread and light loaves, false measures

---

* Chambers's "Domestic Annals of Scotland," vol. ii. p. 42.
† *Ibid.*, vol. ii. p. 242.

and weights, were common.   In all these particulars the magistrates were negligent, so that the people were abused and neglected." *

One does not see how, under the head of morals, the people of the Ages of Faith were superior to the people of to-day.   When we consider that the competition was much less severe than it is now; that the size of the towns was many degrees smaller than at present; and that the opportunities of escaping observation and punishment now afforded by our immense cities were then correspondingly less, we must admit that the average of morality was singularly low, although the average of religious belief and zeal was singularly high.   The few extracts quoted above give a most inadequate impression of the general violence, grossness, cruelty, and licence of the period during which every effort was made and almost every other worthy object was sacrificed with a view to making the people devoutly Christian.   We have surely a right to say, after so large and protracted an experiment, that the moralizing element in Christianity has been over-estimated.   Here was Christianity at work without any competing principle; it was zealously supported by the secular power; yet we find crimes of " uncommon turpitude " co-existing with " extra-ordinary religious purism."   It is not an answer to say that but for Christianity matters, bad as they were, would have been worse; and for this good reason, that a great improvement in decency, order, and civilization generally, coincided in Scotland with a marked decline in religious fervour, such as set in about the middle of the last century.   What is true and quite fair to allege is, that the Scottish people in the seventeenth century were in that stage of semi-barbarism in which no moral principle is able to take a firm hold.

* Chambers's " Domestic Annals of Scotland," vol. ii. p. 240.

Only the slow growth of knowledge and industry can civilize such a people. But this is the doctrine of evolution, not of grace. The latter, as emanating from Almighty power, can no more be arrested or withstood by imperfect development in the race, than by moral degradation in the individual. At least, that is the theory. In practice, we may observe, the growth of morality depends on conditions widely remote from those which favour the vigour and tenacity of theological beliefs. As already shown, Christianity preaches salvation in the next world, not morality in this; and according to the rules laid down, we may not doubt that numbers of the Scotch, in the darkest period, after the commission of every crime against human ethics, were at last touched by grace and were saved, or at least should have been. The point does not admit of verification, and we therefore cannot tell whether celestial happiness did supervene as a compensation for the miseries of a barbarous existence on earth. The fact remains, that those miseries were not mitigated, but were often very much increased by a fanatical belief in the words of Scripture. The cruelty and injustice perpetrated in obedience to the disgusting superstition about witchcraft, a thoroughly scriptural tenet, fill up one of the most horrible pages in the history of mankind. Sorcerers were burnt in batches of four, five, and even of nine at a time on the Castle Hill. But the more zealous spirits were not satisfied. "There is much witchery up and down our land," says Robert Baillie; "the English be but sparing to try it, but some they execute." * Our sympathy is justly given, in the first instance, to the wretched victims; but the mental anxiety and terror of their persecutors must have been no light burden.

* Chambers's "Domestic Annals of Scotland," vol. ii. p. 244.

We will now, for a few moments, turn our attention to Spain, the single European country which rivalled Scotland in its zeal for religion.

One of the liveliest accounts of that interesting nation will be found in the letters of a French lady, who went to Spain in 1679 to attend upon the young queen Henriette, the daughter of the unfortunate Henrietta of England, sister of Charles II. I confine my extracts to the matter in hand—the union, or rather, the disconnection of morality and religion.

" The frequent assassinations in this country, on account of some affront or other, seem to authenticate these facts. If a man receives a box on the ear or a stroke in the face with a hat, nay, with a handkerchief or a glove ; if he be called a drunkard ; or a reflecting word happens to pass on his wife's virtue, these must be wiped off with no less than the blood of the aggressor, and that by assassination. For they say it is not just that, after a signal affront received, the offended party should put his life in an equal balance with the offender. They are so tenacious of revenge that they will not lay aside an injury for twenty years after : if they happen to die before they accomplish it, they will recommend the same upon their death-beds to be executed by their children. I had it from credible hands that a certain person of note, dreading the revenge of his enemy, went to the West Indies, where he staid twenty years, till hearing that both he and his son were dead he returned to Spain, yet not without changing his name for his greater security ; but in vain, for, notwithstanding all his precaution, the grandson of his enemy, though not above twelve years of age, found means to hire a ruffian, who assassinated him soon after his return.

"Most of their assassins are natives of the city of

Valentia, a wicked generation, who will venture at anything for money, and are always provided with firearms that will discharge without noise, and stilettoes. . . . I was told that a certain Spaniard of note having agreed with one of these Bandoleroes, as they call them, of Valentia, for a certain sum of money to dispatch his enemy, but a reconciliation being made soon after betwixt them, he acquainted the Bandolero with it, desiring him not to put his design into execution though at the same time he allowed him the money as a voluntary gift. But the assassin replied that he scorned to have any of his money without deserving it, to do which he must either kill him or his enemy. The gentleman being willing to preserve his own life, was forced to let him put in execution what he had designed against the other, unless he would have resolved to seize him, a thing of dangerous consequence in Spain, where these ruffians are so numerous and so closely united that they are sure to revenge the quarrel of any of their companions, which makes Spain the most doleful theatre of tragical scenes in the universe.

"What is more surprising than all the rest is, that as well those who leave no stone unturned to put their revenge in practice, as those who put them in execution, should engage themselves in certain devotions for the success of their enterprises, at the very time they are going to give the mortal wound to an innocent person of their own religion and country." *

Now as regards the Spanish observation of the seventh commandment. "The Spaniards are so kind-hearted to one another in love-affairs, that if a man meets his mistress in a place where he has no opportunity of conversing with

* "The Ingenious Letters of the Lady's ——— Travels into Spain," Harris's Collection, ii. p. 756, ed. 1705.

her in private, he need only go into the next house and to request the master (whether he know him or not) to give him the opportunity of talking with a lady of his acquaintance in private in his house, and he is sure it will scarce ever be refused." What is meant by the euphemistic term " talking," is made clear by the following strange disclosure. " I remember that, talking the other day with the Marchioness d'Alcannizas, one of the greatest and most virtuous ladies of the court, she frankly told us that if a gentleman should be alone with her for half an hour in a convenient place, and not ask her the last favour, she should think he despised her, though she should, at the same time, not grant his request."

Again, we have to notice the co-existence of a very low moral tone with the most exalted religious zeal, and passionate religious belief.

It is unnecessary to proceed through the previous centuries with so much detail, otherwise it would be easy to show that the sixteenth century was far more immoral, in the widest sense of the word, than the seventeenth. The court of the later Valois is painted for us by the garrulous Brantôme ; and one fails to see how it differed, except for the worse, from the Court of Caligula or Commodus.

The Italians were more refined, but even more wicked, and impressed the English of Elizabeth's reign, by no means a squeamish or fastidious folk, with a " sense of the rottenness of the country whence they obtained their intellectual nourishment, with a sense of frightful anomaly, of putrescence in beauty and splendour, of death in life, and life in death." * No one would expect better things of the fifteenth century, in which the Wars of the Roses in England, and the final struggle against English domination in

* " Euphorion," by Vernon Lee.

France, had the usual effect of protracted warfare in injuring morality.

That the fourteenth century, the era of the great Schism, of the captivity of the Popes at Avignon, and of the Black Death, should have been a period of extraordinary licence and crime cannot surprise us. Both civil and ecclesiastical government were impaired by the events of the time, and pestilence is usually followed by moral irregularities.

So, we pass these ages over, and stop for a moment in the thirteenth century, the age *par excellence* of beautiful things, when chivalry is supposed to have been in its noble prime, when the Church exerted a calm and serene sovereignty over the kneeling nations, when mediæval art reached its supreme and chaste perfection, when the philosophy and theology of the Latin Church culminated in works almost as intricate and wonderful as the maze of pinnacles, flying buttresses, arches, and columns which, surviving still in the cathedrals of Amiens or Chartres, sing us a deceptive siren song of beauty which lures us to their epoch as to a Golden Age. It was very far from a golden age. On the contrary, it was an age of violence, fraud, and impurity, such as can hardly be conceived now. We will take it in its ideal moment, in the reign of St. Louis, the best of kings, and perhaps the best man who ever lived. We will take as a witness one of his most trusted and valued friends, Eude Rigaud, Archbishop of Rouen, and we will see what he says of the morals of the clergy of his own diocese which, like a good pastor as he was, he was constantly visiting for the purpose of discipline and reform.

The *Registrum Visitationum*, or the diary of the pastoral visits of Archbishop Rigaud, forms a quarto volume of upwards of six hundred closely printed pages. It extends from the year 1248 to 1269. Rigaud had been a Franciscan monk, a student at Paris of scholastic philosophy under our famous countryman, Alexander of Hales, and at an early period acquired reputation as a preacher of uncommon eloquence. A tradition obtained that he had been elevated to the archiepiscopal see of Rouen, where he had gone to preach, on account of the impression produced by his piety and learning on the Chapter. Rigaud wished to refuse the proffered dignity, but his professions were disregarded, the Pope, Innocent IV., relieved him of his vows to reject ecclesiastical honours, and he was consecrated archbishop in the month of March, 1248. In the month of July, in the same year, he began his pastoral visitations. He travelled about from monastery to monastery, and sometimes was entertained at the expense of the monks, but more often at his own. Indeed, the religious houses seem frequently to have been in debt, and hardly in a position to give worthy hospitality to so great a lord as an archbishop. He often discovered, both among the secular and the regular clergy, very unclerical habits and amusements, sometimes innocent, at other times very much the contrary. He found the nuns of St. Arnaud had fallen into the evil practice of singing the Psalms and Hours to the Virgin with unbecoming haste— "cum nimia festinatione et precipitatione verborum," and ordered, very properly, that one verse should not be begun till a previous one had been finished. The nuns, moreover, did not observe the rule of silence; and ate meat in the infirmary as often as three times a week. A sick sister would have two or three healthy friends to see her, and regale them with a more dainty repast than the usual convent fare. They all had a measure of wine, but some drank more than others, which was not allowed. Some even gave wine to persons outside the convent, without obtaining leave; for this offence they were made to go without wine the next day. The nuns also had a fondness for linen chemises and sheets, which were against the rule, and these luxuries were forbidden. On the whole, the convents for women, which Rigaud visited, seem to have been fairly correct, and certainly did not afford examples of the gross licentiousness of the monks and priests. Many of the latter fell under episcopal censure for irregularities which would not nowadays be considered very serious, and give a notion of a rollicking, schoolboyish tone, which has an odd effect. Riding about on horseback in an unclerical garb is noted with disapprobation, and seems to have been a common fault. Buying and selling horses was hardly so venial in a priest; no more, perhaps, was the keeping of dogs for hunting purposes. But it was easy to do much worse. One is surprised to find charges of drunkenness constantly recurring. Frequenting taverns and playing at dice were certainly unbecoming in a clergyman, especially when carried so far as to cause the priest to leave or lose his clothes in the public-house, "aliquando amittit vestes suas in tabernis." One is glad to see that Archbishop Rigaud would not stand such indecorum, and deprived the in- cumbent who had been guilty of it of his living. But these transgressions are insignificant, both in number and gravity, compared with the incessant sin of incontinency, which is alleged on nearly every page in the most aggravated form. Priest after priest is charged with immoral conduct, some with married women, some with keeping two mistresses at once, one with incest with his own niece.*

---

* "Item presbyter de Mesnilio David est inobediens et habet pueros suos secum, et concubinam alibi : item duæ se invenerunt in domo ipsius et se verberaverunt invicem. Item presbyter de Sancto Richario infamatus de quadam conjugata, parochiana sua. Item presbyter Sancti Remigii notatus de ebriositate, non defert capam, ludit ad talos,

Without a certain monotony of repetition, it is impossible to convey the impression produced by this protracted catalogue of clerical disorders. "We found the priest of Nesle in ill repute, on account of a certain woman who is said to be pregnant by him; he also trades, and ill-treats his father, who is the patron of the church he holds. This parson fought with a certain knight with a drawn sword amid a clamour and concourse of his friends and relations." *

"The priest of Gonnetot was charged with criminality with two women, and he went to the Pope about the matter, and when he returned he is said to have offended again. The priest of Wanestanvilla was accused with reference to a woman, one of his own parishioners, and her husband on that account departed over sea. He kept her eight years, and she is pregnant; he also plays at dice and drinks too much; he frequents the taverns, does not abide in his church, and goes with a hawk on his fist whenever he likes. Also the priest of Bray-sur-Seine is accused with reference to a certain woman; and because she refused to live in the presbytery, he went to live with her, and had his food and corn brought to her house. Also the priest of Saint-Just haunts taverns, and drinks till he is full up to the throat. Also Lawrence, priest of Longœil, keeps the wife of a man who is abroad; she is called Beatrice Valeran, and he has a son by her.† We found that the priest of Panlyu was famed for incontinency with a maidservant of his, and likewise with two other women, who afterwards bore him two sons; also he is noted for inebriety; he sells his wine, and makes his parishioners drunk. The priest of Auberville is

frequentat tabernam, et ibi multociens verberatur. Item Magister Walterus presbyter de Grandi Curia, infamatus est de propria nepte et de nimia potatione."—"Regest. Visitationum Arch. Rothomagensis," par Th. Bonnin, Rouen, 1852, pp. 20, 21.

* *Ibid.*, p. 19. † *Ibid.*, p. 29.

seriously noted for incontinency, and he married a certain woman with one of his servants, in order that he might have free access to her. Also he had relations with a certain Englishwoman, whom he kept a long time, and sinned with her again after being corrected by the archdeacon; also with the daughter of a poor woman who lives hard by the cross." *

Although the nuns, compared with the priests, appear to have been well-behaved, we occasionally meet with convents in which there were great disorders. "We visited the convent of the Blessed Mary of Almeneschiis. There are thirty-three nuns. All are possessed of property: they have saucepans, copper-kettles, and necklaces. They contract debts in the village, and eat and sit at tables in groups. Each nun has money given her to provide for her table and her kitchen. Many are absent from Compline and Matins, and drink after Compline. Sister Theophana is given to drink. They have no regular time for confession or communication. Sister Hola lately had a boy by one Michael of Val Guido. Secular persons freely enter the cloister and talk with the nuns. They never dine in the refectory. Dionisia Dehatim is accused of ill-conduct with Nicholas de Bleve. They quarrel finely in the cloister and the choir. Alice, the cantatrix, had a boy by a man named Christian. Also the prioress formerly had one boy. They have not got an abbess, as the last recently died."† A most improper set of ladies, certainly, considering their vows of poverty, chastity, and obedience. The strange thing is that Archbishop Rigaud did not visit them, so far as appears, with any censure; perhaps their wealth and social position made it impolitic to do so. Indeed, the grosser sins of the flesh

* "Regest. Visitationum Arch. Rothomagensis," p. 25.
† *Ibid.*, p. 82.

are treated with what we should consider singular mildness. Early lapses from virtue, and even later ones, are pardoned on promise of reform. Only in the case of hardened and persevering sinners are strong measures taken. "We warned them," says Rigaud—and in one case "them" included Master Walter, the priest of Grandcure, who cohabited with his niece—"we warned and threatened them that if we found them again accused of similar misdeeds we would punish them severely."[*] And it would not be right to suspect the archbishop of a weak toleration of vice for acting so leniently. The number of offenders was so great that if he had suspended or expelled them all, he would have had few or no priests left to serve the diocese. He probably did the best which the circumstances permitted; which was, on proof of repeated guilt, to obtain from the culprit a written promise of reform, together with an undertaking to leave his church and the country in case of a relapse into his former depravity. Rigaud has preserved for us a great number of these documents, signed, sealed, and sworn to, by the penitents, and they are extremely curious. In the first place, they show beyond doubt or cavil that the charges were true. *Habemus confitentes reos.* In the next place, the poor priests seem heartily ashamed and sorry, and own without ambiguity, in often crude language, the faults they have committed; though probably the drawing up of these confessions was not entrusted to them, but confided to the sterner pens of the archbishop's secretaries; they acknowledge that if they fall again they will have nothing to say for themselves; that they will give up their curacies without the noise or fuss of a trial—*sine strepitu judicii*—and go away. This appears to have been a great point, to get rid of them quietly; no doubt because a refractory or litigious

* "Regest. Visitationum Arch. Rothomagensis," p. 21.

priest, especially by appealing to Rome, could give rise both to trouble and scandal.*

The next witness I would like to call was a cardinal, an intimate friend and co-reformer of the great Hildebrand, Pope Gregory VII., the Blessed Peter Damiani. Unfortunately, the very nature of the crimes with which he charges the clergy is so monstrous, that it is impossible, even "in the obscurity of a learned language," as Gibbon said, to give an idea of their character. Dean Milman can only distantly refer to Peter Damiani's "odious book," the "Liber Gomorrheanus;" and quotes the title of the first chapter as an adequate indication of its contents. Any modern must

---

* "Universis presentes litteras inspecturis, Radulphus rector ecclesiæ de Sana Villa Rothomagensis diocesis, salutem. Noverit universitas vestra quod cum super irregularitate commissa a me, ut dicebatur, pro eo quod, suspensus et excommunicatus, dicebar celebravisse divina: item super crimine fornicationis et adulterii quod dicebar commisisse cum Robina penildore de Nova-villa: item super eo quod dicebar lusor ad taxillos, et frequentator tabernarum: item super eo quod dicebar capellanum capellæ de Rocherobiis vulnerasse graviter cum falcone in capite; essem apud bonos et graves, et maxime apud revérendum patrem Odonem, Dei gratia, Rothomagensem archiepiscopum adeo diffamatus, quod dictus pater, nolens dissimulare premissa, nolebat super premissis ad inquisitionem contra me procedere, et secundum inquisitionis exigentiam me canonicæ subicere ultioni. Tandem ego, quærens a dicto patre non judicium sed veniam, promisi, sine vi, sine dolo dicto patri spontaneus, quod prædictam ecclesiam meam resignabo, et habebo pro resignata, quandocunque dicto patri placuerit; volens et concedens quod idem pater possit me privare eadem ecclesia sine strepitu judicii et juris solemnitate in aliquo non observata, quandocunque suæ sederit voluntati. Renunciavi autem spontaneus quoad premissa exceptioni de vi et de metu et litteris a sede apostolica contra premissa concedendis seu etiam impetrandis, et omni auxilio juris canonici vel civilis competenti seu competituro per quod dictæ resignatio et privatio impediri valeant vel differi. Juravi præterea spontaneus, tactis sacrosanctis evangeliis, me contra premissa vel aliquod premissorum per me nec per alium non venturum" ("Regest. Visitationum Arch. Rothomagensis," p. 658).

follow his example. It must suffice to say, that nothing in
Aristophanes, Athenæus, or Petronius, gives a picture of
more bestial depravity than the one drawn by a prince of
the Church of the manners of his clerical contemporaries.
It is "unspeakable," and with that remark we must leave
the subject. But what about grace, what about belief in
God, Christ, and the Bible? What about the deterrent
effect of the fear of hell, of the purifying effect of the hope
of heaven? These are questions to which an answer were
desirable.

And now, what is the moral to be drawn from this unpleasant but necessary review? We have seen that not in
one country nor in one age, but all through the Ages of
Faith, the most flagrant breaches of the moral law are quite
compatible with the most fervent and complete belief in
God, in the Bible, and, in short, in Christianity. The usual
answer to this objection is that these people may have had
faith, but it was not living and saving faith. They believed
like the devils, and perhaps did not always tremble like
them as well. So let it be. Mere faith, unless it be of a
particular kind, is not enough. The heart must be touched
by grace, as well as the mind disposed to assent to certain
dogmatic propositions. But agnostics say no more and no
less. The touching of the heart is everything, and assent
to propositions next to nothing. It is abundantly plain that
assent to Christian dogmas offers the slenderest guarantee
that it will have the desired effect in touching the heart.
There never was a moment, from the first teaching of
Christianity till the present day, when sincere pastors have
not deplored the condition of the greater part of their flocks.
That the whole world lieth in wickedness is the constant
burden of their complaint. Could better proof be required
or given that the supposed connection between belief and

morality is illusory? And it is easy to see that this is not an accidental but a necessary result. By laying all the emphasis of its teaching on repentance and the subjective attitude of the soul towards God, and not on good works performed to individuals and society, Christianity has not applied its force in the right direction for producing the maximum of morality. As this was not its aim, it cannot be censured for not having attained it. But it is open to us to point out that this misdirection of force largely accounts for the low morality of the past, and is one of the chief causes of the decline of theology in the present. It is proved by an experience of eighteen hundred years, that the tremendous sanctions which Christianity wields are inoperative on the majority of minds. They do not realize them ; the threats are not heard, as it were, by the inward spirit. The immediate connection between wrong-doing and going to hell is not grasped. Hell is a long way off, is not visible, and its deterrent efficacy is weakest when the attraction of sinful pleasure is strongest. Only minds of a fine, imaginative power, and naturally tender consciences, seize the whole import of the Christian message. This fact alone would put Christianity at a disadvantage in dealing with the bulk of mankind. Few persons care for remote dangers or evils ; they banish them from their minds, as suggesting gloomy thoughts, and trust to the chapter of accidents to escape them entirely. When preachers enlarge every Sunday on the peril of the unrepenting sinner's condition, and tell him that he may at any moment be summoned before the dread tribunal of an angry God, the young and the strong and the giddy accord to them but a languid assent. They feel in robust health, sudden death by accident or disease is the great exception, and pleasure is very delightful, and within reach. It is a maxim of jurisprudence that prompt punishment for wrong-doing is vastly more efficacious than even severer penalties long delayed. Suppose ordinary crime were punished, not with the greatest dispatch compatible with justice, but at a remote period in after-life, say, twenty or thirty years after its commission, would not the deterrent effect of the criminal law be even less than it is ?   But this is by no means all. In addition to this disadvantage, Christian priests have one and all placed a greater one in their own way as teachers of morality, by their doctrine of repentance and consequent salvation.   When, like St. Alphonso de' Liguori, or Mr. Spurgeon, they teach that any amount of crime and sin can be expunged in a moment by sincere contrition and turning to God, even in the last hour, they remove from the cause of morality in this world all the force and urgency of their exhortations, and transfer them to celestial happiness beyond the grave.   If they had been able to preach that good works, and good works only, would take men to heaven, they would have occupied a relatively strong position.   If they could have said to men, "It matters not how sorry you are for having done amiss, you must smart for it all the same," they would have had a powerful lever to keep men in the right way.   But they were tied down by the terms of the divine deed and testament, and forced to use very different language.   The lamentable doctrine of Original Sin, and all that flowed from it, the washing away of sins, flight from the wrath to come, forced them to show that, after all, heaven was open, if certain conditions were complied with, heartfelt repentance, turning to Jesus, confession of sins, receiving the sacrament ; and that, in that case, previous crime or virtue made no difference ; all men justly lay under the sentence of God's wrath, and if He chose to pardon, it was only out of the unspeakable riches of His grace.   It was not for man to make terms. So that by exaggerating human depravity and making all men worthy of hell, they came to admit very bad characters into heaven. And quite rightly, from one point of view. Salvation was their object, not morality. They have not aimed at it, and they have not attained it.

CHAPTER VII.

WHAT CHRISTIANITY HAS DONE.

In attempting to estimate the past, we are exposed to two opposite temptations, either of which may lead us into serious error. We may be so impressed by the recent advance of knowledge, and the enlarged power of man over nature, the pomp and brilliancy of modern material progress, that we turn with disdain from the humbler science and performance of our ancestors, and, comparing their poverty with our own riches, complacently draw flattering conclusions to our own advantage. This disposition is a common mark of energetic but uneducated minds, of people who have made their way in the world by force of character, and who nourish a sort of grudge against learning and scholarship. On the other hand, it is a tone so repulsive to minds which have made themselves acquainted with the past, that these are apt to fall into the opposite extreme, and to see with over-clearness the seamy side of the present. The wealth and noisy progress of the present do not impress persons of this type with much respect. They pronounce them to be vulgar and commonplace, and purchased at far too great a cost ; nay, by the ruin of numerous lovely and precious things, which the present age does not miss, only because it is too deeply buried in sordid cares and frivolous pleasures to know anything about them. If one class points to the triumph of industry and the victories of steam, the other draws attention to the meanness of our Art, and the foul defacement of natural beauty, and even the pollution of the air we breathe and the water we drink by factories, tall chimneys, and the ubiquitous screaming tyrant, the railroad. The admirers of the present look out upon the world, which it is their intention to subdue, as conquerors. They are always for " opening up " new countries, which they say conduces to trade and the spread of civilization. The lovers of the past reply that the march of the so-called civilization should rather be called the spread of ruin, vice, and disease ; that the traders look upon the world rather as buccaneers than as honest men, that they regard it as their oyster which they mean to open with a steam hammer. The interchange of taunts and reproaches goes on in *amœbic* response, as of peasants in an idyll, and no doubt will not readily be brought to a close. It is referred to here in order to exhibit the difficulty of a task which, at one time or another, we are nearly all of us compelled to undertake, to estimate and fairly judge the past, if for no other purpose than lighting up and enabling us to direct the present.

A clear perception of the road we have travelled is one of the best indications of our probable course in the future, whether that course be a straight line or a curve. It is obvious, if society be an organism, and few nowadays would deny the fact, that, in order to understand it, we must study its life, behaviour and habits, on the most extended scale. The present is a transitory phase, which is as insufficient for this purpose as a day or an hour would be for the biological study of one of the higher animals. Both those who wish to break with the past and ignore its teaching as so much dross—the revolutionists ; and those who on various grounds can think of nothing better than an impossible return to it—the reactionaries; will find, and indeed have found already, though the extremes of neither party are very docile to the lessons of experience, that knowledge alone can throw light on our path, and that to take sentiment or passion as our guide is to court catastrophe. Revolutionists, who are too impatient and headstrong to wait for the slow but sure effects of evolution, and reactionaries, who are too selfish or stupid to admit the changes which evolution demands, are equal enemies to progress and human well-being. Incessant and minute change is one of the conditions of life, but great and sudden change is disease, and no change at all is incipient death. One of the numerous misfortunes which afflict mankind is the difficulty of inculcating this truth; it appears to be profoundly offensive to the vulgar of all classes, the majority of the race. A salutary change, let us suppose, is obviously required; it is announced and advised by a reflective individual or group here and there. If they are not too obscure and insignificant to fail wholly in attracting notice, a clamour arises against their monstrous and unheard-of opinions; for critical turning-points occur in the speculative as well as the practical order; modes of thought and doctrines at times need reforming as much as institutions; they cannot be listened to, they are subversive, atheistic, destructive of man's best interests, and so forth. The change does not take place, or oftener it is not overtly admitted as needed or salutary; it is kept down and arrested, as far as possible, even ignored. But it is going on underground, as it were; its partisans increase, and their anger also, till at last comes a time when the dammed-up current has accumulated an energy which overpowers all obstacles, and it dashes furiously forward, scattering devastation along its course. This is the abstract history of all revolutions in Church or State, in thought or practice.

These considerations, even if they be deemed over-trite and obvious, are not out of place as introductory to the subject of this chapter; an attempt to estimate the action of Christianity in the past. In the last chapter it was viewed in relation to its effect on morals; and facts were adduced which seemed to show that in that respect its operation had been far less salutary and decided than it is customary to assume. At the same time it was shown that morality was never the special objective of Christianity, and therefore any failure to foster morality could not justly be made a reproach against it. No system can be blamed for not accomplishing what it never attempted to do. Luther would have read the previous chapter without discomposure. He would have said, " No doubt ; the object of Christianity is to save men's souls in the next world, not to make them moral in this. And it does save. That is all I want." On this ground his position is unassailable. Modern apologists have usually forsaken his inaccessible heights, and put in claims, which seem to be more than disputable, for their religion as a guardian of morality. But this is only one side of a large subject. A doctrine so wide and powerful as the Christian has many other sides, and its energy as a social factor is not to be limited to one point of view. Christianity has had an immense influence on politics, literature, and philosophy ; it has moulded the minds and characters of many of the most distinguished persons who have adorned the human race. But neither its blind friends nor its blind foes can be expected to do it justice, and possibly full justice will never be done to it till it has ceased to exist. Still, an estimate of its value as a social doctrine must ever appear as one of the most important problems presented by history, an attempted solution of which is almost imposed on serious students who are sufficiently withdrawn from theological prepossessions to regard Christianity neither with love nor hatred, but with that sympathy and respect justly due to one of the greatest phases of human evolution.

In the learned and profound investigations of continental scholars concerning the origin of Christianity and the growth of the early Church, sufficient attention has not always been accorded to the precise time and place in the order of human evolution in which that religion arose. This is not intended as a reproach to such illustrious men as Strauss, F. C. Baur, Keim, Hausrath, and Renan. They had more immediate work of a specialist kind to do, and might well leave the *placing* of Christianity in world-history to others. But the point is of great importance. It may with reason be doubted, if the fact is as often remembered as it should be, that Christianity arose amid the corruption and decay of the greatest civilization which the human race had seen, amid the death-throes of the ancient world. From the fact that the New Testament was written before that corruption and decay had assumed their final and fatal form, that St. Paul lived and preached in Antioch the Beautiful ; visited Athens while its citizens still retained enough of the old inquiring spirit to " spend their time in nothing else but either to tell or to hear something new ; " and at last came to martyrdom in Rome while the deceptive bloom of imperial splendour still flushed the cheek of the dying mistress of the world—it is often assumed that this proud heathenism and pagan glory were overthrown by the meek and unlearned disciples of the Galilean prophet of God. Nothing can be less true than this assumption. The soft autumnal calm, and purple tints as of an Indian summer, which lingered, up to the Antonines, over that wide expanse of empire, from the Persian Gulf to the Pillars of Hercules, and from the Nile to the Clyde, broken as it was by the year of Revolution of A.D. 69 and the black tyranny of Domitian's reign, was only a misleading transition to that bitter winter which filled the half of the second and the whole of the third century, to be soon followed by the abiding dark and cold of the Middle Ages. The Empire was moribund when Christianity arose. Indeed, Rome had practically slain the ancient world before the Empire replaced the effete Republic. The barbarous Roman soldier who killed Archimedes absorbed in a problem, is but an instance and a type of what Rome had done always and everywhere by Greek art, civilization and science. The Empire lived upon and consumed the capital of preceding ages, which it did not replace. Population, production, knowledge, all declined and slowly died. The Christian apologists, headed by St. Augustine, were justly indignant at the pagan slander which attributed the fall of the Empire to the spread of Christianity. Their answer to the objection was complete, as we can see far better even than they did themselves. But what they could not be expected to see, and what we can see very well, is, that the fall of the Empire, including the loss and ruin of the old philosophy and knowledge, was an indispensable condition of the spread of Christianity. If the blood of the martyrs was truly said to be the seed of the Church, the decay of knowledge was an equally needed pre-requisite. It will not be denied that this decay of knowledge was present and startlingly rapid. After the silver age which ended nobly with Tacitus and the younger Pliny, Latin pagan literature almost ceases to exist; and the falling off in the form is not more striking than in the value and quality of the contents. All superstitions revived and flourished apace in the ever-waning light of knowledge. A shudder of religious awe ran through the Roman world, and grew more sombre and searching with the progressive gloom and calamities of the time. A spirit wholly different from the light-hearted scepticism of the Augustan age and later Republic stirred men's hearts, and the strongest minds did not escape it. "The pagans were not one whit behind the Christians as regards belief in miracles and in a future life."[*] The sun of ancient science, which had risen in such splendour from Thales to Hipparchus, was now sinking rapidly to the horizon ; and when it at last disappeared, say, in the fifth century, the long night of the Middle Ages began.

But it was in this period of decaying knowledge and civilization that the Christian religion was elaborated and constituted in the historical form which it practically still wears. The creeds and chief dogmas of the Church were worked out in the period which extends from the Council of Jerusalem to the Councils of Nice, Chalcedon, Alexandria, and Ephesus. No evolutionist would think of speaking in any but respectful terms of the great churchmen who laid down the lines along which European thought was destined to travel for a thousand years. The sneering tone of sceptics in the last age is wholly out of place, and arose from pure ignorance of the laws which govern social and intellectual development. The Nicene Creed in the fourth century after Christ was as natural and legitimate a product of the conditions of the time, as was the Socratic philosophy in the fourth century before Christ. What we have to note is, that the Nicene Creed was the product of an age of decay, of disaster, and approaching death, so far as civilization and science were concerned. In every light,

* Hausrath, ''Neutestamentliche Zeitgeschichte," vol. iii. p. 489.

one of the most memorable, and in many respects one of
the most noble of human compositions, it yet, as it could
not fail to do, bears the marks of its birth-time ; and that
time was one of extreme calamity, of growing gloom, ignorance and misery. Within two centuries of its promulgation,
the Græco-Roman world had descended into the great
hollow which is roughly called the Middle Ages, extending
from the fifth to the fifteenth century, a hollow in which
many great, beautiful, and heroic things were done and
created, but in which knowledge, as we understand it, and
as Aristotle understood it, had no place. The revival of
learning and the Renaissance are memorable as the first
sturdy breasting by humanity of the hither slope of the great
hollow which lies between us and the ancient world. The
modern man, reformed and regenerated by knowledge,
looks across it, and recognizes on the opposite ridge, in the
far-shining cities and stately porticoes, in the art, politics,
and science of antiquity, many more ties of kinship and
sympathy than in the mighty concave between, wherein
dwell his Christian ancestry, in the dim light of scholas-
ticism and theology.

The birth of Christianity being on this wise, viz. having
taken place in an era of decay and death of art and philosophy, of knowledge, of wealth, of population, of progress
in every form, and the absence of these things having
been one of the chief negative conditions of its growth and
prosperity, we must look for the sources of its nourishment
in another direction than these ; not in knowledge, or the
eager questioning spirit which leads to knowledge, but in
the humble spirit which believes and accepts on trust the
word of authority ; not in regulated industry, which aims at
constant increase and accumulation of wealth, but in the
resigned poverty which, scorning this world, lays up riches

in heaven; not in political freedom and popular government, which aims at the progressive well-being of all, but in the stern rigour of arbitrary power, which coerces the vicious and refractory into a little order during their brief sojourn on earth. In the decline and fall of Rome, or, as it would be better to say, in the final ruin of ancient civilization, the conditions favourable to this order of beliefs or doctrines spontaneously emerged. It is obvious that there could be no question of free institutions or settled industry in an age chastened by every scourge of war, pestilence and famine; by arbitrary tyranny and military despotism. Knowledge, again, is even more sensitive than capital to the influence of public and widespread calamities, inasmuch as the love of knowledge is rarer and feebler than the love of wealth in most minds. To a man of the fifth century, on the look out for any sphere of activity for his energies, no prospect presented itself in the least similar to what such a man would see now, or would have seen in Athens under Pericles, or in Rome under the Scipios. Public life existed as little as it does at this day in Russia. The pursuit of knowledge for knowledge's sake was out of place in a time when daily existence was not safe from the swords of successive barbarian hordes, or, failing these, from the more cruel onslaught of the merciless tax-collector. That is to say, all the outlets through which modern energy is chiefly expended were then closed; a man could not serve the state as a citizen, he could not serve knowledge as a man of science, he could not augment wealth as an artisan or master of industry.

There was only one thing left for him to do—to serve God.

The last and perhaps the most important legacy left by the ancient philosophy to the world was the doctrine of monotheism, the belief in a single supreme God. The evolution of this capital idea has never yet been traced with the care it supremely deserves. The common notion that it was wholly derived from the Jews is quite unfounded. The germs of it may be found in Greece in the earliest speculations of the Ionic and Eleatic philosophers. It gradually made its way, by the force of its inherent rationality, against manifold opposition, and among the Stoics reached a distinctness and elevation little, if at all, inferior to the highest Jewish conception of Jehovah. The Christian deity was. a union of the two monotheistic conceptions, the Greek and the Jewish. Each element was necessary for the conception to attain its full universality and power. The Jew never quite transcended his notions of a tribal God, who had been in an exclusive way the God of his fathers from the beginning ; the God of Abraham, Isaac, and Jacob, in whom he had a sort of ancestral right of property, who was bound to him, and to whom he was bound, by covenants and mercies and promises, such as no other nation ever imagined. The Jew was, therefore, on a footing of familiarity and intimacy, so to speak, with his God, to which the metaphysical Greek, with his wide discourse of reason, never attained. To the Jew, God is the great companion, the profound and loving, yet terrible, friend of his inmost soul, with whom he holds communion in the sanctuary of his heart, to whom he turns, or should turn, in every hour of adversity or happiness. Hear the Psalmist : " O God, thou art my God ; early will I seek thee. My soul thirsteth for thee, my flesh also longeth after thee, in a barren and dry land where no water is. For thy lovingkindness is better than the life itself : my lips shall praise thee. Have I not remembered thee in my bed, and thought upon thee when I was waking ? Because thou hast been my helper, therefore under the shadow of thy wings will I rejoice."* On the other hand, the very closeness and specialty of the Jew's relation to Jehovah, made his conception of the deity unsuitable to the office of a cosmopolitan God. I venture to suggest that perhaps the opposition of Peter and the Judaizing Christians to the wider views of St. Paul, arose as much from a reluctance to part with their national God, as from the narrow, ceremonial scruples to which it is ascribed. The Greek was as inferior to the Jew in the depth and intensity of his religious sentiment, as he was superior in mental reach and philosophic power. For him, God is the deity of the intellect rather than of the heart; He is the symbol of "eternal law all-ruling,"† and the Hellene all but attained to the impersonal and unknowable reality behind phenomena, which the last word of recent philosophy propounds as the only rational object of worship.

When these two, each in its way, powerful and stimulating notions of God coalesced into one, as they did in the teaching of St. Paul, the effect on the moral and spiritual world was as that of a new force, a new centre of gravity to which all thoughts and feelings naturally tended with an irresistible attraction. The rationality of monotheism as compared with polytheism, of the idea of one all-ruling deity, instead of the anarchy of a crowd of gods and goddesses thwarting each other, recommended the doctrine to all superior minds, as infinitely truer, simpler, and better. Knowledge had progressed far enough to make the uniformity of nature a credible result of the operations of an

* Psalm lxiii. 1-4, 7, 8 (Prayer-book Version.

† " . . . ἐπεὶ οὔτε βροτοῖς γέρας ἄλλο τι μεῖζον
οὔτε θεοῖς, ἢ κοινὸν ἀεὶ νόμον ἐν δίκῃ ὑμνεῖν."

Cleanthis Hymn., 37, 38.

eternal mind ; but it had not gone far enough to exclude the notions of miracle and of providential interference on the part of the deity with human affairs. Moreover, the God of the Jews had become, through St. Paul, the God of the universe, and the " Father of all ; in every age, in every clime adored." The influence of the combined ideas on contemporary minds, as it is shown in the writings of the Fathers, is very striking. A tone of exultation and radiant joy seems to possess them when they refer to the new-found, central object of their worship, which contrasts not only with the sad, desponding tone of the pagans, but even with Israel's delight in Jehovah, which is rarely without a touch of gloom and foreboding, and with the meek resignation of the Middle Ages, which tremble even more than they believe. Compare the *Te Deum* of St. Ambrose with the *Dies Iræ* of Thomas of Alano. The two hymns are parallel, often nearly identical, in thought, but profoundly divergent in sentiment. The one bright, full of hope and trust in God ; the other sombre and anxious and care-laden, almost to the verge of despair. Such was the difference between the fifth and the thirteenth centuries. The earlier Christians, reminded, no doubt, by the paganism which still survived, are never weary of setting forth the superior grandeur and consolation of their faith as compared to that of polytheism ; and it is quite easy even for us to see how incalculably the religious sentiment must have been intensified, when its scattered rays, dispersed among a crowd of deities, were all united in the barely tolerable splendour of one Almighty God and Lord. Nowhere does the passionate adoration, and flow of unbounded devotion, show itself with more fervour and power than in the Prayer for all Conditions of Men in the Alexandrian Liturgy. The original makes the fragments of it which have survived in modern

Liturgies appear very pale and tame. Here is a short specimen :—

"O King of Peace, give us thy peace, keep us in love and charity, be our God, for we know none beside thee : we call upon thy name ; grant unto our souls the life of righteousness, that the death of sin may not prevail against us or any of thy people. Visit, O Lord, and heal those who are sick, according to thy pity and compassion ; turn from them and from us all sickness and diseases, restore them to and confirm them in their strength. Raise up those who have lingered under long and tedious indispositions; succour those who are vexed with unclean spirits. Relieve those who are in prisons or in the mines, under accusations or condemnations, in exile or in slavery, or loaded with grievous tribute." *

With these intense and absorbing feelings running in a deep but, after all, narrow channel, the Western European world turned to meet and advance into that dread and frightful time designated as the Fall of the Roman Empire. How a fragment or a germ of civilization escaped destruction in that great catastrophe it is not easy to say. It is admitted on all hands that a great debt is owing to the Christian bishops of those days, who were the only officials clothed with authority and honour, who survived the wreck of the Roman bureaucracy. Although this fact redounds rather to the credit of episcopacy than of Christianity, still a fair criticism must admit that as without the previous dignity and prestige obtained by the Christian religion, bishops would not have been there, or in a position to discharge their functions, the final result must be credited to the new faith. It is the more incumbent upon us to acknowledge and assert this, as at a later date the part played by

* Bunsen, "Analecta Ante-Nicena," pp. 24, 109.

Christianity in politics was very nearly wholly evil.   In attempting to estimate, as was proposed, the utility of Christianity in the past, it will simplify our task if we divide the subject under three heads, and consider its Political, Philosophical, and Spiritual action in the world.

1. The Political action of Christianity. Owing to well-known historical reasons, the natural and legitimate action of the politics suggested or approved in the New Testament was a long time in showing itself. The courtliness of the bishops who incensed Constantine and Theodosius, was evidence that Christian prelates, as such, had no objection to arbitrary power. But that is hardly a reproach, when nothing but arbitrary power was possible. Under the Catholic feudal *régime* the Church was more often in an attitude of hostility to the secular power than in alliance with it. While the Church was the rival of the State, and bid high for supremacy, it could not coalesce with the State, and support its despotic pretensions. But when, at the end of the Middle Ages, the monarchies of Europe definitively got the upper hand, and aimed straight at arbitrary power, the Church, so far from opposing, was only too ready to help them. A number of texts, which had been overlooked before, were cited to prove the absolute duty of every Christian man to yield passive obedience to kings and governors. It was one of the most critical turning-points in human evolution. In the sixteenth and seventeenth centuries the battle of freedom was fought out. All the monarchies of Europe were moving with rapid strides towards despotism. Nothing can deprive the Dutch of the honour of having been the first to step into the breach and defend, against apparently overwhelming odds, the cause of liberty. The English followed them, nobly but somewhat tardily, under Cromwell. All through this bad time, the

Christian Church threw its whole weight on the side of oppression; and the point to be noticed is, that it had the fullest scriptural warrant for its action, and could not conscientiously have done otherwise. We have all long ago forgotten the opposition of our Jacobites to freedom, and the narrow escape we had of falling under arbitrary power. The weak and worthless Stuarts, with their immense ambition and feeble faculties, were not the chief danger. That lay in the adherence to their pretensions of such saintly men as Bishop Ken, and such noble champions of moral purity as Jeremy Collier. And these men, as they believed all scripture, believed also these texts: "Let every soul be subject unto the higher powers. For there is no power but of God: the powers that be are ordained of God." "Submit yourselves to every ordinance of man for the Lord's sake." "Servants, be subject to your masters with all fear; not only to the good and gentle, but also to the froward." Professor Sewell, commenting on these passages, says with complete truth, "It is idle, and worse than idle, to attempt to restrict and explain away this positive command. And the Christian Church has always upheld it in its full extent. With one uniform, unhesitating voice it has proclaimed the duty of passive obedience." *

It may be objected that the Puritans and other Christian sects have taken a different view of their religious duties, and shown themselves brave champions of civil freedom. To which it may be replied, that the Puritans, when they were oppressed by Laud and Charles, showed the common human faculty of looking away from and ignoring inconvenient facts which told against them and their cause; they passed over these parts of scripture. Even Locke, in his answer to Filmer, never attempted to expound these

* "Christian Politics," p. 111.

formidable texts in a sense favourable to his arguments; like the able controversialist that he was, he felt that the less said on that subject the better. But further, the Puritans, by their partiality for the Old Testament, became almost Jewish in sentiment, and imbibed a portion of the anti-monarchical spirit of the Hebrew prophets and priest-hood. It was not one of these who would have said, "Let every soul be subject unto the higher powers." And yet, again, the Puritans, when they became supreme in America, showed that they could be as oppressive and intolerant as any Catholics or Anglicans in Europe.

It is not necessary to expatiate at any length on the import and effect of this authentic Christian and scriptural teaching. We can easily afford to let bygones be bygones. But when the most immodest and unfounded claims are put forward in behalf of Christianity as an unfailing and universal benefactor to mankind, we may certainly be allowed to point out that for two centuries it was a consistent and determined enemy of human liberty and welfare. It took the side of the Stuarts, Bourbons, and Hapsburgs against their subjects, and it was bound to do so by its own principles. An agnostic may pardon this, as one of those errors of which the past is full. But a Christian, who believes in the perennial value and beneficence of his doctrine, must, one would think, experience certain qualms in moments of retrospection.

2. The influence of Christianity on speculative thought has been far more salutary than it has been on politics, and this not from any accidental circumstance, but in conse-quence of essential qualities in the doctrine itself. It cannot be a mere accident that of the three monotheistic religions, Christianity alone has produced elaborate systems of theology, which in depth and compass can compare with

any systems of philosophy, ancient or modern. The Jews
and Mahometans have each had their disputes and controversies inside their own confessions, from which the
odium theologicum has not been wanting; but their puny
differences cannot be compared to the splendid, far-reaching discussions which have repeatedly filled the Christian
Churches with the most vigorous and brilliant intellectual
life. The subject cannot be treated adequately here. It
will suffice to point to the intellectual revival which followed
the spread of Christianity, and gave to the world the whole
literature of the Fathers, Greek and Latin, in the third,
fourth, and fifth centuries, at the very time when pagan
literature had fallen into sterility and decrepitude. Even
Gibbon, no favourable witness, acknowledges this. Of all
writers who have used Latin as their mother tongue, it is
no exaggeration to say that St. Augustine is by far the most
original, suggestive, and profound. He is a genuine thinker,
not a mere rhetorician like Cicero, Seneca, and the rest.
The controversies of the fourth century, which have given
rise to much tasteless ridicule, notably the Arian controversy, and the witticism suggested that it was preposterous
that the world should be divided into hostile camps by a
diphthong, these controversies were mentally the most
stimulating discussions, not only which the age admitted
of, but which have ever occupied men's minds. All the
faculties of the reason and logical understanding were
brought into play, subtlety the most acute, and discourse
of reason the most lofty. When the western world sank
into barbarism in the sixth, seventh, and eighth centuries,
theological controversy largely ceased; it was a sufficient
task for the West to keep alive, and intellectual luxuries
had to be dispensed with. But the moment the warmth of
reviving civilization returned to the stiffened minds of the

West, deep and searching controversies recommenced. It would be interesting to show how all this mental activity sprang immediately or remotely from the central Christian doctrine, the Divinity of Christ. A long struggle was needed to establish that doctrine, but it was worthy of a long struggle. The difference between "homoousion" and "homoiousion" is only that of a single letter, but as Emile Saisset well said, "Probe the matter to the bottom; between Jesus Christ, man, and Jesus Christ, man-God, there is infinity; there is, if one may so speak, the whole thickness of Christianity." The subsequent controversies, the Monothelite, the Monophysite, and others, are obviously due to the same origin; and all through the following ages, the Scholastic period, the Reformation, the Jansenist and Jesuit epoch, down to Strauss and Moehler, the same great doctrine has been, in a greater or lesser degree, a potent stimulus at once of philosophical inquiry and historical research.

3. It is in the action of Christian doctrine on the human spirit, that we see its power in the highest and most characteristic form. Neutral or injurious in politics, favourably stimulating in the region of speculative thought, its influence on the spiritual side of characters, naturally susceptible to its action, has been transcendent, overpowering, and unparalleled. The restriction to characters "naturally susceptible" will probably be resented, but it cannot be denied. The great mass of men have at all times been feebly sensitive to the higher spiritual influences of Christianity. It is a fact which all preachers of every denomination are for ever denouncing and lamenting. The true Christian saint is the rarest product in every Christian Church. What is even more noteworthy is, that the terrible menaces of God's wrath and damnation which, till quite recent times, have been universally believed by

Christian men, have been equally inoperative; and this to such a degree, that the truly converted and repentant sinners, those who have set about working out their salvation in fear and trembling, have ever been lost in wonder and horror at the reckless folly of the bulk of mankind in leading the lives they did, coupled with their nominal beliefs. Convinced and earnest Christians are always compelled to regard it as madness, or a superlative proof of Satan's power. Volumes of quotations could be given from the highest and best authorities in support of this, as every one conversant with religious literature will be aware. I will restrict myself to two, taken from the works of illustrious men, each in his own confession among the brightest examples of Christian virtue, Blaise Pascal, and Richard Baxter. Pascal says :—

"Rien n'est si important à l'homme que son état; rien ne lui est si redoubtable que l'éternité. Et ainsi, qu'il se trouve des hommes indifférents à la perte de leur être, et au péril d'une éternité de misères, cela n'est point naturel. Ils sont tout autres à l'égard de toutes les autres choses : ils craignent jusqu'aux plus légères ; ils les prévoient, ils les sentent ; et ce même homme qui passe tant de jours et de nuits dans la rage et dans le désespoir pour la perte d'une charge, ou pour quelque offense imaginaire à son honneur, c'est celui-là même qui sait qu'il va tout perdre par la mort, sans inquiétude et sans émotion. C'est une chose monstrueuse de voir dans un même cœur et en même temps cette sensibilité pour les moindres choses, et cette étrange insensibilité pour les plus grandes. C'est un enchantement incompréhensible, et un assoupissement surnaturel, qui marque une force toute-puissante qui le cause." ("Pensees," chap. I.)

Baxter says, "Can you make so light of heaven and hell?

Your corpse will shortly lie in the dust, and angels or devils will shortly seize upon your souls, and every man or woman of you will shortly be among other company and in another case than you are now. . . . O what a place you will be in of joy or torment; O what a light will you shortly see in heaven or hell; O what thoughts will shortly fill your hearts with unspeakable joy or horror! What work will you be employed in? To praise the Lord with saints and angels, or cry out in the fire unquenchable with devils? And should all this be forgotten? And all this will be endless and sealed up by an unchangeable decree. Eternity, eternity will be the measure of your joys or sorrows, and can this be forgotten? And all this is true, sirs, most certainly true. When you have gone up and down a little longer, and slept and awaked a few times more, you will be dead and gone, and find all true that I now tell you; and yet you can now so much forget it. You shall then remember that you heard this sermon, and that this day, in this place, you were reminded of these things, and perceive these matters a thousand times greater than either you or I could here conceive; and yet shall they be now so much forgotten?" *

That these are only fair samples of the tremendous stimulants applied by preachers to awaken Christian sinners to a sense of their guilt and danger, will be admitted, I suppose, on all hands; and yet it is equally admitted that they are practically of very slight effect. Baxter, a few pages before, had declared that "the most will be firebrands in hell for ever." And no theologian with a character to lose, till quite recent times, would have had a doubt about it. On theological grounds the matter is sufficiently perplexing. True believers, like Pascal and Baxter, have at

* Baxter's "Call to the Unconverted."

all times found that in this particular the conduct of men was hardly to be explained. If they believed God's promises and threats, why were their lives such a practical denial of faith in them? The real answer, which divines could not be expected to give, was that the bulk of men had neither sufficient logic, imagination, or tenderness of heart and conscience to assimilate the whole importance and bearing of the Christian scheme. A strong head, which accepted the premises of the Christian doctrine, would not hesitate to work out the conclusions. But the majority of men have not strong heads. A powerful imagination, which realized the awful prospect of a future judgment, and the eternity of bliss or woe consequent upon it, would be only too much appalled by the thought; as cases of religious madness sufficiently show. The truly meek and tender-hearted, again, have a natural turn for piety; as we see by the negroes, who seem to obtain a saintly spirit of detachment and self-renunciation with far greater ease than the more energetic races of Western Europe. But when among the Western Europeans the saintly character, under the combined influences of education and natural endowment, is evolved, the result, as might be supposed, is far more striking, on account of their superior fibre and temperament and general brain-power. The true Christian saint, though a rare phenomenon, is one of the most wonderful to be witnessed in the moral world; so lofty, so pure, so attractive, that he ravishes·men's souls into oblivion of the patent and general fact that he is an exception among thousands or millions of professing Christians. The saints have saved the Churches from neglect and disdain. The hope, even the assertion, has always been that all men could be like them, if only—the condition is not easily reduced to words, and cannot be stated in a manner generally satisfactory, but the implication always is that but for some fault in man, or the wiliness of Satan, sanctity might be universal. It would be as rational to say that the poetry of Shakespeare, the music of Beethoven, and the geometry of Lagrange, were accessible to all men. The genuine saint is a moral genius of a peculiar kind; he is born, not made; though, like all men of genius, he is sure sooner or later to acquire the best education and that most adapted to his powers. Saintliness is not confined to Christianity. There have been Pagan and Mahometan· saints; and it would not be easy to find, even in the Christian Calendar, men more naturally saintly than Marcus Aurelius and Abu Beker. What needs admitting, or rather proclaiming, by agnostics who would be just is, that the Christian doctrine has a power of cultivating and developing saintliness which has had no equal in any other creed or philosophy. When it gets firm hold of a promising subject, one with a heart and a head warm and strong enough to grasp its full import and scope, then it strengthens the will, raises and purifies the affection, and finally achieves a conquest over the baser self in man, of which the result is a character none the less beautiful and soul-subduing because it is wholly beyond imitation by the less spiritually endowed. The " blessed saints," are artists who work with unearthly colours in the liquid and transparent tints of a loftier sky than any accessible or visible to common mortals.

Perhaps there is a certain rashness in attempting to illustrate these remarks by concrete instances of saintly detachment and self-renunciation. Hagiology is not a favourite form of literature nowadays; and it must be admitted that in the lives of many saints, especially of mediæval times, unpleasant traits and circumstances connected with the

superstitions of the age are often found in close neighbourhood with virtues the most beautiful and attractive. Equity
demands that we should make the same allowance for men's
erroneous moral conceptions of duty, as we do for their
erroneous conceptions of intellectual truth, in accordance
with the standards and culture of the times. We do
not think worse of a philosopher's intellect, who lived in
antiquity or the Middle Ages, because he held a number of
absurd opinions and theories in astronomy, chemistry, and
biology. Those who believe in the empirical origin of
moral truth, are bound to be consistent and show the same
charity in the one case as in the other. If we take the case
of Saint Louis, King of France, we must admit that a man
of a more saintly character never, perhaps, existed. If we
consider the temptations to which his high position necessarily exposed him, and the completeness with which he
surmounted every unholy and selfish thought or act, it is
difficult not to regard him as the best man that ever lived.
Yet it is obvious that in many instances his notions of duty
were very wrong or perverted. But though his conscience
may not have been always enlightened, his heart was ever
right. His abortive and ruinous crusades were the cause
of vast misery and harm ; but we cannot wonder that so
devout a man strove to carry out one of the great religious
ideas and duties of the time, and none the less so because
symptoms were arising that the paramount nature of the
duty was beginning to be questioned. In his private life
he saw sometimes amiss—saw duties where none existed.
I refer to his exaggerated submission to the imperious
temper of his mother, his excessive and often repulsive self-
mortifications. But this being fully allowed, there remains
a clear surplus of untarnished virtue rarely surpassed.

There are few tests of a man's spiritual condition more

searching and decisive than the temper with which he bears unmerited insult and railing speech. I do not refer to mere self-command, to the self-respect which forbids an answer in kind, and imposes an external calmness of manner on a swelling indignation within. The man of the world, when it suits him, can attain to this much, which yet is not little, considering the common'. "impotentia" of mankind. The question is not one of self-mastery under, but of superiority to, insult, which feels no anger or resentment at insolence or contempt; and this not from an abject and craven spirit, but from living in a plane of feeling up to which personal insult does not reach. This equanimity in no wise prejudges the question whether injurious language should not be reproved, and in some cases punished, as by a judge for a contempt of court. We are only concerned with that serenity of spirit which is not touched or wounded by opprobrious speech, and all will admit that it is a very rare gift. The following anecdote told of St. Louis, shows the way in which he endured insult :—

As he was sitting in the Court of Parliament, the highest tribunal in France, a woman named Sarrette, who was interested in a suit then being heard, and perhaps dissatisfied with the decision, exclaimed to the king, " Fie, fie ! a fine king of France you are ; much better were it if another were king. You are only the king of the monks and friars, and the wonder is you are not turned out of the kingdom." The ushers wanted to strike the woman, and expel her from the court. But Louis would not allow it, and said, " What you say is very true, and I am not worthy to be king. It would have been much better had it pleased God that another had been put in my place, who knew better how to govern the kingdom ;" and he ordered his chamberlains to give the woman money. In this last act most moralists would admit that Louis was mistaken. To reward a scold for unseemly conduct in a court of justice cannot be considered justifiable. A fine and imprisonment might have taught Sarrette a useful lesson; it is clear that she needed one. As a jurist the king was to blame. But the meekness of spirit, which could suggest such an answer to a king and judge, in reply to a gross insult, was surely very wonderful.

Louis's justice, temperance, and entire self-abnegation in every relation of life are too well known from one of the most charming of mediæval chronicles, the "Mémoires" of Joinville, to make it needful to dwell upon the subject. But to the above-cited example of his humility, it may be well to add an equal proof of his firmness, and that in presence of that very priesthood to whom he was accused of being submissive. "I saw him another time," says Joinville, "at Paris, where all the bishops infcrmed him that they wished to speak with him; and the king went to the Palace—the law-courts—to hear them. There was Guy, Bishop of Auxerre, who spoke to him as follows, in the name of all the prelates: 'Sire, the lords who are here, the archbishops and bishops, have charged me to tell you that the Christian faith is perishing in your hands.' The king made the sign of the cross, and said, 'But tell me how this comes to pass.' 'Sire,' resumed the bishop, 'the reason is that people nowadays think so lightly of excommunication, that they allow themselves to die rather than be absolved, and will not give satisfaction to the Church. The bishops request you, sire, for the love of God, and because it is your duty, to give orders to provosts and bailiffs that all who have remained excommunicated for a year and a day should be constrained, by the seizure of their goods, to receive absolution.' To which the king replied, that he would willingly command it in those cases in which guilt was clearly proven. Whereupon the bishop answered, that the bishops would not consent, at any price, to that condition, and that the royal power had no right to take cognizance of ecclesiastical causes. Then the king said that he would not interfere; and that it would be against God and reason to force people to obtain absolution when the clergy did them wrong. 'And I will give you an example of this,' he went on to say—'the case of the Earl of Brittany, who pleaded in a state of excommunication for seven years against the prelates of his province, and with such effect that the Pope has condemned them all. If, therefore, I had compelled the Earl of Brittany to seek absolution in the first year, I should have sinned against God and him.' And the prelates had to submit," says Joinville; "and I never heard that the subject was brought up again." There was no false humility here, but, on the contrary, rare strength, for all it was so softly spoken. Some years after, Louis published the famous Pragmatic Sanction, the French equivalent to our English Statute of Præmunire, which laid the foundation of the liberties of the Gallican Church in opposition to the See of Rome.

I do not merely admit, but strongly maintain, that St. Louis was a man of such moral elevation and tenderness of nature, that in whatever age of the world he might have lived, and whatever creed he had held, he would have been distinguished as just, upright, and self-sacrificing in an unusual degree. But I think it equally certain that living when he did, at the brightest moment in the Ages of Faith, when the emotional effect of Christianity was at its height, and least disturbed by intellectual opposition, his *spirituality* was intensified by his creed, till he seems more like one of the angels who bow before the Great White Throne than a denizen of common earth. And this is the legitimate and consistent result of Christian training carried to its final perfection by lofty and heroic spirits ; a complete transcending, not only of the sin and corruption of the world, but a passing away from and beyond the world, and human needs and relations, an upward ascent towards the City of God, even before the end of life. The highest crown the Christian can win is that of martyrdom, suffering death for the faith ; by which no benefit is ever supposed to be conferred on men except, perhaps, the example left for imitation by others. The true Christian martyr does everything for Christ. He forsakes all to follow Him, and goes to his doom rejoicing that he has been found worthy to suffer for His name. The original mould in which Christianity was cast cannot be altered; that of a small congregation of meek and lowly men, exposed to the assaults of the "power of darkness," which was allowed to prevail for a season. For them the world was no continuing city, for they sought one to come. In the "tabernacle of this present life they did groan, being burdened," and were "willing rather to be absent from the body and to be present with the Lord." The notion that the world can ever be a place of peace and virtuous happiness is never countenanced in the New Testament. The Christian is always considered as one in the midst of a hostile and evil society, from which he must keep apart ; and, if only he is prepared, the sooner he can leave it the better. We find, accordingly, martyrs almost without exception professing, no doubt sincerely, the utmost gratitude for being delivered from this mortal life. As Sir Thomas More said, "St. Cyprian, that famous bishop of Carthage, gave his executioner thirty pieces of gold, because he knew he should procure unto him an unspeakable good turn;" and More himself, when about to suffer, and the executioner asked him forgiveness, kissed him, and said, "Thou wilt do me this day a greater benefit than ever any mortal man can be able to give me." Heroic constancy, even to death, is the note of the martyr, and indeed of every true Christian. And it is this transcendental character of Christian perfection which has ever made it at once such an imperfect fosterer of morality, and such a stimulator of spirituality and heroic passion. No vestige of self may be suffered to remain in the true confessor's heart, in which every human desire must be burnt up by love of the Redeemer. A man must "*hate* his father, and mother, and wife, and children, and brethren, and sisters, yea, and his own life also," to be a true disciple of Christ. How utterly unequal average human nature is to this transcendent pitch of self-sacrifice, the past and present record of Christianity sufficiently proves. But *some* have been equal to it, and the heroism of the saints has been illuminated by a radiance which seemed to descend direct from heaven. At all times and in all sects, the blood of martyrs has been the seed of the Church. To men, constituted as they are, the voluntary and deliberate laying down of life by confessors for conscience' sake, is always the most impressive and soul-subduing of spectacles, conquering even the cruelty of the persecutors who are consenting unto their deaths. The "face of an angel," remarked in the protomartyr Stephen, is not to be forgotten, and works miracles of conversion and remorse in the solitude of the conscience, when the ghastly scene of stoning without the city, or the burning in the market-place, returns to the memory in the silent watches of the night; and the faith and meekness of the sufferer rise up like accusers from the world of spirits. The meekness and docility of the victims are a cardinal point. All bravado and self-assertion dim the lustre of the martyr's crown. "It has been a reproach to the sufferers in the Marian persecution that, smitten on one cheek, they did not invariably turn the other cheek to the smiter;" and the remark is true. If we compare the carriage of Rowland Taylor with that of Sir Thomas More we are sensible of the difference. There can be no question as to the single-hearted piety and self-devotion of either. But More, partly perhaps by reason of his superior culture and humanist sense of the "becoming," showed a sweet resignation which contrasts favourably with the boisterous humour and self-consciousness of Taylor. "His degradation was performed by Bonner : the usual mode being to put the garments of a Roman Catholic priest on the clerk-convict, and then to strip them off. Taylor refused to put them on, and was forcibly robed by another; and then, when he was thoroughly furnished therewith, he set his hands to his side and said, 'How say you, my lord, am I not a goodly fool? How say you, my masters, if I were in Cheap should I not have boys enough to laugh at these apish toys?" The final ceremony was for the bishop to give the heretic a blow on his breast with his staff. The bishop's chaplain said, 'My lord, strike him not; for he will sure strike again.' 'Yes, by St. Peter will I,' quoth Dr. Taylor. 'The cause is Christ's, and I were no good Christian if I would not fight in my master's quarrel.' So the bishop laid his curse on him, and struck him not. When he went back to his fellow-prisoner, Bradford, he told him how the chaplain had said he would strike again, and 'by my troth,' said he, rubbing his hands, 'I made him believe I would do so indeed !'"

The saintly spirit would seem to be wanting here.

Indeed, the temper which has fitted men for martyrdom has always been liable to the perversion of a fierce fanaticism and stubbornness, in which meek resignation is replaced by a savage combativeness regardless of consequences. In his subsequent behaviour, Taylor rose to a much higher strain. The scene on the February morning, by St. Botolph's church, where his wife and children had waited for him, "suspecting that he might be carried away;" the dialogue in the gloom, "for it was a very dark morning, and the one could not see the other," reach the extreme of tragic pathos. "His daughter Elizabeth cried, saying, 'O my dear father! Mother, mother, here is my father led away!' Then cried his wife, 'Rowland, Rowland, where art thou?' Dr. Taylor answered, 'I am here, dear wife,' and stayed. The sheriff's men would have led him forth, but the sheriff said, ' Stay a little, masters, I pray you, and let him speak to his wife.' Then came she to him, and he took his daughter Mary in his arms, and he and his wife and Elizabeth knelt down and said the Lord's Prayer. At which sight the sheriff wept apace, and so did divers others of the company." It is needless to repeat further one of the best-known scenes in English history. The point to be noticed is, that Taylor rose to the height of saintliness in proportion as he laid aside his haughty carriage. His answer to the sheriff, who asked him, after his martyr's ride through Essex to Suffolk, how he fared : "Well, God be praised, master sheriff, never better ; for now I know I am almost at home;" and his meek expostulation to the miscreant who threw a fagot at him, "which brake his face, so that the blood ran down his visage :" "O friend, I have harm enough ; what needed that?" attain to the summit of Christian resignation.

The death of Sir Thomas More has ever been regarded

as one of the most sublime examples of Christian fortitude on record. His perfect sweetness and self-possession have melted all hearts. He did nothing to provoke his fate, but on the contrary, everything that his conscience allowed him in order to escape it. At no time was he aggressive or self-asserting. When condemned, his carriage was at once meek and manly.

"When Sir Thomas was come now to the Tower-Wharfe, his best-beloved childe, my aunte Rooper, desirous to see her father whome she feared she should never see in this world after, to have his last blessing, gave there attendance to meete him; whome as soone as she had espyed, after she had receaved upon her knees his fatherlie blessing, she ranne hastilie unto him; and without consideration or care of herselfe, passing through the midst of the throng and guarde of men who with billes and halberds compassed him round, there openly in the sight of them all embraced him, not able to say anie word, but: *Oh, my father; oh, my father!* He liking well her most naturall and deare affection towards him, gave her his fatherlie blessing; telling her, that whatever he should suffer, though he were innocent, yet it was not without the will of God; and that she knew well enough all the secrets of his hart, counselling her to accommodate her will to God's blessed pleasure, and bade her be patient for her losse. She was no sooner parted from him and gonne ten steppes, when she not satisfied with the former farewell, like one who had forgotte herselfe, ravished with the intire love of so worthie a father, having neither respect to herselfe nor to the presse of the people about him, suddenly turned back, and ranne hartilie to him, tooke him about the necke and diverse times togeather kissed: whereat he spoke not a word, but carrying still his gravity, tears fell also from his eyes; yea, there were very few in all the troupe who could refrain thereat from weeping, no not the guards themselves." *

To give one more instance of Christian martyrdom; none the less tragic, because it was enacted, not amid the tumult and profanity of a public execution, but in the inner chamber of a man of genius. At thirty years of age, Blaise Pascal determined to "give up the world," and began that course of mortification and prayer which, there can hardly be a doubt, shortened his days. He forsook his scientific labours, by which he had won, as a youth, a foremost rank among the mathematicians of Europe, devoted himself to reading the Scriptures and meditating his great work on the Christian religion; of which only fragments, in the form of the immortal "Thoughts," were ever achieved. The physical privations and pain to which he subjected his emaciated body are described at length by his sister, Madame Périer, in a biography which for simple grace and pathos rivals the best of Walton's "Lives." To avoid wandering and worldly thoughts when engaged in conversation, "he took an iron girdle full of sharp points, which he placed next to his flesh; and when conscious of an impulse to vanity, or even a feeling of pleasure in the place where he happened to be, he struck the girdle with his elbow in order to increase the pain of the punctures." He ate a certain regulated quantity of food, whether hungry or not, never exceeding it, however good his appetite, and never eating less, however great his loathing; and this, on the ground that taking food was a duty, which was never to be accompanied by any sensual pleasure. When his sufferings were acute, and his friends expressed commiseration, he would answer, "Do not pity me; illness is the state natural

* "Life of Sir Thomas More, Knt.," by his great-grandson, Thomas More, Esq., p. 264, ed. 1726.

to Christians, because it places us in the condition we ought
ever to be in—suffering evils, deprived of all the pleasures of
sense, freed from all the passions which afflict us throughout
life, without ambition, without cupidity, in the continued
expectation of death." He mortified his affections not less
than his body, and said that we should never allow any one
to love us with fondness ; in fostering such attachments we
occupied hearts which ought to be given solely to God ;
that it was robbing Him of that on which He set most
store.   " It is not right that others should attach themselves
to me.   Even if they do it willingly and with pleasure, I
should deceive those in whom I excited such a feeling.
Am I not about to die ?—the object of their love then will
perish. As I should warn people against believing a falsehood,
however profitable to me, I should warn them not to attach
themselves to me ; for their duty is to spend their lives in
striving to please God, or in seeking Him." At his death
there was found sewn up inside the lining of his doublet,
two small pieces of parchment and paper, on which were
written in identical words a series of brief sentences, of
which the meaning was misconceived by Condorcet, who
first published them.   The supposition was, that it was a
" mystic amulet," which Pascal had worn next his person
out of superstitious motives.   Its real character is perfectly
clear : a solemn record of the hour and date of his conversion to God and to a life of asceticism :—

The year of grace, 1654.

Monday, 23rd of November, St. Clement's Day, pope and martyr,
and others in the martyrology.

Eve of St. Chrysogonus, martyr, and others.

From about half-past ten at night, till half an hour past midnight.

Fire.

'God of Abraham, God of Isaac, God of Jacob ; not of philosophers
and learned men.

Certitude, certitude. . Feeling, joy, peace.
God of Jesus Christ.
Deum meum es Deum vestrum.
Thy God shall be my God——
Oblivion of the world and everything save God.
He is only to be found by the way taught in the Gospel.
Greatness of the human soul.
Righteous Father, the world has not known thee, but I have known thee.
Joy, joy, joy ! tears of joy.
I have left him ————————————————————————————————
Dereliquerunt me fontem aquæ vivæ.
My God, wilt thou forsake me ?————————————————
May I not be separated from him for ever.
——
This is life eternal, to know thee, the only true God, and Jesus Christ,
whom thou hast sent.
Jesus Christ————————————————————————————————————
Jesus Christ————————————————————————————————————
I have left him : I have fled from him, denied him, crucified him.
May I never be separated from him.
He can only be kept by the way taught in the Gospel.
Renunciation entire and sweet.
Entire submission to Jesus Christ and to my director.
Eternal joy for one day's suffering on earth.
Non obliviscar sermones tuos.   Amen.

"What a noble mind is here o'erthrown," will probably
be the thought of many readers.   And yet, why should that
thought arise?   Doctrinal differences apart, can there be
a doubt in any candid mind, that Pascal strove with all
the force and sincerity of his powerful mind and passionate
nature to attain Christian holiness, and that he threw himself at the foot of the cross as completely and unreservedly
as a human being could?   Are his austerities and mortifications objected to?   The *form* of his asceticism may be
questioned by different schools of theology ; but no earnest,
thorough-going Christian exists, who does not *deny* himself
one way or another, and admit asceticism in principle.
Indeed, asceticism represents a tendency in human nature

far wider than Christianity, and though liable to frightful perversions, is one of the noblest qualities possessed by man. It is one of the higher forms of courage, which not only endures or disdains suffering, but positively courts it, and finds a passionate and fiery joy in the sharp sting of pain. If man had instinctively the universal horror of pain, which some moralists suppose him to have, he would never have been a hunter or a warrior. The delight of self-mastery in some natures, easily gets the upper hand, and leads, according to circumstances, to the voluntary search for danger and suffering, or to the stern refusal of sensuous pleasure. "Quæ major voluptas quam fastidium omnis voluptatis?" asks Tertullian. The spirit of self-sacrifice is just as much a factor of human nature, as the spirit of self-indulgence, though, like all the higher gifts, less common. The deplorable thing is, that the precious gift should be wasted and thrown away on useless objects. The hero who suffers to save others, contributes a direct and tangible good to the world by his action, and even a higher good indirectly by his example. The ascetic who tortures himself to please a cruel god, does equal harm in both ways, to himself and others. Even the old Hebrew saw this when he wrote that his Lord "would have mercy, and not sacrifice." As regards Christian asceticism, especially in the grosser forms of physical, self-inflicted torture, it is a subject which has not received, it would seem, the attention it deserves from Church historians. It arose early in the Church, which like the austerer philosophic sects, the Stoics and Cynics, was led, by the calamities of the decaying Roman Empire, to take a gloomy and despondent view of the moral government of the universe, and to see the finger of an angry God in the incessant woes with which mankind were then scourged. And, indeed, it is not easy to see, on

Christian principles, how voluntary and unmerited suffering can be supposed to be displeasing to God. The whole scheme of Redemption supposes that God was so pleased with the sufferings of the innocent Christ, that, in considera·tion for them, He forgave guilty man. The sufferings of Jesus were entirely voluntary; His buffetings, scourgings crucifixion, were all endured to expiate man's sin; the ransom for his disobedience, the precious blood-shedding which obtained innumerable benefits. If Christians would imitate Christ, should they not do so in this particular, the most characteristic of His office? If agony unspeakable, borne by the Divine Son, the Lamb without blemish, was well-pleasing to His father, why should it be otherwise in sin-stained man? Protestant notions on this subject may be more rational, but they are far less scriptural. The whole idea of Christianity, as given in the New Testament, is steeped in suffering. "Blessed are they that mourn;" "Blessed are they which are persecuted for righteousness' sake." Why? Because "great is their reward in heaven." The worship of the Man of Sorrows was not intended for the tender and the comfortable. "Whosoever will come after me, let him deny himself, and take up his cross, and follow me. For whosoever will save his life, shall lose it; but whosoever shall lose his life for my sake and the gospel's, the same shall save it." Those who assume a tone of sneering and contempt, for the mortifications of the Catholic saints, show that they are true heretics in the primitive sense of the word, inasmuch as they choose and select those words and parts of Scripture only which suit their preconceived views. Let us be rationalists by all means; but let us be consistent rationalists, and consider the Bible as an interesting fragment of ancient Semitic literature. Those who profess to regard it as the Word of

God, and yet ignore and neglect some of its clearest precepts, are not consistent. Any vitality which the Catholic revival of these latter years may have had in Europe or America, is clearly traceable to its superior deference to the paramount and universal authority of those Scriptures which all Christians admit as binding in the last court of appeal.

To return, however, to our more immediate subject—the spirituality of mind stimulated by Christianity, in the higher types of the Christian character.

Within quite recent times, three women have died, who, for complete detachment and recollection, for profound sincerity and devotion to the Cross, may justly be regarded as the equals of any of the saints of old. I do not for a moment pretend to say that there have not been others equally devoted and sincere. Probably there have been many, to me unknown. But these are incontestably eminent enough in Christian virtue, to serve as types of that spirituality which is the most characteristic result of profound Christian belief consistently carried out. The result is in many ways touching, and beautiful in the extreme. It is such flowers of exquisite perfume and beauty, grown in the garden of the soul, which still arrest the attention of a rationalistic age. And nothing can show how far the modern world has drifted away from the old Christian point of view, than the fact that these three sweet saints have made so slight an impression upon it. Had they lived and worked as they did, in the Ages of Faith, their tombs would already have become sacred shrines, to which troops of pious pilgrims would be crowding to kneel and pray. Sister Agnes Jones, Mother Margaret Hallahan, and Sister Dora Pattison, are the three pious women to whom I refer. Their lives have been written by loving hands;

and, in the long series of religious biographies, more touching and graceful portraits would not easily be found. Amid many points of difference as to theological opinion, social position, and character, they yet had striking points of likeness. The passionate love and affection with which they inspired all who came within their influence, show what warm-hearted, generous natures they possessed. Language seems to fail their biographers in attempting to render the devotion with which they were regarded. A dying pauper in the Liverpool workhouse, said he thought he was in heaven when Agnes came to his bedside. A patient of Sister Dora stood "up and reverently pulled his forelock as if he had pronounced the name of a saint or angel," every time he mentioned her. Of Margaret it is written, "What struck me most in our dearest mother, was her largeness of heart, and the total absence of self in all her words and actions." A common trait of these remarkable women was a splendid physique and immense bodily strength. Agnes, the least distinguished in this respect, was yet capable of enduring extraordinary bodily fatigue. "After a whole night on duty in St. Thomas's Hospital, she thinks it lazy to go to bed, and spends the day in walking and paying visits." * Of Dora, the surgeon of the Epidemic Hospital said: "Sister Dora could sit up all night and work all day with little or no rest; and, as far as I could judge, she was neither physically nor mentally the worse for it. Her strength was superhuman. I never saw such a woman." And this will not appear an overstatement in the light of the following anecdote. "A delirious patient, a tall, heavy man, in the worst stage of confluent small-pox, threw himself out of bed in the dead of night, and with a loud yell rushed to the door before she could stop him. She had no time

* "Life," by her sister, p. 160.

for hesitation, but at once grappled with him, all covered as he was with the loathsome disease. Her combined strength and determination prevailed, and she got him back into bed, and held him there by main force until the doctor arrived in the morning."* Margaret, if possible, was still stronger. Her biographer says : " Possessed of extraordinary muscular power, she was rather proud of hearing herself called as strong as Samson ; and when about seventeen years of age, seeing some men hesitate to lift a great iron stove, she thought to put them to shame, and carried it unassisted to the top of the house." All three were brave, but Dora was lion-hearted beyond compare, and would face drunken ruffians in the slums of Walsall, into which the police would only venture with caution.

All had powerful minds, though in no one of them had education been carried very far. Indeed, Margaret was wholly illiterate, and never mastered orthography, geography, or arithmetic. Agnes had the usual education of a young lady of family and position forty years ago. Dora probably was the best trained of the three. But native vigour of mind supplied all defects, and each showed a great faculty of government and organization, though in different degrees. Agnes, who died young, had not time to show her full power ; but the last three years of her life, in charge of the Liverpool workhouse, with its fifteen hundred inmates, testified to her gifts in that direction. Dora was a lovely, fascinating despot, bending all hearts and wills by her supreme charm and force. Margaret was a born ruler, with thoroughly imperial qualities, who could have governed a state in perilous times as well as she governed her convents. If one might venture, in short, to imitate the nomenclature applied to the great Scholastics, we might

* " Life," by Miss Lonsdale, p. 159.

call Agnes, the Soror Angelica, so ineffably meek, resigned, and nunlike she was, for all her Protestant training; Dora, the Soror Practica, with her unequalled power of achieving work, whatever it might be; Margaret, the Soror Dominatrix, by reason of her grand and imposing mind and character, which, in spite of her low birth and want of culture, made her more than the equal of the scholars, nobles, and ecclesiastics of her own Catholic Church.

Now, is it not evident that all these women were simply women of extraordinary genius? Dora's conversation was bewitching; her alternate humour and pathos were the delight and solace of her nurses and patients; and made an observer say that it was easy to see that she might have been a great novelist, if she had not chosen to be something greater and better. Margaret, though she could not spell the simplest words, showed, in her incessant correspondence, great powers of style. Agnes, though inferior to either in these respects, always writes with a simple, clear, and direct vigour which proves what a calm, strong brain she had. No one of them gave a thought to literature, but one sees that literature was easily within their reach, if they had aimed at it. Their distinction was founded on character, the supreme quality; warm, fearless hearts, exquisite tenderness of conscience, passionate self-sacrifice, and devotion to duty. Christians by training and inclination, they realized in their fervent hearts the meaning and purport of the gospel. According to the terms of their belief, "they forsook all and followed " Christ in their several ways—the Evangelical Agnes, the High-Church Dora, the Catholic Margaret. But even their pious biographers admit that, apart from the gifts of grace, which they were not likely to undervalue, their natural powers and endowments were extraordinary. Of Margaret it is said, that even at the first meeting, the most prominent features of her character could not escape notice; "the firm will, the clear and rapid judgment, the boundless power of sympathy, which won her the title of 'everybody's mother.'" Miss Lonsdale tells us how "a hard, sarcastic Scotchman," who was a professed unbeliever, remarked of Dora, whose patient he had been, "She's a noble woman, but she'd have been that without her Christianity." That is just the simple fact of the matter. Such heads and hearts as these are the property of no creed; they are the choice products of that maligned human nature, which theologians tell us is cursed and lost, unless it believes this or that article of faith. If the saintliness of these holy women depended upon their creed, why do not the thousands and millions who hold the same creed exhibit a like saintliness? "God did not give them the grace," is the theological answer; and some are still satisfied with it. But the answer is evidently becoming unreal and meaningless. The doctrine of heredity and variation has deprived it of all weight. Strong minds and fervent hearts, like strong bodies, depend upon organization; on the constitution and quality of the brain. But brains "are begotten, not made," and grace never made a weak brain strong.

The contemplation of these remarkable women suggests one or two more interesting points of view.

1. An experience of some eighteen centuries may be considered conclusive as to the limited hold which Christianity is capable of taking on mankind at large. From the days of St. Paul to the present time, the apathy and worldliness of the great mass of men and women calling themselves Christians, has been the constant lamentation of all sincere preachers. Indeed, the parable of the Sower clearly announces that the fact was to be expected. The seed

falls in four different places, and only in one does it bear fruit—where it fell on *good* ground. The Wicked one, the want of root, the cares of this world, and deceitfulness of riches, prevent its growth in the other places, which are evidently supposed to cover by far the larger area; and the parable of the Marriage of the King's ·Son, with its conclusion, "Many are called but few are chosen," leaves no doubt on the matter. The obvious deduction is, that Christianity is only adapted to a very limited number of minds; that, for one reason or another, the many, called as they may be, will not "hear the word and understand it." And this is exactly what has happened without interruption, for nearly two thousand years; Christendom has never been evangelized, nor near being evangelized. Even the smallest and most select communities of religious persons have their backsliders and formalists, who are, to use Mr. Spurgeon's words, as religious as the seats they sit on. The high Calvinists boldly face the difficulty, and say, "No doubt; the great mass of mankind are predestined from all eternity to damnation; it is only the elect who are really Christians, and go to heaven." Calvinism is out of fashion now, and reproached with suggesting very unpleasant notions as to the moral character of the Deity; but it is consistent and scriptural; I do not say sensible or orthodox. So far from Christianity being the universal religion it is affirmed to be, it is not even adapted to the majority of its own believers. You must have a very fine and peculiar organization to be a true Christian; a special genius, which generally declares itself in early life, as special genius is apt to do. A Sister Agnes or Mother Margaret take to vital religion with the spontaneous affinity that Mozart took to music, Newton to mathematics, and Keats to poetry. Religious genius, in its highest form, is as rare, perhaps more rare, than genius in any other form ; and exalted piety is as unattainable to the common herd as exalted poetry. Bishop Ullathorne, who must have had large opportunities of seeing nuns and others who aimed with special earnestness at a religious life, yet declares of Margaret that she was distinguished from every other holy soul that he had been acquainted with, by three extraordinary gifts, which he mentions : her peculiar love of God ; the pain it cost her to turn from Him to self-introspection ; and her angelic purity. "Rare as suns," he says, "are those souls which seem to act on other souls like a sacramental power, shedding the rays of their own inward sense of God and vital warmth of spirit into the souls that come within the sphere of their action." * And similar testimony as to the rarity of the endowments of Sisters Dora and Agnes are forthcoming from those who have had wide experience of religious persons. Yet, good as these pious women were, I suppose no priest or theologian would say that they had attained the furthest limit of Christian perfection. They all thought in their humility that they had fallen far short of it. What hope, then, is there for souls less richly endowed ?

And let us observe, how this pursuit of a spirituality utterly beyond attainment by ordinary mortals, beautiful as it is when attained, operates injuriously on the morality of average men and women. The standard proposed is so exalted, that instead of attracting the ordinary person to aim at reaching it, it discourages and repels him. He is inwardly conscious that he cannot possibly reach it, even if he tries ever so much. His preacher will probably tell him that, if he trusts in his own strength, he can do nothing ; but that if he will only put all his trust in God and Christ,

* Preface to " Life of Mother Margaret."

the end will be attained.   But that is just what he is unable
to do.   He is exhorted to exert a spirituality of mind
which, by the hypothesis, he has not got.   It is like telling
a man that, if he will only fly, he will reach great altitudes.
He has not the wings.   Even the saints have generally had
long periods of probation and wrestlings with God, before
they could attain to that detachment, spirituality and perfect
faith, which enabled them to perform the act of complete
self-renunciation required.   Yet it is recommended to the
common multitude, as if it were the easiest thing in the
world.

And what is the result? Setting apart the openly profane
and wicked, who do not give a thought to the subject ; and,
without denying it, simply ignore Christianity ; the bulk of
worldly, unconverted believers pass their time in a middle
state between sin and repentance ; believers, but not doers,
of the Word ; wishing they could . embrace their religion
with entire earnestness, but too well aware that, constituted
as they are, they are unable to do so.   Of course, reference
is made only to the true-hearted, honest folk who transgress
from weakness, and not to the spiritually dead Pharisee who
has no doubt about *his* righteousness.   Such are, on all
hands, admitted to be worse than the publicans and harlots.
But the mass of common-place people who go to church or
chapel, who are neither very good nor very bad, neither
exceptionally clever nor stupid, the enormous middle class
of mediocrities, fairly just, conscientious, and kind-hearted,
can it be denied that they are constantly deterred from
embracing a serious view of life's duties, just because a
standard of such exalted perfection is proposed to them,
that they know it is no use attempting to reach it.   They
perhaps try, and fail, and they are more disheartened than
before.   They then live with a mildly evil conscience,

knowing that they ought to do better. But they are at once told that that is not enough ; that they must do their best ; that they must be perfect, as their Father which is in heaven is perfect. Then they do less than they could, out of sheer, weary dejection. In what other art or science do teachers begin by placing the most arduous problems before their pupils ? Young mathematicians are not set to work on the Differential Calculus in their first lessons; young artists are not expected to draw like Andrea, and colour like Titian. But the young catechumen is told that the first thing he must do is " to renounce the devil and all his works, the pomps and vanities of this wicked world, and *all* the sinful lusts of the flesh." For the first precept of the first lesson, this must be admitted to be rather hard. How many saints, after a long life's progress in holiness, have been equal to it ? To renounce the devil and all his works cannot be easy, if all that we are told of Satan's power be true. But the "good child" is told that he must do this at once. By a subsequent after-thought on the part of the compiler, the learner is warned that he cannot do this and a great many other things *of himself;* he needs God's special grace, " which he must learn to call for by diligent prayer." Probably, to nine children out of ten " diligent prayer," commanded in this way, appears even more obscure and meaningless than renouncing the pomps and vanities of this wicked world. How cruel and heedless to place the last stage of spiritual evolution at the threshold of the neophyte's progress. The whole Catechism and the larger part of sermons and Christian teaching are pervaded by the double error of supposing that the highest religious emotions are attainable by all, and that they may be *inculcated* at the earliest period of life. " My duty towards God, is to believe in him, to fear him, and *to love him with all my heart, with all my mind, with all my soul, and with all my strength."* Perhaps the most prompt and certain way of checking an emotion in others, is to tell them that it is their *duty* to feel it. Tell any one he *ought* to feel grateful, and you will probably make him ten times more ungrateful than he was before. We may be sure that no one ever loved God, for being told that it was his duty to love him. Wise and good mothers, by gentle and indirect precept and very direct example, have led their little ones to piety ; but then they used the subtle language of the heart. The unreality and inefficacy of sermons, chiefly depend on the transcendent disproportion between the doctrine preached, and the capacity to receive it by the audience addressed. A mixed congregation, consisting of men whose thoughts are absorbed in business, and women occupied with dress and frivolities, are spoken to in language which would not be inadequate to the spiritual needs of angels. The result is a discrepancy between faith and practice, which the profane are not slow to tax with hypocrisy. Neither religion nor morals gain by such exaggerations ; only the scoffers at all goodness, who delight in pointing out that so-called religious people are no better than their neighbours. To get the best you can out of men, you must not ask more than they can give. But if you ask for that in the proper way, nearly all but the thoroughly bad will respond. By asking for the impossible, you get little or nothing, or worse than nothing ; a conviction that religion is grimace, and a disbelief in the possibility of virtue.

And now let us contemplate these three saints from another side ; that of the value of their work, its usefulness in this world, and its power of diminishing human suffering.

Before I go further, I shall be met with a refusal to allow the question to be stated in this way. It will be said, that these ladies considered far more the souls than the bodies of their patients, pupils, nurses, or nuns, as the case may be ; that although they strove earnestly to heal the sick, none more so, yet their real and main object was to win souls to Christ. I am not inclined to deny so obvious a fact ; but it is one with which I cannot deal, because, as regards the result of their labours in that direction, I can form no opinion. It is wholly beyond my power to verify any statement on that head. Of the numbers who died in their presence, soothed and comforted, beyond doubt, by their assured faith, their fervent prayers, and "tranquil, regardant faces," I cannot tell whether any or none ever passed "to where beyond these voices there is peace." The point must be left undecided, to say the least, for want of evidence of an objective kind, as distinguished from evidence of a subjective kind, reposing entirely on faith. Believers must be satisfied with their own belief, until they can advance arguments far more cogent than any which they have hitherto produced in support of it. Agnostics cannot be expected to argue on principles which they reject. But this does not wholly remove a common ground on which discussion can take place. The temporal work of these good women is offered to us, as a proof of what the divine spirit can do when it finds fitting channels. Now, I will vie with any one in celebrating the unselfish devotion, the self-sacrifice, the warm love and sympathy which they all showed in assuaging human suffering, bodily or mental. I cannot read their lives without tears, and the admiration I feel for them may be truly called passionate. I regard them as inexpressibly lovely and attractive human souls, who, led on by their own warm women's hearts, nearly, if not entirely, conquered self, and became like the beautiful alabaster box of ointment of spikenard, very costly and precious, which, when poured out, filled the house with the odour of the ointment. But this profession does not preclude me from pointing out, that if the question is of diminishing human suffering, these pious workers did not take up the problem with any full sense of its magnitude ; did not begin high enough up in their efforts to stop the stream of evil and pain. While the value of good nursing can hardly be exaggerated, it can never be more than an adjunct of practical medicine. It is in biological and pathological research, with the object of discovering and destroying the germs and origin of disease, that science now justly rests its main hope of serving humanity. And is there not already ample reason for looking on this hope as well-founded? The anecdote, quoted a few pages back, of Sister Dora grappling with the delirious patient in his loathsome condition from confluent small-pox, presents a graphic and even sensational picture of self-devotion for the welfare of a fellow-creature. The deed was heroic and admirable, whether the sufferer's life was ultimately saved or not. But now, regard the method of science in encountering disease, and this particular malady of small-pox. A man of genius, with his eyes open, observes that milkmaids inoculated with cow-pox are not susceptible to the graver contagion, and Jenner, after careful and elaborate experiments, announces the discovery of vaccination. There is nothing to appeal to the dramatic sympathies in this, nothing to stir emotion in the ordinary spectator. On the contrary, at the time it was considered to afford material for ridicule as a sample of scientific absurdity. But which method has been most profitable to humanity? Have all the self-sacrifices of all the Doras and Sisters of Mercy in the world, spared mankind a tithe of the suffering which has been prevented by vaccination? The epidemic of small-pox at Walsall, in which Sister Dora played so noble a part, appears formidable and shocking to us, with our modern ideas of the subject. But, in the last century, before Jenner, it would, in the dimensions it had, have been considered beneath notice. Half the population might have been swept away without attracting particular attention. That was the way with small-pox, and people were resigned. It was the finger or the wrath of God, chastening men for their sins.

Now, as one might expect in these biographies, in no one instance is scientific inquiry ever mentioned as a duty of the slightest importance or value. It would be simple indeed to look for anything of the kind in such a quarter. The point of view is wholly different. God present everywhere, doing or permitting all that happens, is the invariable presumption. Sister Dora on one occasion offered to pay a visit to a friend, "But," she added, " of course, if the Master comes and calls for me, and sends us in more cases, I cannot come." The " Master," of course is God; and the cases were cases of small-pox, which he was supposed to send on the one hand, and to call Dora to nurse on the other. This is the prevailing tone. But in neither of the Protestant lives is there any direct railing at science. In the Catholic life it is very different. There we meet the flash of anger and hatred for science, characteristic of the theologian who fears that his God is in danger. Considering her entire want of scientific or philosophical culture, Mother Margaret showed great penetration in her remark on this subject. When she first caught sight of the Britannia Bridge, she exclaimed, " Oh, how wonderful! But if men do such things as these, they will begin to think they have no need of God." And her biographers tell us she felt a certain satisfaction when some of the wonderful modern discoveries came to nought. She was glad to hear that the laying of the first Atlantic cable had failed; and, what is still worse, and is a stain on her memory, she was even pleased that, " in spite of storm-signals and meteorological theories, the wrecks on the English coast increased, instead of diminishing in number." * " I like these learned gentlemen to know," she would say, " that God is master." Professor Huxley once likened the temper excited in some portions of the clerical world by the recent growth of physical science, to the anger and alarm with which the savage views the progress of an eclipse ; and that the comparison was just, these sentiments of Mother Margaret sufficiently show. It is a favourite theme with theologians to maintain that the love of God leads to the loftiest and purest love of man, and 1 John iv. 20 is quoted with effect. But a long experience has shown that a verse of the Psalms is often a truer statement of the actual fact. " Shall I not hate them, O Lord, that hate thee?" Can we doubt that Mother Margaret, who, for all her warm-heartedness, could rejoice in so dreadful a thing as shipwrecks, just because, in her narrow bigotry, she thought they were a rebuke to men of science, could also have assisted at an Auto da Fé without compunction, if told it was required by the interests of her creed?

The particular case we have been considering is significant enough in itself, as typical of the different methods of theology and science, in their contention against human suffering. But it suggests much wider issues ; the whole question of the great campaign against vice, evil, and misery. The principle of Christian charity is to palliate and assuage physical and social evils in their last and extreme form. If you meet a beggar, give him alms ; if

* " Life," p. 231.

you have no money, divide your cloak with him, as did St. Martin. Feed the hungry, clothe the naked. In a word, run with prompt love and sympathy to succour every case of mortal distress that comes within your reach. Do this in remembrance of Christ, and be blessed. He would be a cold and shallow student of history who ventured to speak of this spontaneous movement of the heart with dis-respect. The Christian care for the sick and infirm was unknown to the pagan world. It was the best and only thing to do under the circumstances. Science was not; and relief, such relief as could be given by poor, unin-structed fellow-men, was all that could be had. But science has slowly and gradually discovered and proved that social and physical evil and pain may not only be soothed, but anticipated and prevented. Not that it neglects palliatives of suffering; on the contrary, it applies them with an efficacy and power utterly beyond the conception of former ages. But it does more; it nips evil in the bud, or rather in the seed, and does not wait for its full efflorescence before it attacks it. Physical, social, and moral evil, disease and sin, it regards as so many pathological conditions, which we may reasonably. hope to correct, modify,. and, ultimately, to suppress. As regards physical disease, this position would hardly be questioned even by the most orthodox. Several of the most formidable afflictions, to which human and animal bodies are subject, have already been got under control. Small-pox and typhoid fever are, we may say, understood and practically mastered; that is, they are not allowed to spread and devastate as they formerly did. A number of other maladies, with which it once seemed hopeless to contend, are even now passing into the class of the controllable disorders, as consumption, rabies, and cholera. Similarly, with regard to pauperism and other social disorders. The prompt and easy narcotic of charity is not to be universally proscribed as uniformly evil, but it is ascertained to be of dangerous application, and liable to aggravate the evil it pretends to cure. Pauperism can only be combated with success, by that knowledge of social and economic laws which corresponds to the knowledge of biological laws in the neighbouring science. It may be proper and wise, in a given case, to divide your coat with a beggar; the only thing that a humane man would or could do. But it is vastly more important to ascertain the social and economic causes of the beggar's existence; and, if he be a common phenomenon, to correct those breaches of the laws of social health which make his emergence possible. Again, with regard to ethics. Moral evil, or sin, can only be successfully corrected by such an investigation and knowledge of man's mental, emotional, and physical constitution, that that part of conduct which is concerned with morals may be directed in a way which conduces to the highest individual and social happiness and well-being. In a word, the Christian principle is to act from spontaneous charity and benevolence with such means as are immediately to hand : to regard evil, pain and disease, as trials sent by God for his own wise ends; chastisements, meant for our rebuke or guidance, to make us turn to him, and leave off caring for a temporal, wicked and miserable world. The principle of science is directly contrary. It has already prevented numberless evils, in a way which would have appeared to our forefathers quite miraculous. Admitting that there will, perhaps, be always a residue of unconquerable evils which science cannot hope to remove, it is maintained that the resignation produced by a clear view of the impossible and inevitable is more complete than that which never wholly renounces the hope of divine aid. Mother Margaret was quite right in her fears ; " But if men do such things as these, they will begin to think that they can do without God." That thought is rapidly spreading over the civilized world.

CHAPTER VIII.

THE results of the previous inquiry would seem to be as follows :—

1. That a wide-spread tendency exists in this, and still more in other countries, to give up a belief in Christianity. And that the scepticism of the present day is very far more serious and scientific than was the deism of the last century.

2. That the supposed consolations of Christianity have been much exaggerated. And that it may be questioned whether that religion does not often produce as much anxiety and mental distress as it does of joy, gladness and content.

3. That by the great doctrine of forgiveness of sins consequent on repentance, even in the last moment of life, Christianity often favours spirituality and salvation at the expense of morals.

4. That the morality of the Ages of Faith was very low ; and that the further we go back into times when belief was strongest, the worse it is found to be.

5. That Christianity has a very limited influence on the world at large ; but a most powerful effect on certain high-toned natures, who, by becoming true saints, produce an immense impression on public opinion, and give that religion much of the honour which it enjoys.

N

6. That although the self-devotion of saints is not only beyond question, but supremely beautiful and attractive; yet, as a means of relieving human suffering and serving man in the widest sense, it is not to be compared for efficiency with science.

It is sufficiently obvious, that, unless the tendencies which we have been considering, meet with a strange and unexpected arrest, the result, in a not distant future, must be a general disappearance of Christianity from among the more advanced populations of the globe. In making this statement, one naturally recalls the grave irony of the Advertisement prefixed to the first edition of Butler's "Analogy," which is often cited as affording a good example of the way in which the hopes of unbelievers may be deceived. "It is come, I know not how," says Butler, "to be taken for granted, by many persons, that Christianity is not so much as a subject of inquiry; but that it is, at length, now discovered to be fictitious. And accordingly they treat it, as if, in the present age, this were an agreed point among all people of discernment; and nothing remained, but to set it up as a principal subject of mirth and ridicule, as it were by way of reprisals, for its having so long interrupted the pleasures of the world." The "people of discernment," it is pointed out, were very much mistaken in their assumption that Christianity was discovered to be fictitious. The "Analogy" was written nearly a hundred and fifty years ago; and, for a fictitious system, Christianity still shows considerable vitality. The number of new churches and chapels built, the zeal and activity of the clergy and missionaries, the propagation of the gospel in foreign parts, and similar facts, are adduced, not without a certain tone of triumph, as sufficient evidence of how groundless and shallow the hopes of the "sceptic" have proved to be in this particular case. Both the original text of Butler, and the modern commentaries upon it, rather show how remote is the scientific and historical point of view from the religious, and what a far-off stage of thought Butler's expressions represent. The word "fictitious" alone, as applied to an ancient and wide-spread religion, jars upon the ear. As if great phases of human thought and feeling could be invented, like a stage play, or concocted by designing priests for the sake of gain. That this really was the current deistical opinion is certain, and it was crudely expressed in the famous, silly verses :—

> " Natural Religion was easy, first, and plain ;
> Tales made it mystery, offerings made it gain ;
> Sacrifices and shows were at length prepared,
> The priests ate roast meat, and the people stared."

A wider knowledge of human nature, past and present, has made such trivial conceptions impossible. No form of the religious sentiment is now regarded as fictitious ; but, on the contrary, as the serious and solid result of the stage of evolution in which it appears. Similarly, with regard to making Christianity a subject of mirth and ridicule. No one with a reputation to lose, would think of speaking with levity of the Christian or any religion. Nothing would be considered better proof of incompetence to handle such subjects than such a tone. The world is older and sadder, and, on the whole, wiser than it was in Butler's day. The alleged interruption of the pleasures of the world by Christianity, is open to question as a matter of fact. Pleasures in abundance, and of a sufficiently coarse kind, were indulged in without difficulty in the Ages of Faith. The " eat, drink, and be merry " temper is generally discountenanced in theory ; and, even in practice, is less rife than it was among our forefathers.

In fact, the result of historical speculation has been, with regard to Christianity, the same as the result of biological speculation has been with regard to man. Both have been taken from the isolation and independence in which they were supposed to exist, with reference to other members of the same order; and have been included in the larger classification, which places man at the head of vertebrate animals, and Christianity at the head of supernatural religions. The biological view has prevailed, one may say, with surprising rapidity, considering the amount of prejudice which had to be overcome. The historical view has naturally triumphed less completely, inasmuch as scientific history is a much younger science than biology. But the end will be the same. Christianity is already classed, by a large and growing number of the most competent historical inquirers, simply as the last and finest specimen of a group of beliefs, which, in one form or another, are co-extensive with humanity and history. If this view should prove to be slower in gaining acceptance than the biological view of the descent of man, the reason will, probably, be not wholly referable to the position of history in the order of the sciences. Distasteful as it was to human vanity to prove that man had descended from an anthropoid ape, which again had descended from a bird or a reptile, the idea still is one which can be put aside, which ordinary folk need not think of in daily life, and which involves no immediate practical consequences to themselves. The final admission, that Christianity is not fictitious, indeed, in Butler's phrase, but simply a form of thought unsuited to a scientific age, and therefore no longer tenable by an educated population, is attended by far greater difficulties. Very obvious practical consequences are involved in such a conclusion, which cannot readily be ignored. If the belief in God,

Christ, and the other articles of the Christian faith must rationally be relinquished, people ask—What are you going to put in their place? What rule of life do you propose to substitute for the one removed? What is the successor to Christianity as a religion? Or, will it have no successor? And some even go so far as to inquire what is to become of those spiritual and religious instincts, which have hitherto found their exercise and satisfaction in a religion now pronounced to be incompatible with the new knowledge. Natural instincts are not to be suppressed by the theories of *savants*, however scientific; and it is argued that the religious sentiment is as much a permanent factor of human nature as the logical intellect; and must, necessarily, survive its endlessly varied and often unstable conclusions.

The religious sentiment, or that group of emotions so called, is one thing, and the Christian or any particular religion is another. The religious sentiment has, during the course of ages, assumed many divergent forms, and at this day is represented in the most dissimilar and diversified beliefs and ceremonies. The original elements of human nature are all capable of morphological development and change in their manifestations, although they remain fundamentally the same. Nothing could well be a more permanent constituent of human nature than the instinct which leads to marriage; but few things have varied more than the institution of marriage. From marriage by capture, through polygamy, polyandry, down to the monogamy of modern states, which still show great differences of detail in their laws on the subject, the legal relation of the sexes have varied with the knowledge, culture, and civilization of the times. It is the same with regard to government and civil institutions, with regard to war and its usages, with regard to the notions of right and wrong. What reason can be given to lead us to suppose that the religious sentiment alone should remain fixed and crystallized in one form, and that a recent one, which supervened in historical times, and was preceded by a great variety of previous forms? Obviously none.

When, therefore, we are asked what religion we propose to substitute in place of the old one, now threatened with extinction, the answer is, that no such pretension is entertained for a moment. Religions are organic growths, and are no more capable of fabrication than animals or plants. The notion that individual men can *found* religions, that is, invent them out of their own heads, and set them going, is on a par with the notion that men can found states, and create policies which last for ages. Both notions were prevalent, and not irrational once, when neither man nor society was conceived as subject to natural laws. So, it was really believed that Lycurgus founded the Spartan State, and Romulus the Roman; that Moses founded Judaism, and Mahomet, Islam. No misconception could be greater, and none is more certain to disappear. That long prepared changes are often suddenly accomplished, under the inspiring leadership of a great man, is beyond question; and it is quite natural that the great man's name should be associated with the change in which he took a prominent part. But he did not make the change, in the sense of founding or beginning something new, which would not have existed without him. His function, and it was great indeed, was to have intellect enough to see the need of change, and courage and Will enough to help it forward, to direct forces which were already at hand. All great changes in Church or State exemplify this truth, in proportion as we are able to observe them with accuracy of detail. Nothing is more certain than that, in one sense

Julius Cæsar overthrew the Republic, and *founded* the Empire of Rome. But how long had such a revolution been preparing? From the days of the Scipios, or of Sulla and Marius. Or, might it not be dated from the earliest constitution of Rome, which rendered a municipal form of government inadequate, and finally impossible for a wide Empire? All great social revolutions result from long precedent, although, perhaps, occult growth, as parturition, in the body physical, pre-supposes embryonic growth. Similarly, with regard to the Reformation. Luther, in vulgar Catholic or Protestant opinion, is credited with the whole glory, or infamy, of the revolt from Rome. But, from the days of Wicliffe and Huss, the entire Church had been seething with projects of reform; and Luther can only claim the honour of having, in the fulness of time, given the critical impulse which liberated forces accumulated during hundreds of previous years.

There can be no question, therefore, of making and offering a New Religion to the world at the present juncture. Our first task must be, to try and discover what is the spontaneous tendency of thought and sentiment on this matter? What is the direction which evolution may be expected to take? If that can be ascertained, a great point will be gained. Three courses are always open to men called upon to deal with great social and moral tendencies. They may be blindly resisted; they may be blindly stimulated and hastened; they may, by careful study and observation of their nature, be largely controlled and directed; that is to say, they may be dealt with in a spirit of reaction, or in a spirit of revolution, or in a spirit of orderly and conscious progress. Reaction, when conducted on a large scale with unflinching vigour, by no means always fails.

The Moslem Obscurantists in Spain succeeded in crushing Arab philosophy.* The Catholic Church has several times extirpated opinions, by the efficient method of killing those who held them. In Spain, Bohemia, Italy, and Belgium, Protestanism was stamped out, like the rinder-pest, by prompt and persevering slaughter. It is a method difficult of prolonged application; and it is generally avenged. The state of religion in Catholic countries, and the animosity felt towards it by large numbers of the proletariat, are not encouraging examples. The Protestants have not been behind the Catholics in their willingness to prosecute, but they have seldom had equal power. In Ireland, however, they nearly reached the highest level of performance in that line. With what disaster to all of us, is now only too apparent.

How evil, on the other hand, the revolutionary spirit can be, has been well shown by France in the eighteenth century, first, in speculation, and afterwards in politics. The precipitate conclusions of the *philosophes*, although proceeding on principles fundamentally sound, as subsequent results have proved, were yet marked by a heat and haste which led to the Romantic reaction, and the Idealist and Transcendental Philosophies, which nearly suspended rational speculation for half a century. It is unnecessary to dwell on the indelible harm done to orderly progress by the violence of the Revolution, which to this day supplies reactionaries with some of their best weapons against a large and generous liberalism. Perhaps the sober, prudent, middle course we have mentioned, which, while frankly accepting and using the new lights obtained, does not exaggerate their illuminating power, is destined in this age to avoid the dangers associated with either of the two extremes.

* See Renan, "Averroes."

The essence of practical religion at all times has been *Sacrifice.* However the origin of religion is to be explained, and anthropologists in later times seem to have elucidated the subject with much success by ancestor worship, the ghost, and other theories, propitiatory sacrifice has been the unfailing mark and memorial of religious belief. It is unnecessary to produce evidence of a statement so redundantly supported. What chiefly deserves notice in this connection, is the progressive change in the character of the sacrifice; corresponding with mental evolution. In earlier times, human sacrifices were, probably, everywhere regarded as the most pleasing and powerful with the deities. Every form of possession valued by primitive people was readily lavished on the altar of the gods, either to avert their wrath or to secure their favour; cattle, firstfruits especially, as at once the most costly to the worshipper and the most acceptable to the Divinity. In time, this gross form of propitiation was transcended; and even the later Jewish prophets speak of it with disdain. As the conceptions of the moral character of the gods grew loftier, the notion of the sacrifices calculated to please them rose in proportion. As men attained to worthier ideas of moral excellence, they recognized that sacrifice of their own baser instincts was likely to be the most pleasing offering to a moral deity. " A wise man," says a passage in the Institutes of Menu, "should constantly discharge all the moral duties, though he perform not constantly the ceremonies of religion; since *he falls low if, while he performs ceremonial acts only, he discharges not his moral duties.*" * And the same law prescribes " content, returning good for evil, resistance to sensual appetites, abstinence from illicit gain, purification, coercion of the organs . . . veracity, and freedom from

* Mill's "History of India," book ii. cap. 6.

wrath."* Yet the cruelty and obscenity of the early Hindu religion are beyond doubt. The frank indecencies and immoralities of primitive creeds are in time explained away by mystical allegories of the most spiritual purity. "The lascivious form of a naked Venus," says Gibbon, referring to the fancies of the Neo-Platonists, "was tortured into the discovery of some moral precept or some physical truth; and the castration of Atys explained the revolution of the sun between the tropics, or the separation of the human soul from vice and error."† The primitive meaning of the phallus in India, according to Mr. Wilson, is entirely forgotten. "The form under which the Lingam is worshipped, that of a column, suggests no impure ideas, and few of the uneducated Hindoos attach any other idea to it than that it *is* Siva; they are not aware of its typical character."‡

The next point is, that primitive religion had little or no connection with human welfare, apart from the action of supernatural beings. Its chief or only object was to guard the worshipper from injuries which came from the spirit-world, or to procure him benefits from the same origin. From a natural, mundane point of view, primitive religion was oftener evil than good. It sacrificed human life and property on the imaginary propitiation of fictitious deities. It is highly probable, indeed, that even the most horrid primitive cults were indirectly beneficial, as means of discipline, and of adapting to social conditions the semi-brutal instincts of prehistoric man. In that respect, primitive religion resembled war; which, destructive as it was in one sense, is still recognized as one of the most educational

* Mill's " History of India," book ii. cap. 6.
† " Decline and Fall," c. xxiii.
‡ Note to Mill's " India," *loc. cit.*

phases which humanity has passed through. But, just as the antagonism between sacrifice and morality was gradually overcome, so the hostility of primitive religion to human welfare was in time replaced by an approximation to concord between them. The angle of divergence became progressively less. Worship of the gods tended more and more to coincide with the welfare of man. The humanization of the various polytheistic religions of the world has been very unequal, both in degree and rapidity, depending as it necessarily must, on the unequal progress in knowledge and civilization. The Hindus in three thousand years have made less progress in purging their primitive beliefs of their cruelty and grossness, than the Romans did in five hundred years. But the general rule holds good, that a progressive people, even without foreign help from more advanced populations, tends to outlive the primitively barbarous and noxious elements of its creed, and to retain those which harmonize with general utility.*

The Christian religion has been no exception to this rule; in fact, it would not be easy to mention a religion which has profited more by the general growth of knowledge and civilization than the Christian. It has been claimed, not without a show of reason, that it is a peculiar and exceptional merit of Christianity, that it has been able to adapt itself to most unequal and divergent stages of culture, and that it has met the wants of barbarous and civilized races with equal success. Though the time is obviously approaching, if it has not been already reached, when its alleged adequacy to the needs of civilized society becomes more and more questionable, it may be frankly admitted that Christianity has surpassed all other religions in its power of keeping up

---

* Polybius's testimony to the value of the Roman religion, as enforcing honesty, is too well known to need quoting (lib. vi. cap. 56).

with human evolution. The fact is, no doubt, owing to the large element of Greek philosophy grafted on Christianity by the Greek and Latin Fathers, and even by St. Paul. The religion would probably not have survived into modern times, unless it had possessed this elasticity and capacity of modification, which have allowed it to exist side by side with the most divergent beliefs on other subjects. A Catholic Christian of the fifth, and one of the nineteenth century, would, if they could meet in the flesh, agree in reference to the Creeds of the Church, but they would be able to agree in little besides. If we could have a conversation with the great St. Augustine, we should soon fail to find common ground for argument, whether as to matters of fact, principles of reasoning, or, even as to the interpretation of scripture; and it may even be doubted if the present able and accomplished pope, who has so deep a veneration for St. Thomas Aquinas, would not find a prolonged discussion on things in general, difficult to maintain with the Angel of the Schools. Yet, St. Augustine, St. Thomas, and Leo XIII., must be admitted to be thoroughly orthodox and authentic Christians. But this flexibility and adaptability of Christianity on the intellectual side, are not the qualities with which we are chiefly concerned at this moment. The point I would bring out, is the incomparably greater emphasis laid by modern Christians, on all that concerns human well-being, than was usually done by their predecessors. In the old days, the Faith, holy living, and especially holy dying, were the great themes of Christian preachers. The true Faith was literally all-important, as, without it, you were hopelessly lost, whatever else you might do or be. Hence, the Faith was to be fought for and suffered for at any cost. Wars, massacres, burnings, tortures, were trivial considerations compared with the one thing needful, which alone could lead to heaven. And we know that these plagues were scattered through many centuries without stint or remorse. After the true Faith was gained, the next chief thing was to make a good use of it, and by a holy life and a repentant death, to save your soul. Earthly miseries, famines, pestilences, ignorance, chronic poverty, were lamentable, no doubt; but the famines and the pestilences were especially so, as manifestations of God's wrath, who was thus chastising a wicked world. Their proper and only antidote was prayer, and repentance, and humiliation before God, who might thereby be induced to stay his hand. Such afflictions were incidental to the lot of man, the appropriate retribution for sin, to be borne with resignation. As for combating them by human means and knowledge, with a view to suppressing them, if such an idea could have emerged, it would have been unquestionably pronounced impious and shocking. The only recognized form of relief was charity; the rich must give of their abundance to the poor, and they would be repaid in heaven. The Church of Rome gave practical effect to this view by the admirable and useful institution of, first, the Frères de la Charité, founded by the Portuguese Johann Ciudad, 1497, and afterwards of the Filles de la Miséricorde, the work of the saintly Vincent of Paul, 1634. Every form of praise and honour is due to those good men and women, who devoted themselves without stint to the relief of human misery, regardless of the more profitable pursuits of Church politics and theological controversy. But the very foundation of these institutions showed that they supplied a great want, which had not been furnished by the Church before; and they were, after all, only a small and subordinate section of the vast hierarchy which had shared the dominion of the world with the temporal power. St. Vincent of Paul met in the ranks of the secular clergy with some of his most stubborn opponents.*

Now, it is hardly too much to say, that in recent times the whole attitude of the clergy in all countries has been changed with regard to social questions. Nearly every form of relief now, in greater or lesser degree, passes through their hands. The improvement of the condition of the poor seems very often to be the chief occupation of many a hard-worked parish priest. To rescue children from vice and temptation, to inform their minds with virtuous principles, to clothe and feed their bodies, to ameliorate the dwellings of their parents, and admit a ray of light and brightness into the squalor of their daily lives,—these, and similar objects, occupy the time and minds of Christian ministers to a degree which was never even remotely approached in the past. In other words, Christian doctrine, or, at least, Christian practice, has been gradually brought into harmony with human and terrestrial wants, so as almost to run parallel with them. The world has much changed. The cessation of religious controversy is a surprising phenomenon. In place of the storm and fury with which polemics formerly filled the air, we have now a great calm. The small sputter of theological disputes, still occasionally heard, is as the explosion of squibs and crackers compared to that of the heavy ordnance in the mighty controversies of old.

Thus, we find two permanent factors running through the religions of the past in all their changes of outward presentation : sacrifices on the part of the worshipper; and a gradual approximation of the service of the gods to the service of man. Neither of these factors is the exclusive property of any one religion ; and both of them in some

* See Feillet, "La Misère au Temps de la Fronde."

degree, perhaps, may belong to all. They are quite capable of detachment and isolation from the surroundings with which they are usually associated in theological creeds. Sacrifice admits of almost infinite degrees both in quality and quantity, from an offering of a pair of turtle doves or two young pigeons, up to a hundred oxen; from the most partial control of the coarsest passions, up to saintly abnegation of every impure or selfish desire. And the spirit of sacrifice, the postponing of self to others, the giving up what the natural man loves and values, whether possessions or cherished lusts, is so little restricted to the worshippers of a God or gods, that it may be said in its highest form to be unattainable by them. The worshipper of a god never quite transcends the hope of a recompense for his devotion; not from men, but from " his Father which seeth in secret," and who shall reward him openly. And this feeling springs inevitably from the very conception of a deity, especially if he be God Almighty. A creature can be on no terms of reciprocity with his Creator; he can only be a recipient from God, never a renderer back of good. The very thought of performing an act of kindness or sympathy to God, is absurd. The infinite disparity between the two beings, man and his Maker, has as a consequence that " every good gift and every perfect gift is *from above.*" Only to his fellows can man be completely altruistic, " hoping for nothing again." That numbers of men and women among the higher races are capable of acts of unalloyed altruism, in which there is not a vestige of after-thought tending to self-advantage, will only be denied by the naturally cynical, or by those educated in an evil religious or philosophic system. The mother who tends her sick child and scorns any counsels to spare her health and strength; the rough miner who bids his mate seize the one chance of escape up the shaft, as he has a wife and children, whereas the speaker is a bachelor ; the surgeon who sucks diphtheric poison from a dying child's throat and dies himself in consequence,—are examples of the love and sacrifice even now to be found in the nobler hearts. And it is denying evolution in fact and theory, to question the certainty that they will become less exceptional than they now are. But, in this capacity of sacrifice regardless of self we have the purest essence of the best religions ; a human quality which exists, which has been evolved in the long travail of the world, but which may be cultivated with prospects of vastly greater increase now that its supreme beauty and price are perceived and valued. When the mental and moral qualities of man are regarded as subject, in common with other forms of life, to the law of heredity and variation, their cultivation and improvement will be conducted on the scientific basis which has already produced such surprising results in other parts of the vegetable and animal kingdoms. The plasticity of human nature is even yet but little appreciated, though what the Spartans, the Stoics, and the Jesuits succeeded in doing with their imperfect empirical methods is suggestive enough. But these, or the two latter, at least, only contemplated the education of the individual. What is wanted is the conscious cultivation, enlightened by science, of society as a whole.

As regards the end to which religions have in an unconscious way more or less tended—the general well-being—there will probably be little difficulty in admitting that it is an object which civilized man has proved himself capable of attaining in a considerable measure already. The superiority of the modern nations, not only to savages, but even to their own not very remote ancestors, is beyond dispute ; and this not only in reference to physical well-being, but to all the higher sentiments and endowments of man. Imperfect as our social state still is, heart-rending as the condition of the poor in town and country must be pronounced to be, it is, nevertheless, vastly in advance of previous conditions; and our own sensitiveness and shame on the subject, though we are not yet sensitive and ashamed enough, are in themselves evidence of improvement. Arduous as the social problem is acknowledged to be, and sore as the suffering is likely to be before it is finally solved, few can deny that it is capable of solution, and that by human means. The abolition of laws which favour the rich and strong, and sacrifice the poor and weak, has, in a small way, begun, and we may depend that in a democracy it will not easily be arrested. A better distribution and a moralization of wealth are approaching with a rapidity which is not exaggerated by the panic fears of the amazed Few, who hear with astonishment and horror that the world is no longer made for idlers only. The period of social revolution into which we are about to enter, will probably be marked by many mistakes, and not a few crimes. Man's capacity for blunder is very great. He smarts for his blunders, and in time corrects them. But the point to be noted is, that the social revolution will be accomplished on secular principles; that this province of practical life is once for all severed from any theological interference. The proletariat of Europe is resolved to have its fair share of the banquet of life, quite regardless of the good or bad things in store for it in the next world.*

---

* See the *Times* (which seldom outruns public opinion), November 18, 1884. In the third leading article it is said, speaking of the East London Mission :—" The great enemy which has to be met in dealing with this class [the poor] is not active hostility, but total and almost impenetrable indifference. Hostility to the clergy, as such, cannot be said to be wide-spread in London. . . . The London artisan looks on

It comes, therefore, to this, that the spirit of sacrifice evolved in the theological stage is now severed from and independent of its parent. Its office is no longer the same. Sacrifice to invisible gods, with prayer sent up to the immortals, imploring pardon, or peace, or some earthly good, have afforded hope and consolation to the sons of men, in the long, dark centuries when knowledge was not ; when visible man and nature were so hostile, that faith and trust in the unseen seemed the only refuge ; that only "beyond the veil" was a sure friend to be found. A bitter experience has at last taught us that the immortals are deaf ; that no prayers, however passionate, are heard, save by the care-laden hearts which utter them.

Thus, the worship of deities has passed into the "Service of Man." Instead of Theolatry, we have Anthropolatry. The divine service has become human service. The accumulated experience of mankind is beginning to bear fruit. Two things have been ascertained with sufficient exactness to serve as guides, both in practice and theory. First, the kind of conduct needed by a social condition such as ours, that is to say, the outlines of a progressive morality suited to the present age, are fairly settled. Secondly, the kind of social condition desired, and already partially in view, which shall supersede the present inferior one, is also in its

the clergyman as at worst a man who is engaged in a work with which he individually has little or no concern ; he does not interfere with the parson, and he hopes that the parson will not interfere with him. . . . Taken in the mass, the lower classes in London are too much occupied in the struggle for existence, and in the attempt to make their lives endurable, to give many thoughts to the other world." The writer contrasts the very different temper of the Parisian *ouvrier*, who "regards the priest as a monster ;" but he admits that there is an element of active hostility to the clergy in our midst.

main features apprehended. The two factors work together to one result, "complete life carried on under social conditions." * The Service of Man consists in furthering both. The higher moralization of the individuals composing the social group will raise the quality of the social group itself, and the improved group will react upon individuals, and enable them to lead higher lives. In a word, we are now in a position to pursue human well-being as a conscious aim, with good prospect of success. We know fairly well the road along which we intend to travel, and we know the kind of human co-operation needed, to enable us to do so ; the type of character and disposition needed to render social help. And we know, further, that society possesses now, in a degree it never possessed before, the means of exacting conformity to this type. Public opinion, as it used to be called, but for which a better expression would be, the "collective conscience," is already able to impose a standard of public and private morals, and to punish, with penalties keenly felt, a manifest inferiority to it. Even in the political world, singleness of purpose, a true public and social spirit, are valued more than great talent and eloquence without them. A life of selfish ease and indulgence is pardoned to great wealth and position with less readiness than formerly ; and, with the growth of democracy, such a temper must necessarily spread, both in extent and intensity.

The remainder of our subject will, therefore, be considered under the two aspects just indicated : (1) the improvement of the individual, and (2) the improvement of society. We can serve men firstly, and perhaps chiefly, by improving ourselves, and this in all respects, physically, mentally, morally. Without a high standard of health,

* H. Spencer's "Data of Ethics," p. 130.

duties become difficult or impossible to perform, and our whole efficiency is lessened. In these days of increased knowledge, when so much of youth, and even of manhood, is taken up with preparatory study and training, the longevity of its worthier members is a distinct gain to society. A vigorous old age is able to accomplish out of all proportion more than several careers, however brilliant, cut short in youth. Few, or none, are now likely to question the value of mental improvement. It remains true all the same that our notions of education are lamentably inadequate, and that the higher forms of it are not even conceived as possible or desirable in our so-called universities. As regards moral training, finally, no one will dispute its paramount necessity; but the subject is obscured, and the result vitiated by the emphasis laid by the religious public, not on morals, but on repentance; not on the vigorous and constant performance of social duty throughout life, but on making our peace with God, some time, it signifies not how short a time, before life closes. What humanity needs is not people who lead unsocial and wicked lives, and are very sorry when about to die; when, by the nature of the case, they can do no more harm nor good; but people who, at an early period, begin to render valuable service to the good cause, and continue rendering more valuable service as they advance in years. We cannot take regrets and repentance in lieu of work; performance only avails. To prevent misconception, even for a moment, it may be added, that by performance, advance in spiritual life is by no means excluded; and that the contemplative life is not placed below the active life, but contrariwise, as will be seen further on.

The improvement of society, again, is an object to which nearly all persons will declare themselves favourable. But many prejudices and passions, largely incompatible with any serious improvement, will need to be overcome, before our advance* in that direction can become as rapid and assured as is desirable.

There will be no want of work for those who wish to engage in the Service of Man.

CHAPTER IX.

ON THE CULTIVATION OF HUMAN NATURE.

FOR this service to be efficient, it is obvious that men must be adequately trained for it. From time immemorial, education for some object or other has been practised by mankind. The young savage is taught to hunt, fish and shoot with persevering assiduity. Every kind of war implies discipline and drill, however rude. Political life, wherever it exists, inevitably leads to an education fitting men for the treatment of public affairs. Besides these partial ends, religion, in all societies above the lowest, is charged with the general and paramount end of training men in the worship and service of the invisible but all-powerful Being or Beings, who are supposed to dispose of human happiness in this world and the next. This has ever rightly been regarded as the most important of all training, because it concerns every one, and incomparably more momentous interests are involved in its efficient carrying out. The cultivation of human nature, in some degree or direction, is as old as humanity.

But the partiality and imperfection of this cultivation are equally old. The daily acquisition of food occupies the whole life of the savage, almost as completely as it does the lives of the birds and animals which he snares and kills. With the growth of knowledge and wealth, wider objects engage man's attention, and exact a corresponding culture to secure their attainment. But these ends, though wider than those of savage life, are still very narrow, consisting in success in petty warfare with neighbouring states, or in party struggles within the primitive city. Even the worship of the gods is stiffly exclusive and partial, and confined to local or tribal divinities, who are " jealous " in the extreme of any rivals in popular reverence.

This imperfection of culture has continued to modern times, though, with every stride in civilization, it has been lessened, and replaced by something better and larger. Yet, it is still obviously local, partial, and imperfect. Nowhere yet does the aim exist to produce the best human being possible ; to train all the faculties of the body, the mind, and the heart, with the sole object of making the most of them. Men are still trained for special trades and professions, for special countries, and, above all, for special religions. And, in the present low development of the human mind and civilization, it cannot be otherwise, or at least, much otherwise. But there can be no doubt that one of the most assured and practical means of improving society, is to improve the individual men and women who compose it. This is strongly but vaguely expressed in the cry for education ; though one is often tempted to think that none needs education more than the popular clamourer for it. Still, a great advance has been made in the mere recognition that the cultivation of individuals, however imperfect, is a matter of primary importance to the general welfare. Deeper views on the subject will come in time.

For the purpose of this essay, we need not regard the subject from this wide and public point of view. We may limit ourselves to the consideration—ample enough—of the change in the theory of human cultivation, likely to follow

the substitution of the service of man for the service of
God ; and we will do so under the three heads—(1) the
body, (2) the mind, and (3) the heart of man.

1. On the first we need not dwell long.   Medical science
has nearly solved the problem of health.   The amount of
exercise and nourishment, the kinds and qualities of foods
and drinks, the limits of work and relaxation, the salubrity
of sites and dwellings and clothing, these and similar topics
connected with the health of the body physical, are so fairly
well understood that any one with a moderately strong constitution, amenable to good advice, may keep in satisfactory
health.   Many of the worst diseases have been almost dis-
armed, though a few, like cancer, are said to be on the
increase ; and there is a great set-off in the fact that the
very success of medical skill and science has produced
serious harm by saving numbers of weak and bad constitutions, which would formerly have perished, but which now
survive to propagate an unhealthy stock ; an evil which will
be probably diminished or removed by stricter views of
marriage and the procreation of children.   The paramount
importance of health for the adequate discharge of public
and private duties, can escape no one.   It is probable that
in a reformed public opinion of the future, a breakdown in
health, when obviously caused by excess or imprudence, or
culpable ignorance, will be regarded as a species of bank-
ruptcy, and severely judged.   A servant of humanity has no
right to be unable to perform his duties to her.

2. Neither need we dwell long on the cultivation of the
mind, interesting as is the subject, and much as there
would be to say about it in another connection.   The
utility of knowledge is now obvious to everybody, and
nearly all departments are fairly well-cultivated, some of
them with splendid results.   Science now is quite able to

take care of itself, and we have no reason to fear that it will not be equal to the task. The great danger is specialism, which cultivates one small segment of the vast circle of knowledge, and remains contentedly ignorant of the rest. Specialism cannot be spared, if only for the reason that he who is not a specialist in some one thing, is likely to be a sciolist in all things. But, next to the sciolist, the pure specialist is, perhaps the least efficient servant of man.

3. I now come to the third, and incomparably the most important, of all the forms of human cultivation,—the cultivation of the heart and feelings.

I have already, in a previous chapter, attempted to show that, as a support of morality, Christian doctrine and practice were inherently defective ; inasmuch as that the true end of Christianity was not morality in this world, but salvation in the next. My object must now be to show that a cultivation of human nature on positive and human principles will have a different result ; first, because of the different end ; secondly, because of the different means and theories adopted with a view to that end.

The cultivation of nature, vegetable or animal, since it has become scientific, has proceeded on the assumption of a universal law of causation, on which were based experiment and proof. The agriculturist and the grazier, aided by the chemist, have discovered the most propitious conditions, foods, soils, stocks, etc., for their special objects in view, and after great time and pains they have fairly mastered the problem. The only part of it which they have not mastered is the meteorological part ; but in other respects their success has been eminently satisfactory. Even pestilences in the animal and vegetable world are stopped, and prevented from spreading, if not from appearing ; as the extirpation of the rinder-pest, the silkworm disease, and perhaps, most remarkable of all, the destruction of locusts in Cyprus, sufficiently show. It was different even in the Augustan age of Rome—

> ". . . alitur vitium, vivitque tegendo,
> Dum medicas adhibere manus ad volnera pastor
> Abnegat, aut *meliora deos sedet omina poscens.*" *

Epidemic diseases were regarded by Jew and Gentile as special proofs of the anger of the Deity; whom men sought by prayer and sacrifice to propitiate, that the plague might be stayed.

> "Help us, O Lares ! help us, Lares, help us !
> And thou, O Marmar, suffer not
> Fell plague and ruin's rot
> Our folk to devastate." †

In these cases, we now look for help to the sanitary inspector, or the veterinary surgeon.

Now, the scientific cultivation of human nature needs the adoption of the same method and principles as have been so fruitful of good results in other departments. We must cease to believe in miracle and divine aid; and, proceeding on the firm ground of cause and effect, not expect to reap except where and when we have ploughed and sown. The theological doctrine of grace, and the metaphysical doctrine of the freedom of the will, are alike fatal to a steady cultivation of human nature from a moral point of view. Both presuppose an unknown factor, whose presence or absence cannot be foreseen, and whose action cannot be measured. "It is here, it is there, it is gone," and no one can tell why. It at once upsets prevision of the future, and cancels all record of and inference from the past.

An authorized expounder ‡ of Catholic doctrine remarks,

---

* Verg., "Georg.," iii. 454.   † "Song of the Arval Brothers."
‡ Power, "Catechism," vol. ii. p. 33.

"Nothing, absolutely nothing, neither little nor much, can be done without the grace of God. We cannot do a good action, nor produce any good fruit conducive to salvation, without the grace of God." "St. Augustine," remarks Canon Liddon, "says there is no reason, apart from the grace of God, why the highest saint should not be the worst criminal." * In an instant, therefore, a criminal may become a saint, or a saint may become a criminal, according to the good pleasure of God, "who hath mercy on whom he will have mercy, and whom he will he hardeneth." If we assume, as we surely may, that the saintly character is marked by rare and precious qualities, we are made to see, on this theory, by what a frail and uncertain tenure they exist. It is hardly necessary to point out that this doctrine must induce an indifference, almost a recklessness, as to the cultivation of human nature, so far as the heart and feelings are concerned. We cannot be sure for twenty-four hours together whether we shall belong to the diabolically wicked or the angelically good.

The analogy between the theological doctrine of grace and the metaphysical tenet of free-will is obvious. They both appeared prominently together in the controversy between Pelagius and St. Augustine. Free-will is a sort of secular correlative of theological grace. It delivers over man, not to the arbitrary inspiration of divine grace given or withheld, but to the arbitrary autocracy of his own power of volition ; which can do with him what it pleases, if it pleases. "According to the doctrine of Free-will, there is an ultimate power of choice in the human will, which, however strongly it may be drawn, or tempted, or attracted to decide one way or another by external appeals or motives, is not *ruled* and *decided* by such motives, but by the will

* "Oxford Sermons," VI.

itself only." *   Again, "While there is life there is hope and there is fear.   The most inveterate habits of vice still leave a power of self-recovery in the man, if he will but exert it; the most confirmed habits of virtue still leave the liability to a fall." †   The close analogy, almost amounting to identity, between the doctrines of Free-will and Grace, is here very clearly shown.   By encouraging the idea that the most inveterate habits of vice can be reformed by an act of will, the paramount importance of habit is masked or even implicitly denied; that is to say, that one of the most important and widely dominant laws of biology is denied, or the moral nature of man is withdrawn from its dominion. If the most confirmed habits of virtue are no guarantee against a "fall" (that means, can be destroyed by an exertion of the wicked will), it is obvious that patient and protracted effort towards self-discipline and the higher life, is so much labour lost.   The subjugation of self and evil desires carried on for years may end in a "fall," and gratification of our most depraved instincts.   And, contrariwise, "inveterate habits of vice" are not the serious danger one might suppose, as the power of self-recovery is always present and capable of throwing them off, if the man will but exert it.   While there is life there is hope and fear; and up to the last the criminal may become a saint, and the saint a criminal, as St. Augustine said.

It is evident that the doctrine of the freedom of the will, supposes the phenomena of the mind to be exempt from the laws and conditions which regulate the rest of nature; and the more courageous metaphysicians do not hesitate to make this assumption: "Can the knowledge of Nature," asks the late Professor Green, " be itself a part of Nature,

---

* Mozley, "Augustinian Doctrine of Predestination," p. 217.
† *Ibid.;* p. 247. .

in that sense of Nature in which it is said to be an object of knowledge ? " * It is not easy to see why the subject which cognizes the object should be less Nature than the object cognized. The image of an object in the mirror which reflects is as much Nature as the object reflected. However, it is not necessary for the purpose in hand to make a flight into the fine æther of Kantian metaphysics. If we consult fact instead of fiction, we shall conclude that moral qualities are, to say the least, as permanent and durable as any biological phenomena. The digestive functions, the circulation of the blood, and the secretions of the body, are not more periodic and permanent than the passions of the mind. Indeed, the latter are the more lasting and persistent of the two groups. The liver of a miser is more likely to break down in the course of his life, than his passion for gold. The muscular heart of the benevolent man may, and often does, fail, before the spiritual heart which makes him unwearied in doing deeds of mercy. The common sense of mankind has always, when not perverted by the necessities of a theory, recognized the permanence of moral qualities, not only in the individual, but in the race—

> " Fortes creantur fortibus et bonis ;
> Est in juvencis, est in equis patrum
> Virtus, neque inbellem feroces
> Progenerant aquilæ columbam." †

That the two doctrines just referred to, of grace and of free-will, have frequently operated to the injury of morality, is proved by examples too numerous to quote. Louis XV., one of the most profligate men in history, was punctilious in his religious exercises ; and, as Carlyle says, used to catechise

* " Prolegomena to Ethics," p. 11.
† " Hor." iv. 4. 29.

the inmates of his harem in the Parc aux Cerfs, "that they might retain their orthodoxy." But the doctrine of grace, which he had no doubt thoroughly grasped, allowed him to feel that he could at any time repent, and that when he did, he would be freed from his sins. In one of the finest historical pictures ever drawn, even by Carlyle, we are admitted to the side of the "sinner's death-bed," to see his anxiety for the sacraments, and how he made the "amende honorable" to God. If it be objected that this is only a sample of Popish superstition, we will take from a sect the most opposed to Catholicism, that of the Scotch Presbyterians, the case of the famous James Erskine of Grange. Dr. Alexander Carlyle, in his amusing autobiography, speaks as follows of this Protestant worthy. Referring to his father's intimacy with Lord Grange (Dr. Carlyle's father, like himself, was a minister of the Church of Scotland), and to their frequent meetings for prayer, he says: "After these meetings for private prayer, however, in which they passed several hours before supper, praying alternately, they did not part without wine. Notwithstanding this intimacy, there were periods of half a year at a time, when there was no intercourse between them at all. My father's conjecture was, that at those times Lord Grange was engaged in a course of debauchery at Edinburgh, and interrupted his religious exercises. For in those intervals, he not only neglected my father's company, but absented himself from church, and did not attend the sacraments, religious services which, at other times, he would not have neglected for the world. Report, however, said that he and his associates passed their time in alternate scenes of the exercises of religion and debauchery; spending their day in meetings for prayer and pious conversation, and their nights in lewdness and revelling. Some men are of opinion that they could not be equally sincere in both. I am apt to think that they were. . . . There is no doubt of the profligacy; and I have frequently seen them drowned in tears during the whole of a sacramental Sunday; when, so far as my observation could reach, they could have no rational object to act a part. The Marquis of Lothian of that day, whom I have seen attending the sacrament at Prestonpans with Lord Grange, and whom no man suspected of plots or hypocrisy, was much addicted to debauchery. The natural casuistry of the passions grants dispensations with more facility than the Church of Rome."*

There are strong rumours that such contradictions between faith and practice were not unknown in Scotland in a more recent past.

Now let us take the milder, but not less instructive case of Dr. Johnson. Few men have had more devout faith in God's grace, and more firm belief in free-will, than Samuel Johnson. He was, in intention at least, highly conscientious. In practice, as he was the first to admit, he often fell short of his standard of duty. We can hardly imagine more fervent prayers and determined resolves than he made with a view to breaking off bad habits and turning over a new leaf. Yet the success was very small, as we learn from the frequent repentances and renewed resolves published by Boswell, *e.g.* :—

"I have now spent fifty-five years in resolving; having, from the earliest time, almost, that I can remember, been forming schemes of a better life. I have done nothing. . . . O God, grant me to resolve aright, and to keep my resolutions, for Jesus Christ's sake. Amen."†

The chief faults with which Johnson reproached himself

---

* "Autobiography of Dr. Alexander Carlyle," p. 13.
† Boswell, anno 1764.

were waste of time, procrastination, and a torpid laziness which made early rising almost an impossibility to him. Against these faults he perpetually made resolutions, and prayed fervently for divine help to keep them. He resolved and prayed in vain; as we know, not only from his own confession, but from abundant other testimony. Boswell is delighted with Johnson's tenderness of conscience, and "fervent desire of improvement." It did not occur to Boswell that he had given, in other parts of his work, ample reasons which accounted for Johnson's failure on this head. Johnson's habits were wholly incompatible with health of mind or body, and they were peculiarly adverse to the alertness of spirit of which he was always lamenting his deficiency. How could a man get up early who always sat up at night as long as he could find any one to keep him company? How could a man retain a prompt and clear energy of mind, ready for all demands, who never scrupled to gorge himself to repletion whenever he had an opportunity. "I never knew," says Boswell, "any man who relished good eating more than he did. When at table, he was totally absorbed in the business of the moment; his looks seem riveted to his plate; nor would he, unless when in very high company, say one word, or even pay the least attention to what was said by others, till he had satisfied his appetite; which was so fierce, and indulged with such intenseness, that, while in the act of eating, the veins of his forehead swelled, and, generally, a strong perspiration was visible." * How much of Johnson's physical suffering and moral deficiencies were owing to his habitual gross feeding, could perhaps only be determined by a physician who had carefully examined the patient; but that his obesity, and shortness of breath, his low spirits and choleric

* Boswell, anno 1763.

temper, were largely attributable to his self-indulgence, there can hardly be a doubt.

If Johnson had been a determinist, and cultivated his nature on rational principles, he would have known that while he retained his usual habits he could not overcome his sloth. A light but nutritious diet, sufficient exercise in the fresh air to induce a pleasant fatigue, frequent cold baths, moderation in all liquors, especially tea, and early hours of going to bed, would probably, in a few months, have enabled him to throw off his lethargy.

The doctrine of determinism is now so generally accepted, that it will not be needful to dwell upon it at any length here. The cumulative argument in its favour, says Mr. Sidgwick, is so strong as almost to amount to complete proof. But its immense importance for the right cultivation of human nature seems still to be overlooked, even by its most illustrious advocates. Even Mr. Sidgwick is of opinion that the decision of the "metaphysical question at issue in this free-will controversy"* does not involve any point of general practical importance. I am unable to accept this view. It appears to me to be one of those cases in which right theory is all-important, as guiding to right practice.

If we admit that "From the universal law that, other things equal, the cohesion of psychical states is proportionate to the frequency with which they have followed one another in experience ; it is an inevitable corollary, that all actions whatever must be determined by those psychical connexions which experience has generated, either in the life of the individual, or in that general antecedent life of which the accumulated results are organized in his constitution,"† we must further admit that any theory which

* "Methods of Ethics," cap. v.
† Herbert Spencer, "Psychology," vol. i. p. 500.

tends to discredit or underrate "habit," tends to make human action uncertain and vacillating, tends therefore to weaken the automatic performance of good actions, which is what the well-being of society demands. The free-will theory openly challenges "habit," and encourages the belief that the most inveterate habit may be broken by an act of volition. The attention is therefore directed to the wrong side of the problem. Instead of vigilantly watching against the slow, insidious growth of evil habits, the failure to carry out good resolutions, the frequent indulgence of vicious tastes; the mind is lulled into a false security by the belief in free-will, imagining itself independent and sovereign, when and while it is being reduced into servitude. The "cohesion of psychical states" is so established by their frequent succession that it becomes organic. If not absolutely inseparable, their cohesion is so strong, that only a violent contrary passion or motive is equal to breaking it. The most hardened lie-a-bed, whom neither duty nor interest can rouse from his slumbers, would promptly sally forth if informed that the house was on fire. It is this fact, viz. that even an inveterate habit may be broken by a gust of passion, or a permanent mood of profound emotion, which has given a semblance of rationality to the doctrine of free-will. No determinist ignores or underrates it. A passion of pure love has often saved a man from a swarm of minor vices. All the famous and sudden religious conversions from evil-living to righteousness, may be traced to the same principle. Ardent love, gratitude, and veneration for Christ, *when* kindled, *are* able to snap the chains of habit, and sometimes to prevent their being welded together again. But it is rash, not to say reckless, to trust to a random cyclone of the nobler passions to save us from our sins. It is of the nature of cyclones to be violent, but of short duration. They may never come; they are apt to be transitory. And then the old cohesion of psychical states reappears, the vicious habit returns, probably, more virulent and domineering for its temporary exile, and the last state of that man is worse than the first.

It is obvious, as already remarked, that the free-will doctrine turns the attention away from the essential and real side of moral cultivation, and directs it to an unreal side. It resembles Sir Kenelm Digby's famous sympathetic powder for the cure of wounds. Digby professed that he would be very sorry not to do his uttermost to make it clear how the powder, "(which they commonly call the powder of sympathy,) doth, naturally and without any magick, cure wounds without touching them, yea, without seeing of the patient;" and he sets forth how the cure "is performed by applying the remedy to the blade of a sword which has wounded a body; so the sword be not too much heated by the fire; for that will make all the spirits of the blood to evaporate; and consequently the sword will contribute but little to the cure. Now, the reason why the sword may be dressed in order to the cure is, because the subtile spirits of the blood penetrate the substance of the blade, as far as it went into the body of the wounded party; and there keep their residence, unless the fire, as I said before, chase them away." Now, the sympathetic powder is hardly more irrational in surgery than the free-will doctrine is in morals. In both cases the attention is directed to the wrong object, and diverted from the right one. While Digby was applying his remedy to the blade of a sword which had caused a wound, he was giving but little care and attention to the wound itself. Indeed, he says that neither the wound nor even the patient need ever be seen. There would have been little hope of the triumphs of modern surgery if this method of treating wounds had prevailed. The real phenomena needing elucidation would not have been studied, and a fiction would have engrossed the attention of the faculty. The believers in free-will have studied ethics and the cultivation of human nature, as Digby studied surgery and the cure of wounds. Their doctrine is the correlative of the sympathetic powder applied to the blade of the sword. The real facts which it behoved them to investigate they have neglected.

Experience shows that moral or immoral action depends upon the previous training and character of the mind, as much as healthy or morbid secretions depend upon the previous habits and constitution of the body. A man with a criminal nature and education, under given circumstances of temptation, can no more help committing crime than he could help having a headache under certain conditions of brain and stomach. Both the crime and the headache result from a series of antecedent causes culminating in these effects. An unhealthy mode of living and, perhaps, a bad constitution lead inevitably to the one; an evil training and, perhaps, a vicious character combined, lead to the other. In neither case can the Will operate directly to suppress either crime or headache at the moment. The physical ailment *may* be removed or mitigated by drugs or reformed habits of living, and the moral evil also *may* be diminished or removed by a complete change in the ethical surroundings of the patient. But neither result is certain; and depends on numerous circumstances, the age of the individual, the inveteracy of the disease, the constitution or character in either case.

All cultivation presupposes, in the vegetable, animal, or human subject, original qualities which justify even an attempt to improve them. There are soils which no farmer in his senses would think of ploughing, manuring, and sowing. There are kinds of vegetables and stocks of cattle which are recognized as unfit for profitable culture. They are left alone, either to die out or to survive in a state of nature. In the same way with human qualities ; some original quality is needed to begin upon. We do not give an elaborate musical education to persons who have no power to distinguish one note from another, nor teach painting to the colour blind, nor mathematics to those arrested by the Ass's Bridge. In other words, cultivation is only rationally applied where there is original quality capable of receiving it.

Certainly, the moral nature of man does not vary less widely than the other parts of his nature. There are men whose quality is to manifest, from their earliest years, a bias to vicious and malignant crime; who have no good instincts on which a moral teacher can work ; who pursue their own selfish gratification at any cost to others. There are also men whose bias is in the contrary direction ; who, without teaching, or in spite of evil teaching, show a generous, upright, unselfish spirit in all their dealings. And these differences are congenital : such persons differ as much as a cachectic constitution differs from a healthy one. Without saying that in the one case, therapeutics, and in the other case, moral training, would be quite without effect, we may be sure that neither therapeutics nor moral training will ever turn the bad into the good, the evil constitution or character into the vigorous and moral.

Before drawing our practical deductions from these facts, let us consider some of these implications.

Nature knows nothing of merit or desert, but only of qualities :

> " Alike to her the better, the worse,
> The glowing angel, the outcast corse."

But for the well-being of man and society, certain qualities in things, animals, and men, are precious in the extreme, as certain other qualities are pernicious. We cultivate the one and discard, or even, if possible, suppress the other. No qualities are so valuable to men in society as the moral qualities in each other's hearts. On nothing does happiness so much depend, both immediately and remotely, as upon the good or bad instincts of the fellow-men by whom we are surrounded. Within certain and not very narrow limits these instincts admit of cultivation; but unless originally present in some degree they cannot be cultivated. Their presence or absence in the individual is no merit or fault of his. Nothing is more certain than that no one makes his own character. That is done for him by his parents and ancestors. The hero was born with his noble and fearless heart; the saint came into the world with his spontaneous aptitude for good works and lofty feeling; and the moral monster, the cowardly, selfish, unscrupulous criminal, was born with his evil passions inherited from progenitors, near or remote. No merit or demerit attaches to the saint or the sinner in the metaphysical and mystic sense of the word. Their good or evil qualities were none of their making. A man inherits his brain as much as he inherits his estate. The strong nature, the vivid imagination, the tender conscience, the firm will, all come by inheritance, as much as money in the funds, or a noble demesne of broad acres. The theological doctrine that there is no such thing as merit in the sight of God, that all we have has been received as a free gift, admits of a plainly scientific expression, as a matter of fact.*

---

* On this point St. Thomas uses almost Positivist expressions :—

"Et ideo meritum hominis apud Deum esse non potest nisi secundum præsuppositionem divinæ ordinationis ; ita scilicet ut id homo conse-

It will perhaps be said that this view does away with moral responsibility; that those who hold it cannot consistently blame any crime or resent any injury; that we should not on this hypothesis reproach a garrotter who half murders us; he is a machine, not a man with free-will, capable of doing and forbearing according to the moral law. It is no more rational to blame him than it would be to blame a runaway locomotive which knocks you down, and mangles or kills you.

To which the answer is, that the sooner the idea of moral responsibility is got rid of, the better it will be for society and moral education. The sooner it is perceived that bad men will be bad, do what we will, though, of course, they may be made less bad, the sooner shall we come to the conclusion that the welfare of society demands the suppression or elimination of bad men, and the careful cultivation of the good only. This is what we do in every other department. We do not cultivate curs and screws and low breeds of cattle. On the contrary, we keep them down as much as we can. What do we gain by this fine language as to moral responsibility? The right to blame, and so forth. Bad men are not touched by it. The bad man has no conscience; he acts after his malignant nature. The fear of sharp punishment may deter him from evil-doing, and quell his selfish appetites; but he will not be converted to virtue by our telling him he has moral responsibility, that he is a

quatur a Deo per suam operationem, quasi mercedem, ad quod Deus ei virtutem operandi deputavit, sicut etiam *res naturales hoc consequuntur per proprios motus et operationes*, ad quod a Deo sunt ordinatæ; differenter tamen, quia creatura rationalis seipsum movet ad agendum per liberum arbitrium, unde sua actio habet rationem meriti; quod non est in aliis creaturis."—"Summæ Theologicæ," Prima Secundæ, Quæstio cxiv. art. prim. But for the arbitrary exception in favour of free-will, this view would coincide with mine.

free agent to choose good or evil, and that he ought to choose the good. His mind is made up to choose the bad. But society, knowing its own interests, has a right to exclude him from its fellowship; not only to prevent and punish his evil actions, but to suppress him in some effectual way, and, above all, prevent his leaving a posterity as wicked as himself.* Society requires good instincts and good actions. It does not want even alternate sins and repentance; it wants performance. The soldier, who deserts in presence of the enemy, is deservedly shot. In civil life, there are forms of criminality which are worse than .desertions; they are open hostilities to the best interests of humanity.

Nothing is gained by disguising the fact that there is no remedy for a bad heart, and no substitute for a good one. Only on good, unselfish instincts can a trustworthy morality repose. "There are many cases," says Mr. Bain, "where a man's social obedience, the fulfilment of his

---

* So Aristotle ("Ethics," lib. x. c. 9) says that some think that legislators ought "ἀπειθοῦσι δὲ καὶ ἀφυεστέροις οὖσι κολάσεις τε καὶ τιμωρίας ἐπιτιθέναι, τοὺς δ' ἀνιάτους ὅλως ἐξορίζειν." Mr. Herbert Spencer, arguing against the modern tendency to promote the "survival of the unfittest," remarks, "It rarely happens that the amount of evil caused by fostering the vicious and good-for-nothing can be estimated. But in America, at a meeting of the States Charities Aid Association, held on Dec. 18, 1874, a startling instance was given in detail by Dr. Harris. It was furnished by a county on the Upper Hudson, remarkable for the ratio of crime and poverty to population. Generations ago there had existed a certain ' gutter-child,' as she would here be called, known as ' Margaret,' who proved to be the prolific mother of a prolific race. Besides great numbers of idiots, imbeciles, drunkards, lunatics, paupers, and prostitutes, ' the county records show two hundred of her descendants who have been criminals.' Was it kindness or cruelty which, generation after generation, enabled them to multiply and become an increasing curse to the society around them?" (" Man versus the State," p. 69.)

bargains, his justice, veracity, respect to other men's rights, costs him a sacrifice with no return, while the omission leads to penalty. Simple prudence would at such a moment suggest the criminal course."[*] And Mr. Herbert Spencer says, "The truly moral deterrent from murder, is not constituted by a representation of hanging as a consequence, or by a representation of tortures in Hell as a consequence, or by a representation of the horror and hatred excited in fellow-men; but by a representation of the necessary natural results—the infliction of death-agony on the victim, the destruction of all his possibilities of happiness, the entailed sufferings to his belongings. Neither the thought of imprisonment, nor of divine anger, nor of social disgrace, is that which constitutes the moral check on theft; but the thought of injury to the person robbed, joined with a vague consciousness of the general evils caused by disregard of proprietary rights. Those who reprobate the adulterer on moral grounds, have their minds filled, not with ideas of an action for damages, or of future punishment following the breach of a commandment, or of loss of reputation; but they are occupied with ideas of unhappiness entailed on the aggrieved wife or husband, the damaged lives of children, and the diffused mischiefs which go along with disregard of the marriage tie. Conversely, the man who is moved by a moral feeling to help another in difficulty, does not picture to himself any reward here or hereafter; but pictures only the better condition he is trying to bring about. One who is morally prompted to fight against a social evil, has neither material benefit nor popular applause before his mind; but only the mischiefs he seeks to remove, and the increased well-being which will follow their removal."[†]

[*] "The Emotions and the Will," chap. x. p. 530. 1859.
[†] "Data of Ethics," pp. 120, 121.

Nothing can be more clearly put. The feeling, sympathetic, generous heart, which recognizes the rights and claims of others, which is pained by their suffering and rejoices in their joy, is declared to be the only trustworthy source of that social morality on which general well-being depends. In this respect, moral conduct regarded as an art, as it is, indeed, incomparably the finest of the fine arts, does not differ from its inferior congeners. No one expects fine pictures or statues from persons devoid of all æsthetic taste, nor oratorios and operas from those deficient in musical ear. If the interest of society requires a due proportion of altruistic sentiment in each of its members, we can only expect them in those individuals who are correspondingly organized. While all the emotions can be cultivated, none can be implanted or directly infused. In this, as in other cases, we can only cultivate the good sorts, the good stock, and eliminate and discourage, as far as possible, the bad.

This view will very probably be regarded by some as giving up the cause of morality altogether. If we cannot preach the categorical imperative of right action to every creature, and assume and expect that every one is capable of performing it, if he chooses to exert his free-will, our preaching is supposed to be vain; an insincere make-believe, itself immoral. This is very probable; and the foolishness of preaching, as often practised, is perhaps only too evident. But it may be remarked that the cause of music is not given up, because a master counsels a pupil without an ear for music to cease attempting to sing. We may preach morality as we choose, but we shall only be successful with the apt scholars, those who have a foundation of good instincts on which to work. It is, no doubt, much simpler to assume that *all* are equally competent; and that, if they do not receive our teaching, it is not because they cannot, but because they will not. Then we arrogate a right to upbraid them, to punish them for their wicked will. They can, if they choose, be quite virtuous and moral. It is an obvious view, recommended by a blunt straightforwardness gratifying to many minds which are disposed to resent and even deny the complexity of nature.

The determinist is not less but more resolute in teaching morality than his free-will opponent. But he demands pupils who can learn. What shall be done with those who cannot learn belongs to another branch of inquiry, and concerns politics rather than morals. But much is gained by discarding the hope of impossibilities, of ceasing to expect grapes of thorns, or figs of thistles. The extirpation of thorns and thistles, in the literal or metaphorical sense, has its difficulties; which we have no ground, however, to regard as insuperable. The object to be obtained is good men with good instincts; not the establishment of a metaphysical theory that all men may be good if they would only choose. So little do we need free-will and deliberate choice between good and evil, that we want a prompt, unreflecting bias towards good. The option between virtue and vice cannot be left an open question. As we see good dogs *chasser de race*, so we need citizens whose leanings are to virtue's side. And we are likely to get them in proportion as we recognize that good men, like poets, are born, not made, and only in a minor degree the product of training; albeit that training, in its own sphere, is of paramount importance.

But training is not often entirely overlooked in practice, even by the partisans of the doctrine of free-will—a fact more creditable to their common sense than their logic. The centre of the problem lies in the question, how can a determinist cultivate virtue or good impulses, seeing that by his principles he cannot choose his desires?   How can he cultivate a sense of duty, if duty depends on altruistic sentiments, of which he is perhaps devoid ?

It would be regarded as a truism rather than a paradox to say that a man cannot cultivate athletics without muscles. Some amount of muscle must be present, on which to begin a course of muscular development.   In the same way some amount of congenital altruism —the tap-root of social morality—must be present, or the cultivation of good impulses, moral sentiments, or the sense of duty, cannot be even attempted.   We should be informed what manner of man the determinist is, who is asked how he can cultivate virtue on his principles.   If he is a base-hearted man, but sufficiently versed in psychology to grasp the full import of the question, he would answer that it was obviously impossible.   He would acknowledge a conscious absence of good impulses, and that his only principle of action was the gratification of self.   If the determinist, on the other hand, were a man of generous nature, full of meekness, courage and love, he would reply, that cultivation, or the satisfaction of those impulses, was the greatest joy he knew; that though often, through slackness of will, infirmity and selfishness, he failed in his duty (of which he was only too conscious), yet he never felt inward peace, except when cultivating the garden of his soul, following the passionate ideal of his heart in all benign works for others, in all purifying discipline of the spirit within him.   Both these men would answer truly ; and the successful cultivation of human nature demands that we should bear in mind the answers of both.   The abstract science of morals needs completing and correcting for the cultivation of human nature, by empirical observation of the peculiarities of individual men.

"Duty" and "debt" are the same word differently written, and both mean that which is "owed." I "ought" is the preterite of I "owe." The French "devoir" is applied to pecuniary debt and moral duty. In Greek ὀφείλω and ὀφείλημα show the same association of ideas. Now, what do we mean by a sense of duty, except a recognition of the claims of others, of neighbour, family, society, or God? In no respect do men differ more than in this sense of duty, because in no respect are men more unlike than in their endowment of egoistic and altruistic impulses. In some persons all sense of the claims of others seems left out from the first. They never seem to regard themselves as owing anything to anybody; but, contrariwise, they consider others always as owing them a great deal. Even borrowed money they repay with pain and regret, and often require the threat or the action of the law to bring them to repayment. This type of character is humourously exemplified in the alleged remark of a spendthrift, who said of a friend less hardened than himself, "He wasted his money in paying his debts;" the use of money being only excusable, it would appear, when no credit was to be obtained. On the other hand, we have natures who not only are prompt in acknowledging claims upon them, who would fast and starve rather than withhold payment when due, but who perceive debts and duties which neither society nor individuals exact from them; who willingly offend the world, and, with open eyes, face its anger and resentment, so they may render it a service which no other is ready to offer. The saints, martyrs, and heroes have been of this type. Resistance to passion or strong temptation can only be rationally expected from a mind which combines a habit of postponing self-gratification to the interests and welfare of others, with an ample endowment of generous and benevolent impulses. The wave of egoistic passion is met by a counter-wave of altruistic emotion, and according to the character and training one or the other prevails. The characteristic feeling of remorse for breach of duty, or gross-gratification of selfish desire, is evidence of this. Genuine remorse, contrition as distinguished from attrition, always arises from a pain of the altruistic feelings, at having returned evil for good, for having injured a loving heart which deserved different treatment at our hands. Remorse is the note of tender and passionate, but ill-governed natures. There is no anguish like it; but it is an anguish of which the cold and the selfish are incapable. So little does it fear or wish to evade punishment, that it seeks it and implores it. The grief over our own hard-heartedness is too acute to be assuaged except by sacrifice and penance; and only in bitter expiation is a slight relief derived for transgression. In religious minds, the reason often gives way when they have been made conscious that they have sinned against and been ungrateful to Christ their Lord, who for them hung upon the tree, was pierced with wounds, reviled, buffeted, and spat upon. Like St. Peter, when they think thereon, they weep. In the naturally generous and tender-hearted, it soon appears and develops with the added years. Education can do much to aid or check its growth. The selfishness of children can be cultivated to any extent. A habit of regard for others may likewise be nurtured. The *proverbial* selfishness of princes largely depends on this fact.

Recognition of the "claims" of others, arising from a sympathetic nature, is the root of duty, but by no means the full-grown tree. The size to which the tree will grow, depends upon the mental power, upon the grasp of ideas, which reveals an almost infinite variety of "claimants." A kind heart coupled with a narrow mind, cannot conceive the higher forms of duty to the State, to humanity, to unpopular causes. Culture and mental force combined, regulate the quality of the duty paid. The difference between abject superstition and lofty piety, depends on the intellect, not on the heart of the worshipper.

In all societies, even the most savage, some duties are inculcated on the young by parents and elders; and certain acts are forbidden or punished, others are applauded and rewarded. The public opinion of society carries on the process. The teaching in childhood, youth, and manhood, is assimilated according to the quality of the learner. The meek, the modest, the kindly, receive in loving trust the word of their elders. They are told they ought to do *this*, that they ought not to do *that*, and they accept the obligation without hesitation or scruple. The *mala prohibita* become to them *mala in se*, and an infraction of the rule laid down appears to them monstrous and profane. In Christian countries duty to God is naturally much insisted on; and if it does not appear to be always attended with the desired success, the reason is not only in the hardness of men's hearts, but also in the intellectual difficulties involved in theism.

But whether the paramount duty be paid to God, to the State, to humanity, to great ideas, or any thing or being beyond self, the germ of it always lies in the unselfish readiness to pay a debt, supposed to be owing to another or others. And it often happens that the supposition is wholly false; that the debt is not owed; that it is imaginary, not real. But the sense of obligation is not concerned with the matter of a given duty, but only with the form. Conscience alone is a deceitful guide; like justice it is blind; it will do evil as readily as good. Its one pre-occupation is to go out of self and pay its debt, duty, reverence, to object, thing or being whom it wishes to serve. And this is so true, that the sense of duty in its intense forms, is not content with simple disregard of self; it insists on hostility to self, on self-mutilation, mortification, as in the severer forms of asceticism.

Passion is by no means the worst enemy to duty; as a strong sense of duty is itself a passion. The passionate natures can often become the most bound by it: witness St. Augustine. The cold heart is the undutiful heart, the heart of stone, which loves neither God nor man.

New duties. The man who recognizes new duties above those he has been taught to observe; who sees, beyond the circle of conventional obligation, the dim forms of new claimants on his heart and service, is a moral inventor, an enlarger of human life. Those who saw the claims of the slave were such; those who see the claims of animals are the same. How many more such have still to be seen!

Reward of virtue. The highest conscience has ever felt that the expectation of reward for virtue was unjustified, and almost incompatible with the idea of virtue: " Not unto us, not unto us." " We are unprofitable servants ; we have done that which was our duty to do." These and similar utterances are the natural and wholesome expressions of the devout heart. And the instinct is right which inspires them. The moment we consider duty as a debt which we owe, we feel it does not admit of reward. Is a man to be paid for paying his debts? How does this view of duty account for resistance to strong temptation ?

The moment we recognize that we can be in the position of owing something to some one person, cause, or idea, it matters not what form the payment may take ; from coin of the realm up to giving away one's life, it is all one ; meeting an obligation which we have recognized we are under. How we came by the sense of this or that particular obligation is immaterial. It may come through many channels; religion, public opinion, *esprit de corps*, or what not. Its fulness and intensity depend far more on the constitution of our minds than on any external influence and teaching. If we are wholly selfish, no teaching will persuade us; if we are generous, loving, and heroic, we move towards self-sacrifice by a natural gravitation. And the point to be especially noticed by those who make virtue to consist in the choice of the better part, after a conflict of motives, is that the greater the virtue the less there is of conscious self-sacrifice. The egoist who will not sacrifice the meanest of his own pleasures or passions for the greatest need of others, and the hero who gives his life for the "sheep," are the opposite poles of humanity. And so little true is it that virtue only exists after it has gained a victory over base temptation, that the very presence or possibility of temptation stains its purity. In ordinary, civilized life this is so. What should we think of a friend or acquaintance, who, we knew, passed his time in hard struggles to conquer the sins forbidden in the sixth, seventh, and eighth commandments? Yet, according to the doctrine of some moralists, the man who dines with us, and has not had a temptation to steal our spoons, and overcome it, is not virtuous; if he has not lusted after the women of our household and subdued his impurity, he is not chaste; if he has not been touched by an impulse to murder us, finally put down, he is not a moral person.

Now, as regards resisting temptation, it is obvious that in proportion as we are tempted to the commission of selfish sin, our character, and, in a minor degree, our education, are at fault. We have started with an overplus of egoistic sentiment, or we have had, by ill-education, the egoistic sentiment unduly cultivated. We shall behave under temptations according to our character. The doctrines we hold will have little weight in the final result, though they will have some. If we experience strong promptings to murder, rape, or theft, the chances are, whether we believe in Hell or Utilitarianism, we shall gratify our passions. If the altruistic element in us is fairly represented, we shall hesitate, or alternately fall into sin and repentance. If self has been "annulled," we shall pass by the temptations, with more or less complete unconsciousness.*

Moralists have been at great pains to show that through virtue lay the only road to final and complete happiness; that, on the other hand, crime and sin inevitably led to pain and misery. It was feared that, if any doubt were allowed to rest on the fact that virtue was its own reward, sensible people would refuse so obviously bad a bargain. As Mr. Leslie Stephen eloquently says : " Here we come to one of the multiform and profound problems which has tortured men in all ages. Virtue—no one denies it—does good to somebody, but how often to the agent ? A belief in justice, as regulating the universe, has been held to imply (I do not ask whether rightly held) that happiness should somehow go along with virtue. To give up the belief in such a supreme regulation, seemed, again, to be an admission that virtue was folly. Yet how can this doctrine be reconciled to the plainest facts of experience ? The lightning strikes the good and the bad ; the hero dies in the ruin of his cause ; the highest self-denial is repaid by the blackest ingratitude ; the keenest sympathy with our fellows implies

* So again St. Thomas :—" Magis est non posse peccare quam non peccare."—" Summæ Theologicæ," Prima Secundæ, Quæstio cxiv. art. prim.

the greatest liability to suffering ; the cold, the sensual, and the systematically selfish, often seem to have the pleasantest lots in life. Great men in despair have pronounced virtue to be but a name ; philosophers have evaded the difficulty by a verbal denial of the plainest truths ; theologians have tried to console their disciples by constructing ideal worlds, which have served for little more than a recognition of the unsatisfactory state of the actual world. The problem so often attacked, will perhaps be solved when we know the origin of evil. Meanwhile we have only to consider in what way it is related to ethical theories." *

This suggestive passage shows very plainly how imperfectly the older speculators grasped the problem with which they had to deal. If virtue depend on a number of good instincts or qualities in the agent's mind or heart, benevolence, sympathy, courage, and resolution, it would seem obvious that no one could be benefited by these precious endowments more than the fortunate owner of them himself. Who derives so much enjoyment from a fine ear for music as the musician who has one ? Who profits by an exquisite sense of colour so much as the artist whom land, sea, and cloud keep in an ecstasy of delight ? Much more, would one say, must the generous and passionate emotions of the heart supply an inward fountain of happiness to the richly endowed natures which possess them. To ask if virtue answers, or " pays," is like asking if fine health and bodily strength pay. Probably no one would be without them if he could help it. And yet there can be no doubt that great strength and fine health often lead their possessor into pain, and even death, by tempting him to overtax his powers. It may be said of all the higher qualities and gifts, that under certain conditions they are capable of

* Leslie Stephen, " Science of Ethics," p. 398.

causing as much pain as pleasure to their owners : but these owners do not wish, therefore, to be rid of them. The musician who is tortured by an organ out of tune, would never think of purchasing peace by the loss or destruction of his musical ear. It is the same with regard to Friendship and Love. Their betrayal probably produces anguish as keen as any known to the human heart. But no one capable of either, would ever regret his capacity for love and friendship. Those who doubt their value, or, with Napoleon, hold that they are " foolish infatuations," are out of court, as they have no personal knowledge of qualities they despise. We need not to be told what manner of man he was who declared that the secret of happiness consisted in a good digestion and a bad heart. And the querist, " Why should I do anything for posterity, seeing that posterity never did anything for me ? " receives even now this answer from Society, and will receive it with greater emphasis in the future : " From you, sir, we expect nothing ; but *you* may expect that your shameless confession of selfishness will not go unpunished." The " unsatisfactory state of the actual world," as Mr. Stephen says, was no doubt a great hindrance in former times to a recognition of the coercive power for good which Society can bring to bear on the selfish and the wicked. But the Christian scheme of rewards and punishments also contributed to the conviction, that only by fear of retribution could men be deterred from evil, and by the hope of recompense be bribed to doing good. A man who did not believe in hell, it was thought, even by good men, had no inducement to practice any virtue or refrain from any vice. Dr. Johnson said he would not believe that Hume's apparent equanimity when dying was sincere, because, on his (Hume's) principles he had no motive to speak the truth. Dr. Young, in his

" Night Thoughts," gave utterance probably to the common sentiment, crude and revolting as it sounds :—

> " ' Has Virtue charms ? '   I grant her heavenly fair ;
> But if unportioned, all will Interest wed.
>
> .   .   .   .   .
>
> A Deity believed, will nought avail ;
> Rewards and punishments make God adored ;
> And hopes and fears give Conscience all her power.
>
> .   .   .   .   .
>
> Who tells me he denies his soul immortal,
> Whate'er his boast, has told me he's a knave.
> His duty 'tis to love himself alone ;
> Nor care though mankind perish, if he smiles." *

The line between " portioned virtue " and " interest," does not appear here to be very clearly drawn, and virtue it is intimated can only be chosen for a valuable consideration. But we must admit all the same, that in this respect the theologians had the best of the argument, till the conception of society as an organism had arisen in speculation, with the momentous consequences which that involves. The health of an organism depends on the health and efficiency of its parts ; and the conduct and morals of the individual are now seen to be no longer the private concern of himself only, but very much also of the society of which he is a member. His vice injures and his virtue benefits the body politic, as far as either influence extends. And this is now so well seen, that perhaps the danger is, as Mr. Mill feared, that society and public opinion are tending to be too coercive and despotic, to the injury of that liberty and individuality which are needed for full and vigorous well-being. We may certainly venture to say this much, that society is now able to make knaves, whether they believe their souls to be immortal or not, feel that crime is

* " Seventh Night," 1169-1182.

connected with misery rather than happiness; and that virtue, perhaps not of the highest, but yet of a fairly high standard, tends directly to the agent's own comfort and peace of mind.

Now, as touching the problem which Mr. Stephen says has tortured mankind for ages, the connection between virtue and happiness, its solution would seem to require a little more precising of what is meant by happiness, than is customary in ethical discussions. Obviously, happiness varies as much as men vary; and what constitutes the happiness of one man makes the misery of another. The healthy and the strong have different sources of happiness from the sickly and the weak. The same man at different periods of life has very different forms of happiness. In other words, happiness is a subjective phenomenon, depending upon the conditions and character of the individual. This being so, if we only consider the agent, without reference to the reaction of society upon him, it is obvious that no one course of conduct can be assumed *à priori* as certain or likely in itself to produce happiness. Virtue may and probably will bring happiness to the virtuous man; but to the criminal and the selfish, virtue will be probably the most distasteful or even painful thing in their experience, while vice will give them unmitigated pleasure. This view, as Mr. Stephen says, "is calculated to shock many respectable people;" but that is not a sufficient reason for rejecting it if it be otherwise supported.

Now, what is a general feature common to all forms of happiness, whether vicious or virtuous? Who are the people who visibly enjoy themselves; who are never or rarely at a loss as to what they shall do with their time? Is it not those persons who have one or more tastes, inclinations or passions, so strongly marked, that they are always ready or ever thirsting for their gratification, which never comes amiss? Even the most sensual and repellent vices, may so fill a mind with intense relish and pleasure, that the sensualist is conscious of nothing but one long draught of voluptuous enjoyment. Satiety may no doubt be rapidly produced, and health ruined by excess; and then the sensualist has a bad time of it; but that is because he has been deprived of his pleasures, and he has nothing to fall back on when his vices have left him. But that fact does not invalidate the statement just made, that a passionate pursuit of some one thing, whatever its character, is the primary condition of that glow of pleasurable feeling which we call happiness. The gambler sitting down to the card-table, the gourmand to his dinner, the book-collector buying choice and rare editions, the artist creating types of beauty, the man of science working out momentous problems, the philanthropist seeking and relieving the wretched, though all enjoying very different kinds of happiness, have this factor in common, that they are pursuing with keen appetite the object they desire. They are free from the aching langour of *ennui;* they escape the hopeless and helpless nausea of the *blasé* mind, which is impotent even to desire. Strong desires or passions, capable of frequent and lasting gratification, are the only materials of happiness.

We have next to notice that the gratification of all the passions is more or less attended with pain. Indeed, it would seem that all intense pleasures need to be tipped with a sharp point of pain to give them their full zest. The fatigue and danger of most manly sports, constitute a large portion of their attractiveness. As gamblers mostly end by losing all their money, their vice must give them more pain than pleasure, but the fact does not deter them from gratifying it. The pains of the drunkard, of the opium eater, of the gourmand, are notorious, but are not often alone sufficient to deter from indulgence in their respective vices. *And to this law the higher and nobler passions offer no exception.* The ambitious man, say a Napoleon, is always exposed to bitter disappointment and mishaps. The agony of a few nights at Fontainebleau, just before his abdication, had so changed Napoleon's countenance that his intimates were shocked by it. Yet the experience was thrown away upon him, and he was ready to recommence the game of ambition, as soon as opportunity offered, by his escape from Elba. Even the peaceful pursuits of literature and science have their acute crises of vexation and frustrated hope. Hume, the most even-tempered of men, was so mortified by the failure of the first volume of his history, that he would have gone abroad, changed his name, and renounced authorship, had not war broken out between England and France. And, to complete the survey, it must be added, that not even the passionate pursuit of holiness itself is without occasional sharp pain; in proof of which it is sufficient to cite the "Acta Sanctorum," *passim.*

A passion for virtue, therefore, is not found to be at any disadvantage, as compared with other passions, in the occasional pain which its gratification involves. If "il faut souffrir pour être belle," it is also true, "il faut souffrir pour être bon;" and it is difficult to see what is gained by attempting to disguise the fact. ·Moralists have been so set upon edification, that they have been over-anxious to persuade men of the desirability of virtue, by expatiating on the sweetness of its pleasures; that virtuous people had an ample *quid pro quo* for their virtue.. And so they have at times, and in one sense always; but they also have dark and bitter moments in which they are ready to faint; doubts within and dangers without, yea, even death itself in isolated desolation, when "all" forsake them and flee; when the hero has nothing to turn to but his own heroic heart. Individuals, if left to themselves, will follow "their own peculiar bent" in their choice of pleasures, whether they be virtuous or vicious, selfish or self-denying, voluptuous or ascetic. But there can be no doubt which class Society, in its own interests, will prefer that its members should choose, viz. the virtuous, the self-denying, and ascetic. Indeed, the most depraved and selfish of men, whatever his own practice, will wish his neighbours to be virtuous. Though he may be unjust and cruel to others, he will resent injustice and cruelty to himself; though a libertine himself, he will probably insist on chastity in his wife, with much emphasis. Thus even the bad are interested on the side of virtue, as far as the conduct of others is concerned. It only needs a little more improvement in society for this to be generally recognized, as it is already partially recognized, for the disfavour of public opinion to be sharply shown to selfish pursuits and passions, and a steady, persistent encouragement of the unselfish and social enjoyments of civic life and duty. A love of good may be cultivated to almost any extent, where the original foundation of an altruistic nature exists. A passionate ideal of excellence can so fill the mind, that no pleasure is felt in anything but in efforts to realize it. "The susceptibility to ideal inflammation is a peculiarity of our nature, varying with constitutions, and affected by various circumstances."* All the desires and passions in characters of normal vigour can, in the proper

* Bain, "The Emotions and the Will," p. 496.

conditions, be thus inflamed, as they can also be starved by systematic discouragement. An ideal society would be one in which an ideal education habitually stimulated and inflamed the good passions, while it starved and discouraged the bad.

THE END.

PRINTED BY WILLIAM CLOWES AND SONS, LIMITED, LONDON AND BECCLES.

1, Paternoster Square,
London.

A LIST OF
KEGAN PAUL, TRENCH & CO.'S
PUBLICATIONS.

CONTENTS.

GENERAL LITERATURE.

A. K. H. B.—From a Quiet Place. A Volume of Sermons. Crown 8vo, 5s.

ALEXANDER, William, D.D., Bishop of Derry.—The Great Question, and other Sermons. Crown 8vo, 6s.

ALLIES, T. W., M.A.—Per Crucem ad Lucem. The Result of a Life. 2 vols. Demy 8vo, 25s.

A Life's Decision. Crown 8vo, 7s. 6d.

AMHERST, Rev. W. J.—The History of Catholic Emancipation and the Progress of the Catholic Church in the British Isles (chiefly in England) from 1771–1820. 2 vols. Demy 8vo, 24s.

AMOS, Professor Sheldon.—The History and Principles of the Civil Law of Rome. An aid to the Study of Scientific and Comparative Jurisprudence. Demy 8vo, 16s.

Ancient and Modern Britons. A Retrospect. 2 vols. Demy 8vo, 24s.

ARISTOTLE.—The Nicomachean Ethics of Aristotle. Translated by F. H. Peters, M.A. Third Edition. Crown 8vo, 6s.

AUBERTIN, J. J.—A Flight to Mexico. With 7 full-page Illustrations and a Railway Map of Mexico. Crown 8vo, 7s. 6d.

AUBERTIN, J. J.—continued.

Six Months in Cape Colony and Natal. With Illustrations and Map. Crown 8vo, 6s.

Aucassin and Nicolette. Edited in Old French and rendered in Modern English by F. W. BOURDILLON. Fcap 8vo, 7s. 6d.

AUCHMUTY, A. C.—**Dives and Pauper, and other Sermons.** Crown 8vo, 3s. 6d.

AZARIUS, Brother.—**Aristotle and the Christian Church.** Small crown 8vo, 3s. 6d.

BADGER, George Percy, D.C.L.—**An English-Arabic Lexicon.** In which the equivalent for English Words and Idiomatic Sentences are rendered into literary and colloquial Arabic. Royal 4to, 80s.

BAGEHOT, Walter. — **The English Constitution.** Fourth Edition. Crown 8vo, 7s. 6d.

Lombard Street. A Description of the Money Market. Eighth Edition. Crown 8vo, 7s. 6d.

Essays on Parliamentary Reform. Crown 8vo, 5s.

Some Articles on the Depreciation of Silver, and Topics connected with it. Demy 8vo, 5s.

BAGOT, Alan, C.E.—**Accidents in Mines:** their Causes and Prevention. Crown 8vo, 6s.

The Principles of Colliery Ventilation. Second Edition, greatly enlarged. Crown 8vo, 5s.

The Principles of Civil Engineering as applied to Agriculture and Estate Management. Crown 8vo, 7s. 6d.

BAIRD, Henry M.—**The Huguenots and Henry of Navarre.** 2 vols. With Maps. 8vo, 24s.

BALDWIN, Capt. J. H.—**The Large and Small Game of Bengal and the North-Western Provinces of India.** With 20 Illustrations. New and Cheaper Edition. Small 4to, 10s. 6d.

BALL, John, F.R.S.—**Notes of a Naturalist in South America.** With Map. Crown 8vo, 8s. 6d.

BALLIN, Ada S. and F. L.—**A Hebrew Grammar.** With Exercises selected from the Bible. Crown 8vo, 7s. 6d.

BARCLAY, Edgar.—**Mountain Life in Algeria.** With numerous Illustrations by Photogravure. Crown 4to, 16s.

BASU, K. P., M.A.—**Students' Mathematical Companion.** Containing problems in Arithmetic, Algebra, Geometry, and Mensuration, for Students of the Indian Universities. Crown 8vo, 6s.

BAUR, Ferdinand, Dr. Ph.—A Philological Introduction to Greek and Latin for Students. Translated and adapted from the German, by C. KEGAN PAUL, M.A., and E. D. STONE, M.A. Third Edition. Crown 8vo, 6s.

BAYLY, Capt. George.—Sea Life Sixty Years Ago. A Record of Adventures which led up to the Discovery of the Relics of the long-missing Expedition commanded by the Comte de la Perouse. Crown 8vo, 3s. 6d.

BENSON, A. C.—William Laud, sometime Archbishop of Canterbury. A Study. With Portrait. Crown 8vo, 6s.

BIRD, Charles, F.G.S.—Higher Education in Germany and England. Small crown 8vo, 2s. 6d.

Birth and Growth of Religion. A Book for Workers. Crown 8vo, cloth, 2s. ; paper covers, 1s.

BLACKBURN, Mrs. Hugh.—Bible Beasts and Birds. 22 Illustrations of Scripture photographed from the Original. 4to, 42s.

BLECKLY, Henry.—Socrates and the Athenians : An Apology. Crown 8vo, 2s. 6d.

BLOOMFIELD, The Lady.—Reminiscences of Court and Diplomatic Life. New and Cheaper Edition. With Frontispiece. Crown 8vo, 6s.

BLUNT, The Ven. Archdeacon.—The Divine Patriot, and other Sermons. Preached in Scarborough and in Cannes. New and Cheaper Edition. Crown 8vo, 4s. 6d.

BLUNT, Wilfrid S.—The Future of Islam. Crown 8vo, 6s.

Ideas about India. Crown 8vo. Cloth, 6s.

BODDY, Alexander A.—To Kairwân the Holy. Scenes in Muhammedan Africa. With Route Map, and Eight Illustrations by A. F. JACASSEY. Crown 8vo, 6s.

BOSANQUET, Bernard.—Knowledge and Reality. A Criticism of Mr. F. H. Bradley's "Principles of Logic." Crown 8vo, 9s.

BOUVERIE-PUSEY, S. E. B.—Permanence and Evolution. An Inquiry into the Supposed Mutability of Animal Types. Crown 8vo, 5s.

BOWEN, H. C., M.A.—Studies in English. For the use of Modern Schools. Ninth Thousand. Small crown 8vo, 1s. 6d.

English Grammar for Beginners. Fcap. 8vo, 1s.

Simple English Poems. English Literature for Junior Classes. In four parts. Parts I., II., and III., 6d. each. Part IV., 1s. Complete, 3s.

BRADLEY, F. H.—The Principles of Logic. Demy 8vo, 16s.

BRIDGETT, Rev. T. E.—History of the Holy Eucharist in Great Britain. 2 vols. Demy 8vo, 18s.

BROOKE, Rev. Stopford A.—**The Fight of Faith.** Sermons preached on various occasions. Fifth Edition. Crown 8vo, 7s. 6d.

The Spirit of the Christian Life. Third Edition. Crown 8vo, 5s.

Theology in the English Poets.— Cowper, Coleridge, Wordsworth, and Burns. Sixth Edition. Post 8vo, 5s.

Christ in Modern Life. Sixteenth Edition. Crown 8vo, 5s.

Sermons. First Series. Thirteenth Edition. Crown 8vo, 5s.

Sermons. Second Series. Sixth Edition. Crown 8vo, 5s.

BROWN, Horatio F.—**Life on the Lagoons.** With 2 Illustrations and Map. Crown 8vo, 6s.

Venetian Studies. Crown 8vo, 7s. 6d.

BROWN, Rev. J. Baldwin.—**The Higher Life.** Its Reality, Experience, and Destiny. Sixth Edition. Crown 8vo, 5s.

Doctrine of Annihilation in the Light of the Gospel of Love. Five Discourses. Fourth Edition. Crown 8vo, 2s. 6d.

The Christian Policy of Life. A Book for Young Men of Business. Third Edition. Crown 8vo, 3s. 6d.

BURDETT, Henry C.—**Help in Sickness—Where to Go and What to Do.** Crown 8vo, 1s. 6d.

Helps to Health. The Habitation—The Nursery—The School-room and—The Person. With a Chapter on Pleasure and Health Resorts. Crown 8vo, 1s. 6d.

BURKE, Oliver J.—**South Isles of Aran (County Galway).** Crown 8vo, 2s. 6d.

BURKE, The Late Very Rev. T. N.—**His Life.** By W. J. FITZPATRICK. 2 vols. With Portrait. Demy 8vo, 30s.

BURTON, Lady.—**The Inner Life of Syria, Palestine, and the Holy Land.** Post 8vo, 6s.

CANDLER, C.—**The Prevention of Consumption.** A Mode of Prevention founded on a New Theory of the Nature of the Tubercle-Bacillus. Demy 8vo, 10s. 6d.

CAPES, J. M.—**The Church of the Apostles:** an Historical Inquiry. Demy 8vo, 9s.

Carlyle and the Open Secret of His Life. By HENRY LARKIN. Demy 8vo, 14s.

CARPENTER, W. B., LL.D., M.D., F.R.S., etc.—**The Principles of Mental Physiology.** With their Applications to the Training and Discipline of the Mind, and the Study of its Morbid Conditions. Illustrated. Sixth Edition. 8vo, 12s.

Catholic Dictionary. Containing some Account of the Doctrine, Discipline, Rites, Ceremonies, Councils, and Religious Orders of the Catholic Church. By WILLIAM E. ADDIS and THOMAS ARNOLD, M.A. Third Edition. Demy 8vo, 21*s.*

Century Guild Hobby Horse. Vol. I. Half parchment, 12*s.* 6*d.*

CHARLES, Rev. R. H.—**Forgiveness,** and other Sermons. Crown 8vo, 4*s.* 6*d.*

CHEYNE, Canon.—**The Prophecies of Isaiah.** Translated with Critical Notes and Dissertations. 2 vols. Fourth Edition. Demy 8vo, 25*s.*

    Job and Solomon ; or, the Wisdom of the Old Testament. Demy 8vo, 12*s.* 6*d.*

    The Psalter ; or, The Book of the Praises of Israel. Translated with Commentary. Demy 8vo.

CLAIRAUT.—**Elements of Geometry.** Translated by Dr. KAINES. With 145 Figures. Crown 8vo, 4*s.* 6*d.*

CLAPPERTON, Jane Hume.—**Scientific Meliorism and the Evolution of Happiness.** Large crown 8vo, 8*s.* 6*d.*

CLARKE, Rev. Henry James, A.K.C.—**The Fundamental Science.** Demy 8vo, 10*s.* 6*d.*

CLODD, Edward, F.R.A.S.—**The Childhood of the World :** a Simple Account of Man in Early Times. Eighth Edition. Crown 8vo, 3*s.*
    A Special Edition for Schools. 1*s.*

    The Childhood of Religions. Including a Simple Account of the Birth and Growth of Myths and Legends. Eighth Thousand. Crown 8vo, 5*s.*
    A Special Edition for Schools. 1*s.* 6*d.*

    Jesus of Nazareth. With a brief sketch of Jewish History to the Time of His Birth. Small crown 8vo, 6*s.*

COGHLAN, J. Cole, D.D.—**The Modern Pharisee** and other Sermons. Edited by the Very Rev. H. H. DICKINSON, D.D., Dean of Chapel Royal, Dublin. New and Cheaper Edition. Crown 8vo, 7*s.* 6*d.*

COLERIDGE, Sara.—**Memoir and Letters of Sara Coleridge.** Edited by her Daughter. With Index. Cheap Edition. With Portrait. 7*s.* 6*d.*

COLERIDGE, The Hon. Stephen.—**Demetrius.** Crown 8vo, 5*s.*

CONNELL, A. K.—**Discontent and Danger in India.** Small crown 8vo, 3*s.* 6*d.*

    The Economic Revolution of India. Crown 8vo, 4*s.* 6*d.*

COOK, Keningale, LL.D.—**The Fathers of Jesus.** A Study of the Lineage of the Christian Doctrine and Traditions. 2 vols. Demy 8vo, 28*s.*

CORR, the late Rev. T. J., M.A.—**Favilla ;** Tales, Essays, and Poems. Crown 8vo, 5*s.*

CORY, William.—**A Guide to Modern English History.** Part I. —MDCCCXV.-MDCCCXXX. Demy 8vo, 9*s.* Part II.— MDCCCXXX.-MDCCCXXXV., 15*s.*

COTTON, H. J. S.—**New India, or India in Transition.** Third Edition. Crown 8vo, 4*s.* 6*d.* ; Cheap Edition, paper covers, 1*s.*

COUTTS, Francis Burdett Money.—**The Training of the Instinct of Love.** With a Preface by the Rev. EDWARD THRING, M.A. Small crown 8vo, 2*s.* 6*d.*

COX, Rev. Sir George W., M.A., Bart.—**The Mythology of the Aryan Nations.** New Edition. Demy 8vo, 16*s.*

Tales of Ancient Greece. New Edition. Small crown 8vo, 6*s.*

A Manual of Mythology in the form of Question and Answer. New Edition. Fcap. 8vo, 3*s.*

An Introduction to the Science of Comparative Mythology and Folk-Lore. Second Edition. Crown 8vo. 7*s.* 6*d.*

COX, Rev. Sir G. W., M.A., Bart., and JONES, Eustace Hinton.— **Popular Romances of the Middle Ages.** Third Edition, in 1 vol. Crown 8vo, 6*s.*

COX, Rev. Samuel, D.D.—**A Commentary on the Book of Job** With a Translation. Second Edition. Demy 8vo, 15*s.*

Salvator Mundi ; or, 'Is Christ the Saviour of all Men ? Tenth Edition. Crown 8vo, 5*s.*

The Larger Hope. A Sequel to "Salvator Mundi." Second Edition. 16mo, 1*s.*

The Genesis of Evil, and other Sermons, mainly expository. Third Edition. Crown 8vo, 6*s.*

Balaam. An Exposition and a Study. Crown 8vo, 5*s.*

Miracles. An Argument and a Challenge. Crown 8vo, 2*s.* 6*d.*

CRAVEN, Mrs.—**A Year's Meditations.** Crown 8vo, 6*s.*

CRAWFURD, Oswald.—**Portugal, Old and New.** With Illustrations and Maps. New and Cheaper Edition. Crown 8vo, 6*s.*

CRUISE, Francis Richard, M.D.—**Thomas à Kempis.** Notes of a Visit to the Scenes in which his Life was spent. With Portraits and Illustrations. Demy 8vo, 12*s.*

CUNNINGHAM, W., B.D —**Politics and Economics :** An Essay on the Nature of the Principles of Political Economy, together with a survey of Recent Legislation. Crown 8vo, 5*s.*

DANIELL, Clarmont.—**The Gold Treasure of India.** An Inquiry into its Amount, the Cause of its Accumulation, and the Proper Means of using it as Money. Crown 8vo, 5*s.*

DANIELL, *Clarmont.—continued.*

> **Discarded Silver: a Plan for its Use as Money.** Small crown 8vo, 2s.

DANIEL, *Gerard.* Mary Stuart: a Sketch and a Defence. Crown 8vo, 5s.

DARMESTETER, *Arsene.*—The Life of Words as the Symbols of Ideas. Crown 8vo, 4s. 6d.

DAVIDSON, *Rev. Samuel, D.D., LL.D.*—Canon of the Bible: Its Formation, History, and Fluctuations. Third and Revised Edition. Small crown 8vo, 5s.

> **The Doctrine of Last Things** contained in the New Testament compared with the Notions of the Jews and the Statements of Church Creeds. Small crown 8vo, 3s. 6d.

DAWSON, *Geo., M.A.* Prayers, with a Discourse on Prayer. Edited by his Wife. First Series. Ninth Edition. Crown 8vo, 3s. 6d.

> **Prayers, with a Discourse on Prayer.** Edited by GEORGE ST. CLAIR. Second Series. Crown 8vo, 6s.

> **Sermons on Disputed Points and Special Occasions.** Edited by his Wife. Fourth Edition. Crown 8vo, 6s.

> **Sermons on Daily Life and Duty.** Edited by his Wife. Fourth Edition. Crown 8vo, 6s.

> **The Authentic Gospel,** and other Sermons. Edited by GEORGE ST. CLAIR, F.G.S. Third Edition. Crown 8vo, 6s.

> **Biographical Lectures.** Edited by GEORGE ST. CLAIR, F.G.S. Third Edition. Large crown 8vo, 7s. 6d.

> **Shakespeare, and other Lectures.** Edited by GEORGE ST. CLAIR, F.G.S. Large crown 8vo, 7s. 6d.

DE JONCOURT, *Madame Marie.*—Wholesome Cookery. Fourth Edition. Crown 8vo, cloth, 1s. 6d; paper covers, 1s.

DENT, *H. C.*—A Year in Brazil. With Notes on Religion, Meteorology, Natural History, etc. Maps and Illustrations. Demy 8vo, 18s.

Doctor Faust. The Old German Puppet Play, turned into English, with Introduction, etc., by T. C. H. HEDDERWICK. Large post 8vo, 7s. 6d.

DOWDEN, *Edward, LL.D.*—Shakspere: a Critical Study of his Mind and Art. Eighth Edition. Post 8vo, 12s.

> **Studies in Literature, 1789–1877.** Fourth Edition. Large post 8vo, 6s.

> **Transcripts and Studies.** Large post 8vo.

Dulce Domum. Fcap. 8vo, 5s.

DU MONCEL, Count.—**The Telephone, the Microphone, and the Phonograph.** With 74 Illustrations. Third Edition. Small crown 8vo, 5s.

DUNN, H. Percy.—**Infant Health.** The Physiology and Hygiene of Early Life. Crown 8vo.

DURUY, Victor.—**History of Rome and the Roman People.** Edited by Prof. MAHAFFY. With nearly 3000 Illustrations. 4to. 6 vols. in 12 parts, 30s. each vol.

Education Library. Edited by Sir PHILIP MAGNUS :—

> **An Introduction to the History of Educational Theories.** By OSCAR BROWNING, M.A. Second Edition. 3s. 6d.

> **Old Greek Education.** By the Rev. Prof. MAHAFFY, M.A. Second Edition. 3s. 6d.

> **School Management.** Including a general view of the work of Education, Organization and Discipline. By JOSEPH LANDON. Sixth Edition. 6s.

EDWARDES, Major-General Sir Herbert B.—**Memorials of his Life and Letters.** By his Wife. With Portrait and Illustrations. 2 vols. Demy 8vo, 36s.

ELSDALE, Henry.—**Studies in Tennyson's Idylls.** Crown 8vo, 5s.

Emerson's (Ralph Waldo) Life. By OLIVER WENDELL HOLMES. English Copyright Edition. With Portrait. Crown 8vo, 6s.

"Fan Kwae" at Canton before Treaty Days 1825-1844. By an old Resident. With Frontispiece. Crown 8vo, 5s.

Five o'clock Tea. Containing Receipts for Cakes, Savoury Sandwiches, etc. Fcap. 8vo, cloth, 1s. 6d. ; paper covers, 1s.

FOTHERINGHAM, James.—**Studies in the Poetry of Robert Browning.** Crown 8vo. 6s.

GARDINER, Samuel R., and J. BASS MULLINGER, M.A.—**Introduction to the Study of English History.** Second Edition. Large crown 8vo, 9s.

Genesis in Advance of Present Science. A Critical Investigation of Chapters I.-IX. By a Septuagenarian Beneficed Presbyter. Demy 8vo, 10s. 6d.

GEORGE, Henry.—**Progress and Poverty :** An Inquiry into the Causes of Industrial Depressions, and of Increase of Want with Increase of Wealth. The Remedy. Fifth Library Edition. Post 8vo, 7s. 6d. Cabinet Edition. Crown 8vo, 2s. 6d. Also a Cheap Edition. Limp cloth, 1s. 6d. ; paper covers, 1s.

> **Protection, or Free Trade.** An Examination of the Tariff Question, with especial regard to the Interests of Labour. Second Edition. Crown 8vo, 5s.

GEORGE, Henry.—continued.

Social Problems. Fourth Thousand. Crown 8vo, 5*s.* Cheap Edition, paper covers, 1*s.*

GILBERT, Mrs. — **Autobiography,** and other Memorials. Edited by JOSIAH GILBERT. Fifth Edition. Crown 8vo, 7*s.* 6*d.*

GLANVILL, Joseph.—**Scepsis Scientifica ;** or, Confest Ignorance, the Way to Science ; in an Essay of the Vanity of Dogmatizing and Confident Opinion. Edited, with Introductory Essay, by JOHN OWEN. Elzevir 8vo, printed on hand-made paper, 6*s.*

Glossary of Terms and Phrases. Edited by the Rev. H. PERCY SMITH and others. Second and Cheaper Edition. Medium 8vo, 7*s.* 6*d.*

GLOVER, F., M.A.—**Exempla Latina.** A First Construing Book, with Short Notes, Lexicon, and an Introduction to the Analysis of Sentences. Second Edition. Fcap. 8vo, 2*s.*

GOODENOUGH, Commodore J. G.—**Memoir of,** with Extracts from his Letters and Journals. Edited by his Widow. With Steel Engraved Portrait. Third Edition. Crown 8vo, 5*s.*

GORDON, Major-General C. G.—**His Journals at Kartoum.** Printed from the original MS. With Introduction and Notes by A. EGMONT HAKE. Portrait, 2 Maps, and 30 Illustrations. Two vols., demy 8vo, 21*s.* Also a Cheap Edition in 1 vol., 6*s.*

Gordon's (General) Last Journal. A Facsimile of the last Journal received in England from GENERAL GORDON. Reproduced by Photo-lithography. Imperial 4to, £3 3*s.*

Events in his Life. From the Day of his Birth to the Day of his Death. By Sir H. W. GORDON. With Maps and Illustrations. Second Edition. Demy 8vo, 7*s.* 6*d.*

GOSSE, Edmund.—**Seventeenth Century Studies.** A Contribution to the History of English Poetry. Demy 8vo, 10*s.* 6*d.*

GOULD, Rev. S. Baring, M.A.—**Germany, Present and Past.** New and Cheaper Edition. Large crown 8vo, 7*s.* 6*d.*

The Vicar of Morwenstow. A Life of Robert Stephen Hawker. Crown 8vo, 6*s.*

GOWAN, Major Walter E.—**A. Ivanoff's Russian Grammar.** (16th Edition.) Translated, enlarged, and arranged for use of Students of the Russian Language. Demy 8vo, 6*s.*

GOWER, Lord Ronald. **My Reminiscences.** MINIATURE EDITION, printed on hand-made paper, limp parchment antique, 10*s.* 6*d.*

Bric-à-Brac. Being some Photoprints taken at Gower Lodge, Windsor. Super royal 8vo.

Last Days of Mary Antoinette. An Historical Sketch. With Portrait and Facsimiles. Fcap. 4to, 10*s.* 6*d.*

GOWER, Lord Ronald.—continued.

Notes of a Tour from Brindisi to Yokohama, 1883-1884. Fcap. 8vo, 2*s*. 6*d*.

GRAHAM, William, M.A.—The Creed of Science, Religious, Moral, and Social. Second Edition, Revised. Crown 8vo, 6*s*.

The Social Problem, in its Economic, Moral, and Political Aspects. Demy 8vo, 14*s*.

GREY, Rowland.—In Sunny Switzerland. A Tale of Six Weeks. Second Edition. Small crown 8vo, 5*s*.

Lindenblumen and other Stories. Small crown 8vo, 5*s*.

GRIMLEY, Rev. H. N., M.A.—Tremadoc Sermons, chiefly on the Spiritual Body, the Unseen World, and the Divine Humanity. Fourth Edition. Crown 8vo, 6*s*.

The Temple of Humanity, and other Sermons. Crown 8vo, 6*s*.

GURNEY, Edmund.—Tertium Quid : chapters on Various Disputed Questions. 2 vols. Crown 8vo, 12*s*.

HADDON, Caroline.—The Larger Life, Studies in Hinton's Ethics. Crown 8vo, 5*s*.

HAECKEL, Prof. Ernst.—The History of Creation. Translation revised by Professor E. RAY LANKESTER, M.A., F.R.S. With Coloured Plates and Genealogical Trees of the various groups of both Plants and Animals. 2 vols. Third Edition. Post 8vo, 32*s*.

The History of the Evolution of Man. With numerous Illustrations. 2 vols. Post 8vo, 32*s*.

A Visit to Ceylon. Post 8vo, 7*s*. 6*d*.

Freedom in Science and Teaching. With a Prefatory Note by T. H. HUXLEY, F.R.S. Crown 8vo, 5*s*.

Hamilton, Memoirs of Arthur, B.A., of Trinity College, Cambridge. Crown 8vo, 6*s*.

Handbook of Home Rule, being Articles on the Irish Question by Various Writers. Edited by JAMES BRYCE, M.P. Second Edition. Crown 8vo, 1*s*. sewed, or 1*s*. 6*d*. cloth.

HARRIS, William.—The History of the Radical Party in Parliament. Demy 8vo, 15*s*.

HAWEIS, Rev. H. R., M.A.—Current Coin. Materialism—The Devil—Crime—Drunkenness—Pauperism—Emotion—Recreation —The Sabbath. Fifth Edition. Crown 8vo, 5*s*.

Arrows in the Air. Fifth Edition. Crown 8vo, 5*s*.

Speech in Season. Fifth Edition. Crown 8vo, 5*s*.

Thoughts for the Times. Fourteenth Edition. Crown 8vo, 5*s*.

HAWEIS, Rev. H. R., M.A.—continued.

Unsectarian Family Prayers. New Edition. Fcap. 8vo, 1s. 6d.

HAWTHORNE, Nathaniel.—Works. Complete in Twelve Volumes. Large post 8vo, 7s. 6d. each volume.

HEATH, Francis George.—Autumnal Leaves. Third and cheaper Edition. Large crown 8vo, 6s.

Sylvan Winter. With 70 Illustrations. Large crown 8vo, 14s.

Hegel's Philosophy of Fine Art. The Introduction, translated by BERNARD BOSANQUET. Crown 8vo, 5s.

HENNESSY, Sir John Pope.—Ralegh in Ireland. With his Letters on Irish Affairs and some Contemporary Documents. Large crown 8vo, printed on hand-made paper, parchment, 10s. 6d.

HENRY, Philip.—Diaries and Letters of. Edited by MATTHEW HENRY LEE, M.A. Large crown 8vo, 7s. 6d.

HINTON, J.—Life and Letters. With an Introduction by Sir W. W. GULL, Bart., and Portrait engraved on Steel by C. H. Jeens. Fifth Edition. Crown 8vo, 8s. 6d.

Philosophy and Religion. Selections from the Manuscripts of the late James Hinton. Edited by CAROLINE HADDON. Second Edition. Crown 8vo, 5s.

The Law Breaker, and The Coming of the Law. Edited by MARGARET HINTON. Crown 8vo, 6s.

The Mystery of Pain. New Edition. Fcap. 8vo, 1s.

Homer's Iliad. Greek text, with a Translation by J. G. CORDERY. 2 vols. Demy 8vo, 24s.

HOOPER, Mary.—Little Dinners: How to Serve them with Elegance and Economy. Twentieth Edition. Crown 8vo, 2s. 6d.

Cookery for Invalids, Persons of Delicate Digestion, and Children. Fifth Edition. Crown 8vo, 2s. 6d.

Every-Day Meals. Being Economical and Wholesome Recipes for Breakfast, Luncheon, and Supper. Seventh Edition. Crown 8vo, 2s. 6d.

HOPKINS, Ellice.—Work amongst Working Men. Sixth Edition. Crown 8vo, 3s. 6d.

HORNADAY, W. T.—Two Years in a Jungle. With Illustrations. Demy 8vo, 21s.

HOSPITALIER, E.—The Modern Applications of Electricity. Translated and Enlarged by JULIUS MAIER, Ph.D. 2 vols. Second Edition, Revised, with many additions and numerous Illustrations. Demy 8vo, 25s.

HOWARD, Robert, M.A.—**The Church of England and other Religious Communions.** A course of Lectures delivered in the Parish Church of Clapham. Crown 8vo, 7*s.* 6*d.*

How to Make a Saint; or, The Process of Canonization in the Church of England. By the PRIG. Fcap 8vo, 3*s.* 6*d.*

HUNTER, William C.—**Bits of Old China.** Small crown 8vo, 6*s.*

HYNDMAN, H. M.—**The Historical Basis of Socialism in England.** Large crown 8vo, 8*s.* 6*d.*

IDDESLEIGH, Earl of.—**The Pleasures, Dangers, and Uses of Desultory Reading.** Fcap. 8vo, in Whatman paper cover, 1*s.*

IM THURN, Everard F.—**Among the Indians of Guiana.** Being Sketches, chiefly anthropologic, from the Interior of British Guiana. With 53 Illustrations and a Map. Demy 8vo, 18*s.*

JACCOUD, Prof. S.—**The Curability and Treatment of Pulmonary Phthisis.** Translated and edited by MONTAGU LUBBOCK, M.D. Demy 8vo, 15*s.*

Jaunt in a Junk: A Ten Days' Cruise in Indian Seas. Large crown 8vo, 7*s.* 6*d.*

JENKINS, E., and RAYMOND, J.—**The Architect's Legal Handbook.** Third Edition, revised. Crown 8vo, 6*s.*

JENKINS, Rev. Canon R. C.—**Heraldry: English and Foreign.** With a Dictionary of Heraldic Terms and 156 Illustrations. Small crown 8vo, 3*s.* 6*d.*

The Story of the Caraffa: the Pontificate of Paul IV. Small crown 8vo, 3*s.* 6*d.*

JOEL, L.—**A Consul's Manual and Shipowner's and Shipmaster's Practical Guide in their Transactions Abroad.** With Definitions of Nautical, Mercantile, and Legal Terms; a Glossary of Mercantile Terms in English, French, German, Italian, and Spanish; Tables of the Money, Weights, and Measures of the Principal Commercial Nations and their Equivalents in British Standards; and Forms of Consular and Notarial Acts. Demy 8vo, 12*s.*

JOHNSTON, H. H., F.Z.S.—**The Kilima-njaro Expedition.** A Record of Scientific Exploration in Eastern Equatorial Africa, and a General Description of the Natural History, Languages, and Commerce of the Kilima-njaro District. With 6 Maps, and over 80 Illustrations by the Author. Demy 8vo, 21*s.*

JORDAN, Furneaux, F.R.C.S.—**Anatomy and Physiology in Character.** Crown 8vo, 5*s.*

JOYCE, P. W., LL.D., etc.—**Old Celtic Romances.** Translated from the Gaelic. Crown 8vo, 7*s.* 6*d.*

KAUFMANN, Rev. M., B.A.—Socialism : its Nature, its Dangers, and its Remedies considered. Crown 8vo, 7s. 6d.

Utopias ; or, Schemes of Social Improvement, from Sir Thomas More to Karl Marx. Crown 8vo, 5s.

KAY, David, F.R.G.S.—Education and Educators. Crown 8vo. 7s. 6d.

KAY, Joseph.—Free Trade in Land. Edited by his Widow. With Preface by the Right Hon. JOHN BRIGHT, M.P. Seventh Edition. Crown 8vo, 5s.

**** Also a cheaper edition, without the Appendix, but with a Review of Recent Changes in the Land Laws of England, by the RIGHT HON. G. OSBORNE MORGAN, Q.C., M.P. Cloth, 1s. 6d. ; paper covers, 1s.

KELKE, W. H. H.—An Epitome of English Grammar for the Use of Students. Adapted to the London Matriculation Course and Similar Examinations. Crown 8vo, 4s. 6d.

KEMPIS, Thomas à.—Of the Imitation of Christ. Parchment Library Edition.—Parchment or cloth, 6s. ; vellum, 7s. 6d. The Red Line Edition, fcap. 8vo, cloth extra, 2s. 6d. The Cabinet Edition, small 8vo, cloth limp, 1s. ; cloth boards, 1s. 6d. The Miniature Edition, cloth limp, 32mo, 1s.

**** All the above Editions may be had in various extra bindings.

Notes of a Visit to the Scenes in which his Life was spent. With numerous Illustrations. By F. R. CRUISE, M.D. Demy 8vo, 12s.

KETTLEWELL, Rev. S.—Thomas à Kempis and the Brothers of Common Life. With Portrait. Second Edition. Crown 8vo, 7s. 6d.

KIDD, Joseph, M.D.—The Laws of Therapeutics ; or, the Science and Art of Medicine. Second Edition. Crown 8vo, 6s.

KINGSFORD, Anna, M.D.—The Perfect Way in Diet. A Treatise advocating a Return to the Natural and Ancient Food of our Race. Third Edition. Small crown 8vo, 2s.

KINGSLEY, Charles, M.A.—Letters and Memories of his Life. Edited by his Wife. With two Steel Engraved Portraits, and Vignettes on Wood. Sixteenth Cabinet Edition. 2 vols. Crown 8vo, 12s.

**** Also a People's Edition, in one volume. With Portrait. Crown 8vo, 6s.

All Saints' Day, and other Sermons. Edited by the Rev. W. HARRISON. Third Edition. Crown 8vo, 7s. 6d.

True Words for Brave Men. A Book for Soldiers' and Sailors' Libraries. Sixteenth Thousand. Crown 8vo, 2s. 6d.

KNOX, Alexander A.—The New Playground ; or, Wanderings in Algeria. New and Cheaper Edition. Large crown 8vo, 6s.

Kosmos ; or, the Hope of the World. 3*s.* 6*d.*

Land Concentration and Irresponsibility of Political Power, as causing the Anomaly of a Widespread State of Want by the Side of the Vast Supplies of Nature. Crown 8vo, 5*s.*

LANDON, Joseph.—**School Management ;** Including a General View of the Work of Education, Organization, and Discipline. Sixth Edition. Crown 8vo, 6*s.*

LAURIE, S. S.—**The Rise and Early Constitution of Universities.** With a Survey of Mediæval Education. Crown 8vo, 6*s.*

LEE, Rev. F. G., D.C.L.—**The Other World ;** or, Glimpses of the Supernatural. 2 vols. A New Edition. Crown 8vo, 15*s.*

LEFEVRE, Right Hon. G. Shaw.—**Peel and O'Connell.** Demy 8vo, 10*s.* 6*d.*

Letters from an Unknown Friend. By the Author of " Charles Lowder." With a Preface by the Rev. W. H. CLEAVER. Fcap. 8vo, 1*s.*

Life of a Prig. By ONE. Third Edition. Fcap. 8vo, 3*s.* 6*d.*

LILLIE, Arthur, M.R.A.S.—**The Popular Life of Buddha.** Containing an Answer to the Hibbert Lectures of 1881. With Illustrations. Crown 8vo, 6*s.*

> **Buddhism in Christendom ;** or, Jesus the Essene. With Illustrations. Demy 8vo, 15*s.*

LONGFELLOW, H. Wadsworth.—**Life.** By his Brother, SAMUEL LONGFELLOW. With Portraits and Illustrations. 3 vols. Demy 8vo, 42*s.*

LONSDALE, Margaret.—**Sister Dora :** a Biography. With Portrait. Twenty-ninth Edition. Small crown 8vo, 2*s.* 6*d.*

> **George Eliot : Thoughts upon her Life, her Books, and Herself.** Second Edition. Small crown 8vo, 1*s.* 6*d.*

LOUNSBURY, Thomas R.—**James Fenimore Cooper.** With Portrait. Crown 8vo, 5*s.*

LOWDER, Charles.—**A Biography.** By the Author of " St. Teresa." Twelfth Edition. Crown 8vo. With Portrait. 3*s.* 6*d.*

LÜCKES, Eva C. E.—**Lectures on General Nursing,** delivered to the Probationers of the London Hospital Training School for Nurses. Second Edition. Crown 8vo, 2*s.* 6*d.*

LYALL, William Rowe, D.D.—**Propædeia Prophetica ;** or, The Use and Design of the Old Testament Examined. New Edition. With Notices by GEORGE C. PEARSON, M.A., Hon. Canon of Canterbury. Demy 8vo, 10*s.* 6*d.*

LYTTON, Edward Bulwer, Lord.—**Life, Letters and Literary Remains.** By his Son, the EARL OF LYTTON. With Portraits, Illustrations and Facsimiles. Demy 8vo. Vols. I. and II., 32*s.*

MACAULAY, G. C.—Francis Beaumont : A Critical Study. Crown 8vo, 5*s.*

MACHIAVELLI, Niccolò. — Life and Times. By Prof. VILLARI. Translated by LINDA VILLARI. 4 vols. Large post 8vo, 48*s.*

Discourses on the First Decade of Titus Livius. Translated from the Italian by NINIAN HILL THOMSON, M.A. Large crown 8vo, 12*s.*

The Prince. Translated from the Italian by N. H. T. Small crown 8vo, printed on hand-made paper, bevelled boards, 6*s.*

MACNEILL, J. G. Swift.—How the Union was carried. Crown 8vo, cloth, 1*s.* 6*d.* ; paper covers, 1*s.*

MAGNUS, Lady.—About the Jews since Bible Times. From the Babylonian Exile till the English Exodus. Small crown 8vo, 6*s.*

MAGUIRE, Thomas.—Lectures on Philosophy. Demy 8vo, 9*s.*

Many Voices. A volume of Extracts from the Religious Writers of Christendom from the First to the Sixteenth Century. With Biographical Sketches. Crown 8vo, cloth extra, red edges, 6*s.*

MARKHAM, Capt. Albert Hastings, R.N.—The Great Frozen Sea : A Personal Narrative of the Voyage of the *Alert* during the Arctic Expedition of 1875-6. With 6 full-page Illustrations, 2 Maps, and 27 Woodcuts. Sixth and Cheaper Edition. Crown 8vo, 6*s.*

MARTINEAU, Gertrude.—Outline Lessons on Morals. Small crown 8vo, 3*s.* 6*d.*

MASON, Charlotte M.—Home Education : a Course of Lectures to Ladies. Crown 8vo, 3*s.* 6*d.*

Matter and Energy : An Examination of the Fundamental Conceptions of Physical Force. By B. L. L. Small crown 8vo, 2*s.*

MAUDSLEY, H., M.D.—Body and Will. Being an Essay concerning Will, in its Metaphysical, Physiological, and Pathological Aspects. 8vo, 12*s.*

Natural Causes and Supernatural Seemings. Second Edition. Crown 8vo, 6*s.*

McGRATH, Terence.—Pictures from Ireland. New and Cheaper Edition. Crown 8vo, 2*s.*

MEREDITH, M.A.—Theotokos, the Example for Woman. Dedicated, by permission, to Lady Agnes Wood. Revised by the Venerable Archdeacon DENISON. 32mo, limp cloth, 1*s.* 6*d.*

MILLER, Edward.—The History and Doctrines of Irvingism ; or, The so-called Catholic and Apostolic Church. 2 vols. Large post 8vo, 15*s.*

The Church in Relation to the State. Large crown 8vo, 4*s.*

MILLS, Herbert.—**Poverty and the State** ; or, Work for the Un-employed. An Inquiry into the Causes and Extent of Enforced Idleness, with a Statement of a Remedy. Crown 8vo, 6s.

MITCHELL, Lucy M.—**A History of Ancient Sculpture.** With numerous Illustrations, including 6 Plates in Phototype. Super-royal 8vo, 42s.

MOCKLER, E.—**A Grammar of the Baloochee Language,** as it is spoken in Makran (Ancient Gedrosia), in the Persia-Arabic and Roman characters. Fcap. 8vo, 5s.

MOHL, Julius and Mary.—**Letters and Recollections of.** By M. C. M. SIMPSON. With Portraits and Two Illustrations. Demy 8vo, 15s.

MOLESWORTH, Rev. W. Nassau, M.A.—**History of the Church of England from 1660.** Large crown 8vo, 7s. 6d.

MORELL, J. R.—**Euclid Simplified in Method and Language.** Being a Manual of Geometry. Compiled from the most important French Works, approved by the University of Paris and the Minister of Public Instruction. Fcap. 8vo, 2s. 6d.

MORGAN, C. Lloyd.—**The Springs of Conduct.** An Essay in Evolution. Large crown 8vo, cloth, 7s. 6d.

MORISON, J. Cotter.—**The Service of Man :** an Essay towards the Religion of the Future. Second Edition. Demy 8vo, 10s. 6d.

MORSE, E. S., Ph.D.—**First Book of Zoology.** With numerous Illustrations. New and Cheaper Edition. Crown 8vo, 2s. 6d.

My Lawyer : A Concise Abridgment of the Laws of England. By a Barrister-at-Law. Crown 8vo, 6s. 6d.

NELSON, J. H., M.A.—**A Prospectus of the Scientific Study of the Hindû Law.** Demy 8vo, 9s.

Indian Usage and Judge-made Law in Madras. Demy 8vo, 12s.

NEWMAN, Cardinal.—**Characteristics from the Writings of.** Being Selections from his various Works. Arranged with the Author's personal Approval. Seventh Edition. With Portrait. Crown 8vo, 6s.

**** A Portrait of Cardinal Newman, mounted for framing, can be had, 2s. 6d.

NEWMAN, Francis William.—**Essays on Diet.** Small crown 8vo, cloth limp, 2s.

New Social Teachings. By POLITICUS. Small crown 8vo, 5s.

NICOLS, Arthur, F.G.S., F.R.G.S.—**Chapters from the Physical History of the Earth :** an Introduction to Geology and Palæontology. With numerous Illustrations. Crown 8vo, 5s.

NIHILL, Rev. H. D.—**The Sisters of St. Mary at the Cross :** Sisters of the Poor and their Work. Crown 8vo, 2s. 6d.

NOEL, The Hon. Roden.—**Essays on Poetry and Poets.** Demy 8vo, 12*s.*

NOPS, Marianne.—**Class Lessons on Euclid.** Part I. containing the First Two Books of the Elements. Crown 8vo, 2*s.* 6*d.*

Nuces: EXERCISES ON THE SYNTAX OF THE PUBLIC SCHOOL LATIN PRIMER. New Edition in Three Parts. Crown 8vo, each 1*s.*

*** The Three Parts can also be had bound together, 3*s.*

OATES, Frank, F.R.G.S.—**Matabele Land and the Victoria Falls.** A Naturalist's Wanderings in the Interior of South Africa. Edited by C. G. OATES, B.A. With numerous Illustrations and 4 Maps. Demy 8vo, 21*s.*

O'BRIEN, R. Barry.—**Irish Wrongs and English Remedies,** with other Essays. Crown 8vo, 5*s.*

OGLE, Anna C.—**A Lost Love.** Small crown 8vo, 2*s.* 6*d.*

O'MEARA, Kathleen.—**Henri Perreyve and his Counsels to the Sick.** Small crown 8vo, 5*s.*

One and a Half in Norway. A Chronicle of Small Beer. By Either and Both. Small crown 8vo, 3*s.* 6*d.*

O'NEIL, the late Rev. Lord.—**Sermons.** With Memoir and Portrait. Crown 8vo, 6*s.*

Essays and Addresses. Crown 8vo, 5*s.*

OTTLEY, H. Bickersteth.—**The Great Dilemma.** Christ His Own Witness or His Own Accuser. Six Lectures. Second Edition. Crown 8vo, 3*s.* 6*d.*

Our Public Schools—Eton, Harrow, Winchester, Rugby, Westminster, Marlborough, The Charterhouse. Crown 8vo, 6*s.*

PADGHAM, Richard.—**In the Midst of Life we are in Death.** Crown 8vo, 5*s.*

PALMER, the late William.—**Notes of a Visit to Russia in 1840–1841.** Selected and arranged by JOHN H. CARDINAL NEWMAN, with Portrait. Crown 8vo, 8*s.* 6*d.*

Early Christian Symbolism. A Series of Compositions from Fresco Paintings, Glasses, and Sculptured Sarcophagi. Edited by the Rev. Provost NORTHCOTE, D.D., and the Rev. Canon BROWNLOW, M.A. With Coloured Plates, folio, 42*s.*, or with Plain Plates, folio, 25*s.*

Parchment Library. Choicely Printed on hand-made paper, limp parchment antique or cloth, 6*s.* ; vellum, 7*s.* 6*d.* each volume.

The Poetical Works of John Milton. 2 vols.

Chaucer's Canterbury Tales. Edited by A. W. POLLARD. 2 vols.

Parchment Library—*continued.*

> **Letters and Journals of Jonathan Swift.** Selected and edited, with a Commentary and Notes, by STANLEY LANE POOLE.

> **De Quincey's Confessions of an English Opium Eater.** Reprinted from the First Edition. Edited by RICHARD GARNETT.

> **The Gospel according to Matthew, Mark, and Luke.**

> **Selections from the Prose Writings of Jonathan Swift.** With a Preface and Notes by STANLEY LANE-POOLE and Portrait.

> **English Sacred Lyrics.**

> **Sir Joshua Reynolds's Discourses.** Edited by EDMUND GOSSE.

> **Selections from Milton's Prose Writings.** Edited by ERNEST MYERS.

> **The Book of Psalms.** Translated by the Rev. Canon T. K. CHEYNE, M.A., D.D.

> **The Vicar of Wakefield.** With Preface and Notes by AUSTIN DOBSON.

> **English Comic Dramatists.** Edited by OSWALD CRAWFURD.

> **English Lyrics.**

> **The Sonnets of John Milton.** Edited by MARK PATTISON. With Portrait after Vertue.

> **French Lyrics.** Selected and Annotated by GEORGE SAINTS-BURY. With a Miniature Frontispiece designed and etched by H. G. Glindoni.

> **Fables by Mr. John Gay.** With Memoir by AUSTIN DOBSON, and an Etched Portrait from an unfinished Oil Sketch by Sir Godfrey Kneller.

> **Select Letters of Percy Bysshe Shelley.** Edited, with an Introduction, by RICHARD GARNETT.

> **The Christian Year.** Thoughts in Verse for the Sundays and Holy Days throughout the Year. With Miniature Portrait of the Rev. J. Keble, after a Drawing by G. Richmond, R.A.

> **Shakspere's Works.** Complete in Twelve Volumes.

> **Eighteenth Century Essays.** Selected and Edited by AUSTIN DOBSON. With a Miniature Frontispiece by R. Caldecott.

> **Q. Horati Flacci Opera.** Edited by F. A. CORNISH, Assistant Master at Eton. With a Frontispiece after a design by L. Alma Tadema, etched by Leopold Lowenstam.

> **Edgar Allan Poe's Poems.** With an Essay on his Poetry by ANDREW LANG, and a Frontispiece by Linley Sambourne.

Parchment Library—*continued.*

Shakspere's Sonnets. Edited by EDWARD DOWDEN. With a Frontispiece etched by Leopold Lowenstam, after the Death Mask.

English Odes. Selected by EDMUND GOSSE. With Frontispiece on India paper by Hamo Thornycroft, A.R.A.

Of the Imitation of Christ. By THOMAS À KEMPIS. A revised Translation. With Frontispiece on India paper, from a Design by W. B. Richmond.

Poems: Selected from PERCY BYSSHE SHELLEY. Dedicated to Lady Shelley. With a Preface by RICHARD GARNETT and a Miniature Frontispiece.

PARSLOE, Joseph.—**Our Railways.** Sketches, Historical and Descriptive. With Practical Information as to Fares and Rates, etc., and a Chapter on Railway Reform. Crown 8vo, 6s.

PASCAL, Blaise.—**The Thoughts of.** Translated from the Text of Auguste Molinier, by C. KEGAN PAUL. Large crown 8vo, with Frontispiece, printed on hand-made paper, parchment antique, or cloth, 12s. ; vellum, 15s.

PAUL, Alexander.—**Short Parliaments.** A History of the National Demand for frequent General Elections. Small crown 8vo, 3s. 6d.

PAUL, C. Kegan.—**Biographical Sketches.** Printed on hand-made paper, bound in buckram. Second Edition. Crown 8vo, 7s. 6d.

PEARSON, Rev. S.—**Week-day Living.** A Book for Young Men and Women. Second Edition. Crown 8vo, 5s.

PENRICE, Major J.—**Arabic and English Dictionary of the Koran.** 4to, 21s.

PESCHEL, Dr. Oscar.—**The Races of Man and their Geographical Distribution.** Second Edition. Large crown 8vo, 9s.

PIDGEON, D.—**An Engineer's Holiday ;** or, Notes of a Round Trip from Long. 0° to 0°. New and Cheaper Edition. Large crown 8vo, 7s. 6d.

Old World Questions and New World Answers. Second Edition. Large crown 8vo, 7s. 6d.

Plain Thoughts for Men. Eight Lectures delivered at Forester's Hall, Clerkenwell, during the London Mission, 1884. Crown 8vo, cloth, 1s. 6d ; paper covers, 1s.

PRICE, Prof. Bonamy. — **Chapters on Practical Political Economy.** Being the Substance of Lectures delivered before the University of Oxford. New and Cheaper Edition. Crown 8vo, 5s.

Prig's Bede : the Venerable Bede, Expurgated, Expounded, and Exposed. By The Prig. Second Edition. Fcap. 8vo, 3s. 6d.

Pulpit Commentary, The. (*Old Testament Series.*) Edited by the Rev. J. S. EXELL, M.A., and the Very Rev. Dean H. D. M. SPENCE, M.A., D.D.

Genesis. By the Rev. T. WHITELAW, D.D. With Homilies by the Very Rev. J. F. MONTGOMERY, D.D., Rev. Prof. R. A. REDFORD, M.A., LL.B., Rev. F. HASTINGS, Rev. W. ROBERTS, M.A. An Introduction to the Study of the Old Testament by the Venerable Archdeacon FARRAR, D.D., F.R.S.; and Introductions to the Pentateuch by the Right Rev. H. COTTERILL, D.D., and Rev. T. WHITELAW, M.A. Eighth Edition. 1 vol., 15*s*.

Exodus. By the Rev. Canon RAWLINSON. With Homilies by Rev. J. ORR, Rev. D. YOUNG, B.A., Rev. C. A. GOODHART, Rev. J. URQUHART, and the Rev. H. T. ROBJOHNS. Fourth Edition. 2 vols., 18*s*.

Leviticus. By the Rev. Prebendary MEYRICK, M.A. With Introductions by the Rev. R. COLLINS, Rev. Professor A. CAVE, and Homilies by Rev. Prof. REDFORD, LL.B., Rev. J. A. MACDONALD, Rev. W. CLARKSON, B.A., Rev. S. R. ALDRIDGE, LL.B., and Rev. McCHEYNE EDGAR. Fourth Edition. 15*s*.

Numbers. By the Rev. R. WINTERBOTHAM, LL.B. With Homilies by the Rev. Professor W. BINNIE, D.D., Rev. E. S. PROUT, M.A., Rev. D. YOUNG, Rev. J. WAITE, and an Introduction by the Rev. THOMAS WHITELAW, M.A. Fifth Edition. 15*s*.

Deuteronomy. By the Rev. W. L. ALEXANDER, D.D. With Homilies by Rev. C. CLEMANCE, D.D., Rev. J. ORR, B.D., Rev. R. M. EDGAR, M.A., Rev. D. DAVIES, M.A. Fourth edition. 15*s*.

Joshua. By Rev. J. J. LIAS, M.A. With Homilies by Rev. S. R. ALDRIDGE, LL.B., Rev. R. GLOVER, REV. E. DE PRESSENSÉ, D.D., Rev. J. WAITE, B.A., Rev. W. F. ADENEY, M.A.; and an Introduction by the Rev. A. PLUMMER, M.A. Fifth Edition. 12*s*. 6*d*.

Judges and Ruth. By the Bishop of BATH and WELLS, and Rev. J. MORISON, D.D. With Homilies by Rev. A. F. MUIR, M.A., Rev. W. F. ADENEY, M.A., Rev. W. M. STATHAM, and Rev. Professor J. THOMSON, M.A. Fifth Edition. 10*s*. 6*d*.

1 Samuel. By the Very Rev. R. P. SMITH, D.D. With Homilies by Rev. DONALD FRASER, D.D., Rev. Prof. CHAPMAN, and Rev. B. DALE. Sixth Edition. 15*s*.

1 Kings. By the Rev. JOSEPH HAMMOND, LL.B. With Homilies by the Rev. E. DE PRESSENSÉ, D.D., Rev. J. WAITE, B.A., Rev. A. ROWLAND, LL.B., Rev. J. A. MACDONALD, and Rev. J. URQUHART. Fifth Edition. 15*s*.

Pulpit Commentary, The—*continued.*

1 Chronicles. By the Rev. Prof. P. C. BARKER, M.A., LL.B.
With Homilies by Rev. Prof. J. R. THOMSON, M.A., Rev. R.
TUCK, B.A., Rev. W. CLARKSON, B.A., Rev. F. WHITFIELD,
M.A., and Rev. RICHARD GLOVER. 15*s.*

Ezra, Nehemiah, and Esther. By Rev. Canon G. RAWLINSON,
M.A. With Homilies by Rev. Prof. J. R. THOMSON, M.A., Rev.
Prof. R. A. REDFORD, LL.B., M.A., Rev. W. S. LEWIS, M.A.,
Rev. J. A. MACDONALD, Rev. A. MACKENNAL, B.A., Rev. W.
CLARKSON, B.A., Rev. F. HASTINGS, Rev. W. DINWIDDIE,
LL.B., Rev. Prof. ROWLANDS, B.A., Rev. G. WOOD, B.A.,
Rev. Prof. P. C. BARKER, M.A., LL.B., and the Rev. J. S.
EXELL, M.A. Sixth Edition. 1 vol., 12*s.* 6*d.*

Isaiah. By the Rev. Canon G. RAWLINSON, M.A. With Homilies
by Rev. Prof. E. JOHNSON, M.A., Rev. W. CLARKSON, B.A.,
Rev. W. M. STATHAM, and Rev. R. TUCK, B.A. Second
Edition. 2 vols., 15*s.* each.

Jeremiah. (Vol. I.) By the Rev. Canon T. K. CHEYNE, M.A.,
D.D. With Homilies by the Rev. W. F. ADENEY, M.A., Rev.
A. F. MUIR, M.A., Rev. S. CONWAY, B.A., Rev. J. WAITE,
B.A., and Rev. D. YOUNG, B.A. Third Edition. 15*s.*

Jeremiah (Vol. II.) and Lamentations. By Rev. T. K.
CHEYNE, M.A. With Homilies by Rev. Prof. J. R. THOMSON,
M.A., Rev. W. F. ADENEY, M.A., Rev. A. F. MUIR, M.A.,
Rev. S. CONWAY, B.A., Rev. D. YOUNG, B.A. 15*s.*

Hosea and Joel. By the Rev. Prof. J. J. GIVEN, Ph.D., D.D.
With Homilies by the Rev. Prof. J. R. THOMSON, M.A., Rev.
A. ROWLAND, B.A., LL.B., Rev. C. JERDAN, M.A., LL.B.,
Rev. J. ORR, M.A., B.D., and Rev. D. THOMAS, D.D. 15*s.*

Pulpit Commentary, The. (*New Testament Series.*)
St. Mark. By Very Rev. E. BICKERSTETH, D.D., Dean of Lich-
field. With Homilies by Rev. Prof. THOMSON, M.A., Rev. Prof.
J. J. GIVEN, Ph.D., D.D., Rev. Prof. JOHNSON, M.A., Rev. A.
ROWLAND, B.A., LL.B., Rev. A. MUIR, and Rev. R. GREEN.
Fifth Edition. 2 vols., 21*s.*

The Acts of the Apostles. By the Bishop of BATH and WELLS.
With Homilies by Rev. Prof. P. C. BARKER, M.A., LL.B., Rev.
Prof. E. JOHNSON, M.A., Rev. Prof. R. A. REDFORD, LL.B.,
Rev. R. TUCK, B.A., Rev. W. CLARKSON, B.A. Third Edition.
2 vols., 21*s.*

1 Corinthians. By the Ven. Archdeacon FARRAR, D.D. With
Homilies by Rev. Ex-Chancellor LIPSCOMB, LL.D., Rev.
DAVID THOMAS, D.D., Rev. D. FRASER, D.D., Rev. Prof.
J. R. THOMSON, M.A., Rev. J. WAITE, B.A., Rev. R. TUCK,
B.A., Rev. E. HURNDALL, M.A., and Rev. H. BREMNER, B.D.
·Third Edition. 15*s.*

Pulpit Commentary, The—*continued.*

2 Corinthians and Galatians. By the Ven. Archdeacon FARRAR, D.D., and Rev. Prebendary E. HUXTABLE. With Homilies by Rev. Ex-Chancellor LIPSCOMB, LL.D., Rev. DAVID THOMAS, D.D., Rev. DONALD FRASER, D.D., Rev. R. TUCK, B.A., Rev. E. HURNDALL, M.A., Rev. Prof. J. R. THOMSON, M.A., Rev. R. FINLAYSON, B.A., Rev. W. F. ADENEY, M.A., Rev. R. M. EDGAR, M.A., and Rev. T. CROSKERY, D.D. 21*s.*

Ephesians, Philippians, and Colossians. By the Rev. Prof. W. G. BLAIKIE, D.D., Rev. B. C. CAFFIN, M.A., and Rev. G. G. FINDLAY, B.A. With Homilies by Rev. D. THOMAS, D.D., Rev. R. M. EDGAR, M.A., Rev. R. FINLAYSON, B.A., Rev. W. F. ADENEY, M.A., Rev. Prof. T. CROSKERY, D.D., Rev. E. S. PROUT, M.A., Rev. Canon VERNON HUTTON, and Rev. U. R. THOMAS, D.D. Second Edition. 21*s.*

Thessalonians, Timothy, Titus, and Philemon. By the Bishop of Bath and Wells, Rev. Dr. GLOAG and Rev. Dr. EALES. With Homilies by the Rev. B. C. CAFFIN, M.A., Rev. R. FINLAYSON, B.A., Rev. Prof. T. CROSKERY, D.D., Rev. W. F. ADENEY, M.A., Rev. W. M. STATHAM, and Rev. D. THOMAS, D.D. 15*s.*

Hebrews and James. By the Rev. J. BARMBY, D.D., and Rev Prebendary E. C. S. GIBSON, M.A. With Homiletics by the Rev. C. JERDAN, M.A., LL.B., and Rev. Prebendary E. C. S. GIBSON. And Homilies by the Rev. W. JONES, Rev. C. NEW, Rev. D. YOUNG, B.A., Rev. J. S. BRIGHT, Rev. T. F. LOCKYER, B.A., and Rev. C. JERDAN, M.A., LL.B. Second Edition. 15*s.*

PUSEY, Dr.—**Sermons for the Church's Seasons from Advent to Trinity.** Selected from the Published Sermons of the late EDWARD BOUVERIE PUSEY, D.D. Crown 8vo, 5*s.*

RANKE, Leopold von.—**Universal History.** The oldest Historical Group of Nations and the Greeks. Edited by G. W. PROTHERO. Demy 8vo, 16*s.*

RENDELL, J. M.—**Concise Handbook of the Island of Madeira.** With Plan of Funchal and Map of the Island. Fcap. 8vo, 1*s.* 6*d.*

REVELL, W. F.—**Ethical Forecasts.** Crown 8vo.

REYNOLDS, Rev. J. W.—**The Supernatural in Nature.** A Verification by Free Use of Science. Third Edition, Revised and Enlarged. Demy 8vo, 14*s.*

The Mystery of Miracles. Third and Enlarged Edition. Crown 8vo, 6*s.*

The Mystery of the Universe our Common Faith. Demy 8vo, 14*s.*

The World to Come: Immortality a Physical Fact. Crown 8vo, 6*s.*

RIBOT, Prof. Th.—Heredity: A Psychological Study of its Phenomena, its Laws, its Causes, and its Consequences. Second Edition. Large crown 8vo, 9s.

ROBERTSON, The late Rev. F. W., M.A.—Life and Letters of. Edited by the Rev. STOPFORD BROOKE, M.A.

    I. Two vols., uniform with the Sermons. With Steel Portrait. Crown 8vo, 7s. 6d.

    II. Library Edition, in Demy 8vo, with Portrait. 12s.

    III. A Popular Edition, in 1 vol. Crown 8vo, 6s.

ROBERTSON, The late Rev. F. W., M.A.—continued.

Sermons. Four Series. Small crown 8vo, 3s. 6d. each.

The Human Race, and other Sermons. Preached at Cheltenham, Oxford, and Brighton. New and Cheaper Edition. Small crown 8vo, 3s. 6d.

Notes on Genesis. New and Cheaper Edition. Small crown 8vo, 3s. 6d.

Expository Lectures on St. Paul's Epistles to the Corinthians. A New Edition. Small crown 8vo, 5s.

Lectures and Addresses, with other Literary Remains. A New Edition. Small crown 8vo, 5s.

An Analysis of Tennyson's "In Memoriam." (Dedicated by Permission to the Poet-Laureate.) Fcap. 8vo, 2s.

The Education of the Human Race. Translated from the German of GOTTHOLD EPHRAIM LESSING. Fcap. 8vo, 2s. 6d.

The above Works can also be had, bound in half-morocco.

*** A Portrait of the late Rev. F. W. Robertson, mounted for framing, can be had, 2s. 6d.

ROMANES, G. J.— Mental Evolution in Animals. With a Posthumous Essay on Instinct by CHARLES DARWIN, F.R.S. Demy 8vo, 12s.

ROOSEVELT, Theodore. Hunting Trips of a Ranchman. Sketches of Sport on the Northern Cattle Plains. With 26 Illustrations. Royal 8vo, 18s.

ROSMINI SERBATI, Antonio.—Life. By the REV. W. LOCKHART. Second Edition. 2 vols. With Portraits. Crown 8vo, 12s.

Rosmini's Origin of Ideas. Translated from the Fifth Italian Edition of the Nuovo Saggio *Sull' origine delle idee.* 3 vols. Demy 8vo, cloth, 10s. 6d. each.

Rosmini's Psychology. 3 vols. Demy 8vo [Vols. I. and II. now ready], 10s. 6d. each.

ROSS, Janet.—Italian Sketches. With 14 full-page Illustrations. Crown 8vo, 7s. 6d.

RULE, Martin, M.A.—The Life and Times of St. Anselm, Archbishop of Canterbury and Primate of the Britains. 2 vols. Demy 8vo, 32s.

SAMUELL, Richard.—**Seven, the Sacred Number:** Its use in Scripture and its Application to Biblical Criticism. Crown 8vo, 10s. 6d.

SAYCE, Rev. Archibald Henry.—**Introduction to the Science of Language.** 2 vols. Second Edition. Large post 8vo, 21s.

SCOONES, W. Baptiste.—**Four Centuries of English Letters:** A Selection of 350 Letters by 150 Writers, from the Period of the Paston Letters to the Present Time. Third Edition. Large crown 8vo, 6s.

SÉE, Prof. Germain.—**Bacillary Phthisis of the Lungs.** Translated and edited for English Practitioners by WILLIAM HENRY WEDDELL, M.R.C.S. Demy 8vo, 10s. 6d.

Shakspere's Works. The Avon Edition, 12 vols., fcap. 8vo, cloth, 18s.; in cloth box, 21s.; bound in 6 vols., cloth, 15s.

Shakspere's Works, an Index to. By EVANGELINE O'CONNOR. Crown 8vo, 5s.

SHELLEY, Percy Bysshe.—**Life.** By EDWARD DOWDEN, LL.D. 2 vols. With Portraits. Demy 8vo, 36s.

SHILLITO, Rev. Joseph.—**Womanhood:** its Duties, Temptations, and Privileges. A Book for Young Women. Third Edition. Crown 8vo, 3s. 6d.

Shooting, Practical Hints. Being a Treatise on the Shot Gun and its Management. By "20 Bore." With 55 Illustrations. Demy 8vo, 12s.

Sister Augustine, Superior of the Sisters of Charity at the St. Johannis Hospital at Bonn. Authorized Translation by HANS THARAU, from the German "Memorials of AMALIE VON LASAULX." Cheap Edition. Large crown 8vo, 4s. 6d.

SKINNER, James.—**A Memoir.** By the Author of "Charles Lowder." With a Preface by the Rev. Canon CARTER, and Portrait. Large crown, 7s. 6d.

*** Also a cheap Edition. With Portrait. Fourth Edition. Crown 8vo, 3s. 6d.

SMEATON, D. Mackenzie.—**The Loyal Karens of Burma.** Crown 8vo, 4s. 6d.

SMITH, Edward, M.D., LL.B., F.R.S.—**Tubercular Consumption in its Early and Remediable Stages.** Second Edition. Crown 8vo, 6s.

SMITH, Sir W. Cusack, Bart.—**Our War Ships.** A Naval Essay. Crown 8vo, 5s.

Spanish Mystics. By the Editor of "Many Voices." Crown 8vo, 5s.

Specimens of English Prose Style from Malory to Macaulay. Selected and Annotated, with an Introductory Essay, by GEORGE SAINTSBURY. Large crown 8vo, printed on hand-made paper, parchment antique or cloth, 12s.; vellum, 15s.

SPEDDING, James.—Reviews and Discussions, Literary, Political, and Historical not relating to Bacon. Demy 8vo, 12*s.* 6*d.*

· —— Evenings with a Reviewer; or, Macaulay and Bacon. With a Prefatory Notice by G. S. VENABLES, Q.C. 2 vols. Demy 8vo, 18*s.*

Stray Papers on Education, and Scenes from School Life. By B. H. Second Edition. Small crown 8vo, 3*s.* 6*d.*

STREATFEILD, Rev. G. S., M.A.—Lincolnshire and the Danes. Large crown 8vo, 7*s.* 6*d.*

STRECKER-WISLICENUS.—Organic Chemistry. Translated and Edited, with Extensive Additions, by W. R. HODGKINSON, Ph.D., and A. J. GREENAWAY, F.I.C. Second and cheaper Edition. Demy 8vo, 12*s.* 6*d.*

Suakin, 1885; being a Sketch of the Campaign of this year. By an Officer who was there. Second Edition. Crown 8vo, 2*s.* 6*d.*

SULLY, James, M.A.—Pessimism : a History and a Criticism. Second Edition. Demy 8vo, 14*s.*

Sunshine and Sea. A Yachting Visit to the Channel Islands and · Coast of Brittany. With Frontispiece from a Photograph and 24 Illustrations. Crown 8vo, 6*s.*

SWEDENBORG, Eman.—De Cultu et Amore Dei ubi Agitur de Telluris ortu, Paradiso et Vivario, tum de Primogeniti Seu Adami Nativitate Infantia, et Amore. Crown 8vo, 6*s.*

—— On the Worship and Love of God. Treating of the Birth of the Earth, Paradise, and the Abode of Living Creatures. Translated from the original Latin. Crown 8vo, 7*s.* 6*d.*

—— Prodromus Philosophiæ Ratiocinantis de Infinito, et Causa Finali Creationis : deque Mechanismo Operationis Animæ et Corporis. Edidit THOMAS MURRAY GORMAN, M.A. Crown 8vo, 7*s.* 6*d.*

TACITUS.—The Agricola. A Translation. Small crown 8vo, 2*s.* 6*d.*

TARRING, C. J.—A Práctical Elementary Turkish Grammar. Crown 8vo, 6*s.*

TAYLOR, Rev. Isaac.—The Alphabet. An Account of the Origin and Development of Letters. With numerous Tables and Facsimiles. 2 vols. Demy 8vo, 36*s.*

TAYLOR, Jeremy.—The Marriage Ring. With Preface, Notes, and Appendices. Edited by FRANCIS BURDETT MONEY COUTTS. Small crown 8vo, 2*s.* 6*d.*

TAYLOR, Sedley. — Profit Sharing between Capital and · Labour. To which is added a Memorandum on the Industrial Partnership at the Whitwood Collieries, by ARCHIBALD and HENRY BRIGGS, with remarks by SEDLEY TAYLOR. Crown 8vo, 2*s.* 6*d.*

THOM, J. Hamilton.—**Laws of Life after the Mind of Christ.** Two Series. Crown 8vo, 7s. 6d. each.

THOMPSON, Sir H.—**Diet in Relation to Age and Activity.** Fcap. 8vo, cloth, 1s. 6d. ; paper covers, 1s.

TIDMAN, Paul F.—**Money and Labour.** 1s. 6d.

TIPPLE, Rev. S. A.—**Sunday Mornings at Norwood.** Prayers and Sermons. Crown 8vo, 6s.

TODHUNTER, Dr. J.—**A Study of Shelley.** Crown 8vo, 7s.

TOLSTOI, Count Leo.—**Christ's Christianity.** Translated from the Russian. Large crown 8vo, 7s. 6d. .

TRANT, William.—**Trade Unions: Their Origin, Objects, and Efficacy.** Small crown 8vo, 1s. 6d. ; paper covers, 1s.

TRENCH, The late R. C., Archbishop.—**Notes on the Parables of Our Lord.** Fourteenth Edition. 8vo, 12s. Cheap Edition, 7s. 6d.

Notes on the Miracles of Our Lord. Twelfth Edition. 8vo, 12s. Cheap Edition, 7s. 6d.

Studies in the Gospels. Fifth Edition, Revised. 8vo, 10s. 6d.

Brief Thoughts and Meditations on Some Passages in Holy Scripture. Third Edition. Crown 8vo, 3s. 6d.

Synonyms of the New Testament. Tenth Edition, En larged. 8vo, 12s.

Sermons New and Old. Crown 8vo, 6s.

On the Authorized Version of the New Testament. Second Edition. 8vo, 7s.

Commentary on the Epistles to the Seven Churches in Asia. Fourth Edition, Revised. 8vo, 8s. 6d.

The Sermon on the Mount. An Exposition drawn from the Writings of St. Augustine, with an Essay on his Merits as an Interpreter of Holy Scripture. Fourth Edition, Enlarged. 8vo, 10s. 6d.

Shipwrecks of Faith. Three Sermons preached before the University of Cambridge in May, 1867. Fcap. 8vo, 2s. 6d.

Lectures on Mediæval Church History. Being the Sub-stance of Lectures delivered at Queen's College, London. Second Edition. 8vo, 12s.

English, Past and Present. Thirteenth Edition, Revised and Improved. Fcap. 8vo, 5s.

On the Study of Words. Nineteenth Edition, Revised. Fcap. 8vo, 5s.

TRENCH, The late R. C., Archbishop.—continued.

Select Glossary of English Words Used Formerly in Senses Different from the Present. Sixth Edition, Revised and Enlarged. Fcap. 8vo, 5*s.*

Proverbs and Their Lessons. Seventh Edition, Enlarged. Fcap. 8vo, 4*s.*

Poems. Collected and Arranged anew. Ninth Edition. Fcap. 8vo, 7*s.* 6*d.*

Poems. Library Edition. 2 vols. Small crown 8vo, 10*s.*

Sacred Latin Poetry. Chiefly Lyrical, Selected and Arranged for Use. Third Edition, Corrected and Improved. Fcap. 8vo, 7*s.*

A Household Book of English Poetry. Selected and Arranged, with Notes. Fourth Edition, Revised. Extra fcap. 8vo, 5*s.* 6*d.*

An Essay on the Life and Genius of Calderon. With Translations from his "Life's a Dream" and "Great Theatre of the World." Second Edition, Revised and Improved. Extra fcap. 8vo, 5*s.* 6*d.*

Gustavus Adolphus in Germany, and other Lectures on the Thirty Years' War. Third Edition, Enlarged. Fcap. 8vo, 4*s.*

Plutarch : his Life, his Lives, and his Morals. Second Edition, Enlarged. Fcap. 8vo, 3*s.* 6*d.*

Remains of the late Mrs. Richard Trench. Being Selections from her Journals, Letters, and other Papers. New and Cheaper Issue. With Portrait. 8vo, 6*s.*

TUKE, Daniel Hack, M.D., F.R.C.P.—Chapters in the History of the Insane in the British Isles. With Four Illustrations. Large crown 8vo, 12*s.*

TWINING, Louisa.—Workhouse Visiting and Management during Twenty-Five Years. Small crown 8vo, 2*s.*

VAUGHAN, H. Halford.—New Readings and Renderings of Shakespeare's Tragedies. 3 vols. Demy 8vo, 12*s.* 6*d.* each.

VICARY, J. Fulford.—Saga Time. With Illustrations. Crown 8vo, 7*s.* 6*d.*

VOGT, Lieut.-Col. Hermann.—The Egyptian War of 1882. A translation. With Map and Plans. Large crown 8vo, 6*s.*

VOLCKXSOM, E. W. v.—Catechism of Elementary Modern Chemistry. Small crown 8vo, 3*s.*

WALPOLE, Chas. George.—A Short History of Ireland from the Earliest Times to the Union with Great Britain. With 5 Maps and Appendices. Third Edition. Crown 8vo, 6*s.*

WARD, Wilfrid.—The Wish to Believe. A Discussion Concerning the Temper of Mind in which a reasonable Man should undertake Religious Inquiry. Small crown 8vo, 5*s.*

WARD, William George, Ph.D.—Essays on the Philosophy of Theism. Edited, with an Introduction, by WILFRID WARD. 2 vols. Demy 8vo, 21*s.*

WARNER, Francis, M.D.—Lectures on the Anatomy of Movement. Crown 8vo, 4*s.* 6*d.*

WARTER, J. W.—An Old Shropshire Oak. 2 vols. Demy 8vo, 28*s.*

WEDMORE, Frederick.—The Masters of Genre Painting. With Sixteen Illustrations. Post 8vo, 7*s.* 6*d.*

WHITMAN, Sidney.—Conventional Cant: its Results and Remedy. Crown 8vo, 6*s.*

WHITNEY, Prof. William Dwight.—Essentials of English Grammar, for the Use of Schools. Second Edition. Crown 8vo, 3*s.* 6*d.*

WHITWORTH, George Clifford.—An Anglo-Indian Dictionary: a Glossary of Indian Terms used in English, and of such English or other Non-Indian Terms as have obtained special meanings in India. Demy 8vo, cloth, 12*s.*

WILSON, Lieut.-Col. C. T.—The Duke of Berwick, Marshal of France, 1702–1734. Demy 8vo, 15*s.*

WILSON, Mrs. R. F.—The Christian Brothers. Their Origin and Work. With a Sketch of the Life of their Founder, the Ven. JEAN BAPTISTE, de la Salle. Crown 8vo, 6*s.*

WOLTMANN, Dr. Alfred, and WOERMANN, Dr. Karl.—History of Painting. With numerous Illustrations. Medium 8vo. Vol. I. Painting in Antiquity and the Middle Ages. 28*s.*; bevelled boards, gilt leaves, 30*s.* Vol. II. The Painting of the Renascence. 42*s.*; bevelled boards, gilt leaves, 45*s.*

YOUMANS, Edward L., M.D.—A Class Book of Chemistry, on the Basis of the New System. With 200 Illustrations. Crown 8vo, 5*s.*

YOUMANS, Eliza A.—First Book of Botany. Designed to Cultivate the Observing Powers of Children. With 300 Engravings. New and Cheaper Edition. Crown 8vo, 2*s.* 6*d.*

YOUNG, Arthur.—Axial Polarity of Man's Word-Embodied Ideas, and its Teaching. Demy 4to, 15*s.*

THE INTERNATIONAL SCIENTIFIC SERIES.

I. **Forms of Water in Clouds and Rivers, Ice and Glaciers.** By J. Tyndall, LL.D., F.R.S. With 25 Illustrations. Ninth Edition. 5*s.*

II. **Physics and Politics;** or, Thoughts on the Application of the Principles of "Natural Selection" and "Inheritance" to Political Society. By Walter Bagehot. Eighth Edition. 4*s.*

III. **Foods.** By Edward Smith, M.D., LL.B., F.R.S. With numerous Illustrations. Ninth Edition. 5*s.*

IV. **Mind and Body:** the Theories and their Relation. By Alexander Bain, LL.D. With Four Illustrations. Eighth Edition. 4*s.*

V. **The Study of Sociology.** By Herbert Spencer. Thirteenth Edition. 5*s.*

VI. **On the Conservation of Energy.** By Balfour Stewart, M.A., LL.D., F.R.S. With 14 Illustrations. Seventh Edition. 5*s.*

VII. **Animal Locomotion;** or Walking, Swimming, and Flying. By J. B. Pettigrew, M.D., F.R.S., etc. With 130 Illustrations. Third Edition. 5*s.*

VIII. **Responsibility in Mental Disease.** By Henry Maudsley, M.D. Fourth Edition. 5*s.*

IX. **The New Chemistry.** By Professor J. P. Cooke. With 31 Illustrations. Ninth Edition. 5*s.*

X. **The Science of Law.** By Professor Sheldon Amos. Sixth Edition. 5*s.*

XI. **Animal Mechanism:** a Treatise on Terrestrial and Aerial Locomotion. By Professor E. J. Marey. With 117 Illustrations. Third Edition. 5*s.*

XII. **The Doctrine of Descent and Darwinism.** By Professor Oscar Schmidt. With 26 Illustrations. Seventh Edition. 5*s.*

XIII. **The History of the Conflict between Religion and Science.** By J. W. Draper, M.D., LL.D. Twentieth Edition. 5*s.*

XIV. **Fungi:** their Nature, Influences, Uses, etc. By M. C. Cooke, M.D., LL.D. Edited by the Rev. M. J. Berkeley, M.A., F.L.S. With numerous Illustrations. Third Edition. 5*s.*

XV. **The Chemical Effects of Light and Photography.** By Dr. Hermann Vogel. With 100 Illustrations. Fourth Edition. 5*s.*

XVI. **The Life and Growth of Language.** By Professor William Dwight Whitney. Fifth Edition. 5*s.*

XVII. **Money and the Mechanism of Exchange.** By W Stanley Jevons, M.A., F.R.S. Eighth Edition. 5*s.*

XVIII. **The Nature of Light.** With a General Account of Physical Optics. By Dr. Eugene Lommel. With 188 Illustrations and a Table of Spectra in Chromo-lithography. Fourth Edition. 5*s.*

XIX. **Animal Parasites and Messmates.** By P. J. Van Beneden. With 83 Illustrations. Third Edition. 5*s.*

XX. **Fermentation.** By Professor Schützenberger. With 28 Illustrations. Fourth Edition. 5*s.*

XXI. **The Five Senses of Man.** By Professor Bernstein. With 91 Illustrations. Fifth Edition. 5*s.*

XXII. **The Theory of Sound in its Relation to Music.** By Professor Pietro Blaserna. With numerous Illustrations. Third Edition. 5*s.*

XXIII. **Studies in Spectrum Analysis.** By J. Norman Lockyer, F.R.S. With six photographic Illustrations of Spectra, and numerous engravings on Wood. Fourth Edition. 6*s.* 6*d.*

XXIV. **A History of the Growth of the Steam Engine.** By Professor R. H. Thurston. With numerous Illustrations. Fourth Edition. 6*s.* 6*d.*

XXV. **Education as a Science.** By Alexander Bain, LL.D. Sixth Edition. 5*s.*

XXVI. **The Human Species.** By Professor A. de Quatrefages. Fourth Edition. 5*s.*

XXVII. **Modern Chromatics.** With Applications to Art and Industry. By Ogden N. Rood. With 130 original Illustrations. Second Edition. 5*s.*

XXVIII. **The Crayfish :** an Introduction to the Study of Zoology. By Professor T. H. Huxley. With 82 Illustrations. Fourth Edition. 5*s.*

XXIX. **The Brain as an Organ of Mind.** By H. Charlton Bastian, M.D. With numerous Illustrations. Third Edition. 5*s.*

XXX. **The Atomic Theory.** By Prof. Wurtz. Translated by G. Cleminshaw, F.C.S. Fourth Edition. 5*s.*

XXXI. **The Natural Conditions of Existence as they affect Animal Life.** By Karl Semper. With 2 Maps and 106 Woodcuts. Third Edition. 5*s.*

XXXII. **General Physiology of Muscles and Nerves.** By Prof. J. Rosenthal. Third Edition. With Illustrations. 5*s.*

XXXIII. **Sight :** an Exposition of the Principles of Monocular and Binocular Vision. By Joseph le Conte, LL.D. Second Edition. With 132 Illustrations. 5*s.*

XXXIV. **Illusions :** a Psychological Study. By James Sully. Third Edition. 5*s.*

XXXV. **Volcanoes : what they are and what they teach.** By Professor J. W. Judd, F.R.S. With 92 Illustrations on Wood. Third Edition. 5*s.*

XXXVI. **Suicide :** an Essay on Comparative Moral Statistics. By Prof. H. Morselli. Second Edition. With Diagrams. 5*s.*

XXXVII. **The Brain and its Functions.** By J. Luys. With Illustrations. Second Edition. 5*s.*

XXXVIII. **Myth and Science :** an Essay. By Tito Vignoli. Third Edition. 5*s.*

XXXIX. **The Sun.** By Professor Young. With Illustrations. Second Edition. 5*s.*

XL. **Ants, Bees, and Wasps :** a Record of Observations on the Habits of the Social Hymenoptera. By Sir John Lubbock, Bart., M.P. With 5 Chromo-lithographic Illustrations. Eighth Edition. 5*s.*

XLI. **Animal Intelligence.** By G. J. Romanes, LL.D., F.R.S. Fourth Edition. 5*s.*

XLII. **The Concepts and Theories of Modern Physics.** By J. B. Stallo. Third Edition. 5*s.*

XLIII. **Diseases of the Memory ;** An Essay in the Positive Psychology. By Prof. Th. Ribot. Third Edition. 5*s.*

XLIV. **Man before Metals.** By N. Joly, with 148 Illustrations. Fourth Edition. 5*s.*

XLV. **The Science of Politics.** By Prof. Sheldon Amos. Third Edition. 5*s.*

XLVI. **Elementary Meteorology.** By Robert H. Scott. Fourth Edition. With Numerous Illustrations. 5*s.*

XLVII. **The Organs of Speech and their Application in the Formation of Articulate Sounds.** By Georg Hermann Von Meyer. With 47 Woodcuts. 5*s.*

XLVIII. **Fallacies.** A View of Logic from the Practical Side. By Alfred Sidgwick. Second Edition. 5*s.*

XLIX. **Origin of Cultivated Plants.** By Alphonse de Candolle. 5*s.*

L. **Jelly-Fish, Star-Fish, and Sea-Urchins.** Being a Research on Primitive Nervous Systems. By G. J. Romanes. With Illustrations. 5*s.*

LI. **The Common Sense of the Exact Sciences.** By the late William Kingdon Clifford. Second Edition. With 100 Figures. 5*s.*

LII. **Physical Expression: Its Modes and Principles.** By Francis Warner, M.D., F.R.C.P., Hunterian Professor of Comparative Anatomy and Physiology, R.C.S.E. With 50 Illustrations. 5*s.*

LIII. **Anthropoid Apes.** By Robert Hartmann. With 63 Illustrations. 5*s.*

LIV. **The Mammalia in their Relation to Primeval Times.** By Oscar Schmidt. With 51 Woodcuts. 5*s.*

LV. **Comparative Literature.** By H. Macaulay Posnett, LL.D. 5*s.*

LVI. **Earthquakes and other Earth Movements.** By Prof. John Milne. With 38 Figures. Second Edition. 5*s.*

LVII. **Microbes, Ferments, and Moulds.** By E. L. Trouessart. With 107 Illustrations. 5*s.*

LVIII. **Geographical and Geological Distribution of Animals.** By Professor A. Heilprin. With Frontispiece. 5*s.*

LIX. **Weather.** A Popular Exposition of the Nature of Weather Changes from Day to Day. By the Hon. Ralph Abercromby. With 96 Illustrations. 5*s.*

LX. **Animal Magnetism.** By Alfred Binet and Charles Féré. 5*s.*

LXI. **Manual of British Discomycetes,** with descriptions of all the Species of Fungi hitherto found in Britain included in the Family, and Illustrations of the Genera. By William Phillips, F.L.S. 5*s.*

LXII. **International Law.** With Materials for a Code of International Law. By Professor Leone Levi. 5*s.*

LXIII. **The Origin of Floral Structures through Insect Agency.** By Prof. G. Henslow.

MILITARY WORKS.

BRACKENBURY, Col. C. B., R.A. — **Military Handbooks for Regimental Officers.**

I. **Military Sketching and Reconnaissance.** By Col. F. J. Hutchison and Major H. G. MacGregor. Fifth Edition. With 15 Plates. Small crown 8vo, 4*s.*

II. **The Elements of Modern Tactics Practically applied to English Formations.** By Lieut.-Col. Wilkinson Shaw. Sixth Edition. With 25 Plates and Maps. Small crown 8vo, 9*s.*

III. **Field Artillery.** Its Equipment, Organization and Tactics. By Major Sisson C. Pratt, R.A. With 12 Plates. Third Edition. Small crown 8vo, 6*s.*

BRACKENBURY, Col. C. B., R.A.—continued.

    IV. **The Elements of Military Administration.** First Part : Permanent System of Administration. By Major J. W. Buxton. Small crown 8vo, 7*s.* 6*d.*

    V. **Military Law:** Its Procedure and Practice. By Major Sisson C. Pratt, R.A. Third Edition. Small crown 8vo, 4*s.* 6*d.*

    VI. **Cavalry in Modern War.** By Col. F. Chenevix Trench. Small crown 8vo, 6*s.*

    VII. **Field Works.** Their Technical Construction and Tactical Application. By the Editor, Col. C. B. Brackenbury, R.A. Small crown 8vo.

BRENT, Brig.-Gen. J. L.—**Mobilizable Fortifications and their Controlling Influence in War.** Crown 8vo, 5*s.*

BROOKE, Major, C. K.—**A System of Field Training.** Small crown 8vo, cloth limp, 2*s.*

Campaign of Fredericksburg, November—December, 1862. A Study for Officers of Volunteers. With 5 Maps and Plans. Crown 8vo, 5*s.*

CLERY, C., Lieut.-Col.—**Minor Tactics.** With 26 Maps and Plans. Seventh Edition, Revised. Crown 8vo, 9*s.*

COLVILE, Lieut. Col. C. F.—**Military Tribunals.** Sewed, 2*s.* 6*d.*

CRAUFURD, Capt. H. J.—**Suggestions for the Military Training of a Company of Infantry.** Crown 8vo, 1*s.* 6*d.*

HAMILTON, Capt. Ian, A.D.C.—**The Fighting of the Future.** 1*s.*

HARRISON, Col. R.—**The Officer's Memorandum Book for Peace and War.** Fourth Edition, Revised throughout. Oblong 32mo, red basil, with pencil, 3*s.* 6*d.*

Notes on Cavalry Tactics, Organisation, etc. By a Cavalry Officer. With Diagrams. Demy 8vo, 12*s.*

PARR, Capt. H. Hallam, C.M.G.—**The Dress, Horses, and Equipment of Infantry and Staff Officers.** Crown 8vo, 1*s.*

SCHAW, Col. H.—**The Defence and Attack of Positions and Localities.** Third Edition, Revised and Corrected. Crown 8vo, 3*s.* 6*d.*

STONE, Capt. F. Gleadowe, R.A.—**Tactical Studies from the Franco-German War of 1870-71.** With 22 Lithographic Sketches and Maps. Demy 8vo, 30*s.*

WILKINSON, H. Spenser, Capt. 20th Lancashire R.V.—**Citizen Soldiers.** Essays towards the Improvement of the Volunteer Force. Crown 8vo, 2*s.* 6*d.*

POETRY.

ABBAY, R.—The Castle of Knaresborough. A Tale in Verse. Crown 8vo, 6s.

ADAM OF ST. VICTOR.—The Liturgical Poetry of Adam of St. Victor. From the text of GAUTIER. With Translations into English in the Original Metres, and Short Explanatory Notes, by DIGBY S. WRANGHAM, M.A. 3 vols. Crown 8vo, printed on hand-made paper, boards, 21s.

AITCHISON, James.—The Chronicle of Mites. A Satire. Small crown 8vo. 5s.

ALEXANDER, William, D.D., Bishop of Derry.—St. Augustine's Holiday, and other Poems. Crown 8vo, 6s.

AUCHMUTY, A. C.—Poems of English Heroism : From Brunanburh to Lucknow ; from Athelstan to Albert. Small crown 8vo, 1s. 6d.

BARNES, William.—Poems of Rural Life, in the Dorset Dialect. New Edition, complete in one vol. Crown 8vo, 8s. 6d.

BAYNES, Rev. Canon H. R.—Home Songs for Quiet Hours. Fourth and Cheaper Edition. Fcap. 8vo, cloth, 2s. 6d.

BEVINGTON, L. S.—Key Notes. Small crown 8vo, 5s.

BLUNT, Wilfrid Scawen. — The Wind and the Whirlwind. Demy 8vo, 1s. 6d.

The Love Sonnets of Proteus. Fifth Edition, 18mo. Cloth extra, gilt top, 5s.

BOWEN, H. C., M.A.—Simple English Poems. English Literature for Junior Classes. In Four Parts. Parts I., II., and III., 6d. each, and Part IV., 1s. Complete, 3s.

BRYANT, W. C.—Poems. Cheap Edition, with Frontispiece. Small crown 8vo, 3s. 6d.

Calderon's Dramas : the Wonder-Working Magician — Life is a Dream—the Purgatory of St. Patrick. Translated by DENIS FLORENCE MACCARTHY. Post 8vo, 10s.

Camoens' Lusiads. — Portuguese Text, with Translation by J. J. AUBERTIN. Second Edition. 2 vols. Crown 8vo, 12s.

CAMPBELL, Lewis.—Sophocles. The Seven Plays in English Verse. Crown 8vo, 7s. 6d.

CERVANTES.—Journey to Parnassus. Spanish Text, with Translation into English Tercets, Preface, and Illustrative Notes, by JAMES Y. GIBSON. Crown 8vo, 12s.

CERVANTES—continued.

Numantia: a Tragedy. Translated from the Spanish, with Introduction and Notes, by JAMES Y. GIBSON. Crown 8vo, printed on hand-made paper, 5*s.*

Chronicles of Christopher Columbus. A Poem in 12 Cantos. By M. D. C. Crown 8vo, 7*s.* 6*d.*

Cid Ballads, and other Poems.—Translated from Spanish and German by J. Y. GIBSON. 2 vols. Crown 8vo, 12*s.*

COXHEAD, Ethel.—Birds and Babies. With 33 Illustrations. Imp. 16mo, gilt, 2*s.* 6*d.*

Dante's Divina Commedia. Translated in the *Terza Rima* of Original, by F. K. H. HASELFOOT. Demy 8vo, 16*s.*

DE BERANGER.—A Selection from his Songs. In English Verse. By WILLIAM TOYNBEE. Small crown 8vo, 2*s.* 6*d.*

DENNIS, J.—English Sonnets. Collected and Arranged by. Small crown 8vo, 2*s.* 6*d.*

DE VERE, Aubrey.—Poetical Works.

    I. THE SEARCH AFTER PROSERPINE, etc. 6*s.*
    II. THE LEGENDS OF ST. PATRICK, etc. 6*s.*
    III. ALEXANDER THE GREAT, etc. 6*s.*

The Foray of Queen Meave, and other Legends of Ireland's Heroic Age. Small crown 8vo, 5*s.*

Legends of the Saxon Saints. Small crown 8vo, 6*s.*

Legends and Records of the Church and the Empire. Small crown 8vo, 6*s.*

DILLON, Arthur.—Gods and Men. Fcap. 4to, 7*s.* 6*d.*

DOBSON, Austin.—Old World Idylls and other Verses. Seventh Edition. Elzevir 8vo, gilt top, 6*s.*

At the Sign of the Lyre. Fifth Edition. Elzevir 8vo, gilt top, 6*s.*

DOWDEN, Edward, LL.D.—Shakspere's Sonnets. With Introduction and Notes. Large post 8vo, 7*s.* 6*d.*

DUTT, Toru.—A Sheaf Gleaned in French Fields. New Edition. Demy 8vo, 10*s.* 6*d.*

Ancient Ballads and Legends of Hindustan. With an Introductory Memoir by EDMUND GOSSE. Second Edition, 18mo. Cloth extra, gilt top, 5*s.*

EDWARDS, Miss Betham.—Poems. Small crown 8vo, 3*s.* 6*d.*

ELLIOTT, Ebenezer, The Corn Law Rhymer.—Poems. Edited by his son, the Rev. EDWIN ELLIOTT, of St. John's, Antigua. 2 vols. Crown 8vo, 18*s.*

English Verse. Edited by W. J. LINTON and R. H. STODDARD. 5 vols. Crown 8vo, cloth, 5*s.* each.

    I. CHAUCER TO BURNS.
    II. TRANSLATIONS.
    III. LYRICS OF THE NINETEENTH CENTURY.
    IV. DRAMATIC SCENES AND CHARACTERS.
    V. BALLADS AND ROMANCES.

FOSKETT, Edward.—**Poems.** Crown 8vo, 6*s.*

GOODCHILD, John A.—**Somnia Medici.** Three series. Small crown 8vo, 5*s.* each.

GOSSE, Edmund.—**New Poems.** Crown 8vo, 7*s.* 6*d.*

    Firdausi in Exile, and other Poems. Second Edition. Elzevir 8vo, gilt top, 6*s.*

GURNEY, Rev. Alfred.—**The Vision of the Eucharist,** and other Poems. Crown 8vo, 5*s.*

    A Christmas Faggot. Small crown 8vo, 5*s.*

HARRISON, Clifford.—**In Hours of Leisure.** Crown 8vo, 5*s.*

HEYWOOD, J. C.—**Herodias,** a Dramatic Poem. New Edition, Revised. Small crown 8vo, 5*s.*

    Antonius. A Dramatic Poem. New Edition, Revised. Small crown 8vo, 5*s.*

    Salome. A Dramatic Poem. Small crown 8vo, 5*s.*

HICKEY, E. H.—**A Sculptor,** and other Poems. Small crown 8vo, 5*s.*

HOLE, W. G.—**Procris,** and other Poems. Fcap. 8vo, 3*s.* 6*d.*

KEATS, John.—**Poetical Works.** Edited by W. T. ARNOLD. Large crown 8vo, choicely printed on hand-made paper, with Portrait in *eau-forte.* Parchment or cloth, 12*s.* ; vellum, 15*s.*

KING, Edward. **A Venetian Lover.** Small 4to, 6*s.*

KING, Mrs. Hamilton.—**The Disciples.** Ninth Edition, and 'Notes. Small crown 8vo, 5*s.*

    A Book of Dreams. Second Edition. Crown 8vo, 3*s.* 6*d.*

LAFFAN, Mrs. R. S. De Courcy.—**A Song of Jubilee,** and other Poems. With Frontispiece. Small crown 8vo, 3*s.* 6*d.*

LANG, A.—**XXXII. Ballades in Blue China.** Elzevir 8vo, 5*s.*

    Rhymes à la Mode. With Frontispiece by E. A. Abbey. Second Edition. Elzevir 8vo, cloth extra, gilt top, 5*s.*

LANGFORD, J. A., LL.D.—**On Sea and Shore.** Small crown 8vo, 5*s.*

LASCELLES, John.—Golden Fetters, and other Poems. Small crown 8vo, 3*s*. 6*d*.

LAWSON, Right Hon. Mr. Justice.—Hymni Usitati Latine Redditi : with other Verses. Small 8vo, parchment, 5*s*.

Living English Poets MDCCCLXXXII. With Frontispiece by Walter Crane. Second Edition. Large crown 8vo. Printed on hand-made paper. Parchment or cloth, 12*s*. ; vellum, 15*s*.

LOCKER, F.—London Lyrics. Tenth Edition. With Portrait, Elzevir 8vo. Cloth extra, gilt top, 5*s*.

Love in Idleness. A Volume of Poems. With an Etching by W. B. Scott. Small crown 8vo, 5*s*.

LUMSDEN, Lieut.-Col. H. W.—Beowulf : an Old English Poem. Translated into Modern Rhymes. Second and Revised Edition. Small crown 8vo, 5*s*.

LYSAGHT, Sidney Royse.—A Modern Ideal. A Dramatic Poem. Small crown 8vo, 5*s*.

MAGNUSSON, Eirikr, M.A., and PALMER, E. H., M.A.—Johan Ludvig Runeberg's Lyrical Songs, Idylls, and Epigrams. Fcap. 8vo, 5*s*.

MEREDITH, Owen [The Earl of Lytton].—Lucile. New Edition. With 32 Illustrations. 16mo, 3*s*. 6*d*. Cloth extra, gilt edges, 4*s*. 6*d*.

MORRIS, Lewis.—Poetical Works of. New and Cheaper Editions, with Portrait. Complete in 3 vols., 5*s*. each.
Vol. I. contains "Songs of Two Worlds." Twelfth Edition.
Vol. II. contains "The Epic of Hades." Twenty-first Edition.
Vol. III. contains "Gwen" and "The Ode of Life." Seventh Edition.
Vol. IV. contains "Songs Unsung" and "Gycia." Fifth Edition.

Songs of Britain. Third Edition. Fcap. 8vo, 5*s*.

The Epic of Hades. With 16 Autotype Illustrations, after the Drawings of the late George R. Chapman. 4to, cloth extra, gilt leaves, 21*s*.

The Epic of Hades. Presentation Edition. 4to, cloth extra, gilt leaves, 10*s*. 6*d*.

The Lewis Morris Birthday Book. Edited by S. S. COPE-MAN, with Frontispiece after a Design by the late George R. Chapman. 32mo, cloth extra, gilt edges, 2*s*. ; cloth limp, 1*s*. 6*d*

MORSHEAD, E. D. A.—The House of Atreus. Being the Agamemnon, Libation-Bearers, and Furies of Æschylus. Translated into English Verse. Crown 8vo, 7*s*.

The Suppliant Maidens of Æschylus. Crown 8vo, 3*s*. 6*d*.

MOZLEY, J. Rickards.—**The Romance of Dennell.** A Poem in Five Cantos. Crown 8vo, 7*s.* 6*d.*

MULHOLLAND, Rosa.—**Vagrant Verses.** Small crown 8vo, 5*s.*

NADEN, Constance C. W.—**A Modern Apostle, and other Poems.** Small crown 8vo, 5*s.*

NOEL, The Hon. Roden.—**A Little Child's Monument.** Third Edition. Small crown 8vo, 3*s.* 6*d.*

 The House of Ravensburg. New Edition. Small crown 8vo, 6*s.*

 The Red Flag, and other Poems. New Edition. Small crown 8vo, 6*s.*

 Songs of the Heights and Deeps. Crown 8vo, 6*s.*

O'BRIEN, Charlotte Grace.—**Lyrics.** Small crown 8vo, 3*s.* 6*d.*

O'HAGAN, John.—**The Song of Roland.** Translated into English Verse. New and Cheaper Edition. Crown 8vo, 5*s.*

PFEIFFER, Emily.—**The Rhyme of the Lady of the Rock, and How it Grew.** Second Edition. Small crown 8vo, 3*s.* 6*d.*

 Gerard's Monument, and other Poems. Second Edition. Crown 8vo, 6*s.*

 Under the Aspens: Lyrical and Dramatic. With Portrait. Crown 8vo, 6*s.*

PIATT, J. J.—**Idyls and Lyrics of the Ohio Valley.** Crown 8vo, 5*s.*

PREVOST, Francis.—**Melilot.** 3*s.* 6*d.*

 Fires of Green Wood. Small crown 8vo, 3*s.* 6*d.*

Rare Poems of the 16th and 17th Centuries. Edited by W. J. LINTON. Crown 8vo, 5*s.*

RHOADES, James.—**The Georgics of Virgil.** Translated into English Verse. Small crown 8vo, 5*s.*

 Poems. Small crown 8vo, 4*s.* 6*d.*

 Dux Redux. A Forest Tangle. Small crown 8vo, 3*s.* 6*d.*

ROBINSON, A. Mary F.—**A Handful of Honeysuckle.** Fcap. 8vo, 3*s.* 6*d.*

 The Crowned Hippolytus. Translated from Euripides. With New Poems. Small crown 8vo, 5*s.*

SCHILLER, Friedrich.—**Wallenstein.** A Drama. Done in English Verse, by J. A. W. HUNTER, M.A. Crown 8vo, 7*s.* 6*d.*

SCHWARTZ, J. M. W.—**Nivalis.** A Tragedy in Five Acts. Small crown 8vo, 5*s.*

SCOTT, E. J. L.—**The Eclogues of Virgil.**—Translated into English Verse. Small crown 8vo, 3*s.* 6*d.*

SHERBROOKE, Viscount.—**Poems of a Life.** Second Edition. Small crown 8vo, 2*s.* 6*d.*

SINCLAIR, Julian.—**Nakiketas, and** other Poems. Small crown 8vo, 2*s.* 6*d.*

SMITH, J. W. Gilbart.—**The Loves of Vandyck.** A Tale of Genoa. Small crown 8vo, 2*s.* 6*d.*

　　The Log o' the "Norseman." Small crown 8vo, 5*s.*

　　Serbelloni. Small crown 8vo, 5*s.*

Sophocles : The Seven Plays in English Verse. Translated by LEWIS CAMPBELL. Crown 8vo, 7*s.* 6*d.*

STEWART, Phillips.—**Poems.** Small crown 8vo, 2*s.* 6*d.*

SYMONDS, John Addington.—**Vagabunduli Libellus.** Crown 8vo, 6*s.*

Tasso's Jerusalem Delivered. Translated by Sir JOHN KINGSTON JAMES, Bart. Two Volumes. Printed on hand-made paper, parchment, bevelled boards. Large crown 8vo, 21*s.*

TAYLOR, Sir H.—**Works.** Complete in Five Volumes. Crown 8vo, 30*s.*

　　Philip Van Artevelde. Fcap. 8vo, 3*s.* 6*d.*

　　The Virgin Widow, etc. Fcap. 8vo, 3*s.* 6*d.*

　　The Statesman. Fcap. 8vo, 3*s.* 6*d.*

TODHUNTER, Dr. J.—**Laurella,** and other Poems. Crown 8vo, 6*s.* 6*d.*

　　Forest Songs. Small crown 8vo, 3*s.* 6*d.*

　　The True Tragedy of Rienzi : a Drama. 3*s.* 6*d.*

　　Alcestis : a Dramatic Poem. Extra fcap. 8vo, 5*s.*

　　Helena in Troas. Small crown 8vo, 2*s.* 6*d.*

TOMKINS, Zitella E.—**Sister Lucetta, and other Poems.** Small crown 8vo, 3*s.* 6*d.*

TYNAN, Katherine.—**Louise de la Valliere, and** other Poems. Small crown 8vo, 3*s.* 6*d.*

　　Shamrocks. Small crown 8vo, 5*s.*

Unspoken Thoughts. Small crown 8vo, 3*s.* 6*d.*

Victorian Hymns : English Sacred Songs of Fifty Years. Dedicated to the Queen. Large post 8vo, 10*s.* 6*d.*

WEBSTER, Augusta.—**In a Day :** a Drama. Small crown 8vo, 2*s.* 6*d.*

　　Disguises : a Drama. Small crown 8vo, 5*s.*

WILLIAMS, James.—**A Lawyer's Leisure.** Small crown 8vo, 3*s.* 6*d.*

WOOD, Edmund.—Poems. Small crown 8vo, 3*s*. 6*d*.

Wordsworth Birthday Book, The. Edited by ADELAIDE and VIOLET WORDSWORTH. 32mo, limp cloth, 1*s*. 6*d*. ; cloth extra, 2*s*.

YOUNGS, Ella Sharpe.—Paphus, and other Poems. Small crown 8vo, 3*s*. 6*d*.

A Heart's Life, Sarpedon, and other Poems. Small crown 8vo, 5*s*. 6*d*.

The Apotheosis of Antinous, and other Poems. With Portrait. Small crown 8vo, 10*s*. 6*d*.

NOVELS AND TALES.

"All But:" a Chronicle of Laxenford Life. By PEN OLIVER, F.R.C.S. With 20 Illustrations. Second Edition. Crown 8vo, 6*s*.

BANKS, Mrs. G. L.—God's Providence House. New Edition. Crown 8vo, 3*s*. 6*d*.

CHICHELE, Mary.—Doing and Undoing. A Story. Crown 8vo, 4*s*. 6*d*.

Danish Parsonage. By an Angler. Crown 8vo, 6*s*.

GRAY, Maxwell.—The Silence of Dean Maitland. Fifth Edition. With Frontispiece. Crown 8vo, 6*s*.

HUNTER, Hay.—The Crime of Christmas Day. A Tale of the Latin Quarter. By the Author of "My Ducats and my Daughter." 1*s*.

HUNTER, Hay, and WHYTE, Walter.—My Ducats and My Daughter. New and Cheaper Edition. With Frontispiece. Crown 8vo, 6*s*.

INGELOW, Jean.—Off the Skelligs : a Novel. With Frontispiece. Second Edition. Crown 8vo, 6*s*.

JENKINS, Edward.—A Secret of Two Lives. Crown 8vo, 2*s*. 6*d*.

KIELLAND, Alexander L.—Garman and Worse. A Norwegian Novel. Authorized Translation, by W. W. Kettlewell. Crown 8vo, 6*s*.

LANG, Andrew.—In the Wrong Paradise, and other Stories. Second Edition. Crown 8vo, 6*s*.

MACDONALD, G.—Donal Grant. A Novel. Second Edition. With Frontispiece. Crown 8vo, 6*s*.

Home Again. With Frontispiece. Crown 8vo, 6*s*.

Castle Warlock. A Novel. Second Edition. With Frontispiece. Crown 8vo, 6*s*.

MACDONALD, G.—continued.

Malcolm. With Portrait of the Author engraved on Steel. Eighth Edition. Crown 8vo, *6s.*

The Marquis of Lossie. Seventh Edition. With Frontispiece. Crown 8vo, *6s.*

St. George and St. Michael. Fifth Edition. With Frontispiece. Crown 8vo, *6s.*

What's Mine's Mine. Second Edition. With Frontispiece. Crown 8vo, *6s.*

Annals of a Quiet Neighbourhood. Sixth Edition. With Frontispiece. Crown 8vo, *6s.*

The Seaboard Parish : a Sequel to "Annals of a Quiet Neighbourhood." Fourth Edition. With Frontispiece. Crown 8vo, *6s.*

Wilfred Cumbermede. An Autobiographical Story. Fourth Edition. With Frontispiece. Crown 8vo, *6s.*

Thomas Wingfold, Curate. Fourth Edition. With Frontispiece. Crown 8vo, *6s.*

Paul Faber, Surgeon. Fourth Edition. With Frontispiece. Crown 8vo, *6s.*

MALET, Lucas.—**Colonel Enderby's Wife.** A Novel. New and Cheaper Edition. With Frontispiece. Crown 8vo, *6s.*

MULHOLLAND, Rosa.—**Marcella Grace.** An Irish Novel. Crown 8vo. *6s.*

PALGRAVE, W. Gifford.—**Hermann Agha :** an Eastern Narrative. Third Edition. Crown 8vo, *6s.*

SHAW, Flora L.—**Castle Blair :** a Story of Youthful Days. New and Cheaper Edition. Crown 8vo, *3s. 6d.*

STRETTON, Hesba.—**Through a Needle's Eye :** a Story. New and Cheaper Edition, with Frontispiece. Crown 8vo, *6s.*

TAYLOR, Col. Meadows, C.S.I., M.R.I.A.—**Seeta :** a Novel. With Frontispiece. Crown 8vo, *6s.*

Tippoo Sultaun : a Tale of the Mysore War. With Frontispiece. Crown 8vo, *6s.*

Ralph Darnell. With Frontispiece. Crown 8vo, *6s.*

A Noble Queen. With Frontispiece. Crown 8vo, *6s.*

The Confessions of a Thug. With Frontispiece. Crown 8vo, *6s.*

Tara : a Mahratta Tale. With Frontispiece. Crown 8vo, *6s.*

Within Sound of the Sea. With Frontispiece. Crown 8vo, *6s.*

BOOKS FOR THE YOUNG.

Brave Men's Footsteps. A Book of Example and Anecdote for Young People. By the Editor of "Men who have Risen." With 4 Illustrations by C. Doyle. Ninth Edition. Crown 8vo, 3*s*. 6*d*.

COXHEAD, Ethel.—**Birds and Babies.** With 33 Illustrations. Second Edition. Imp. 16mo, cloth gilt, 2*s*. 6*d*.

DAVIES, G. Christopher.—**Rambles and Adventures of our School Field Club.** With 4 Illustrations. New and Cheaper Edition. Crown 8vo, 3*s*. 6*d*.

EDMONDS, Herbert.—**Well Spent Lives:** a Series of Modern Biographies. New and Cheaper Edition. Crown 8vo, 3*s*. 6*d*.

EVANS, Mark.—**The Story of our Father's Love,** told to Children. Sixth and Cheaper Edition of Theology for Children. With 4 Illustrations. Fcap. 8vo, 1*s*. 6*d*.

MAC KENNA, S. J.—**Plucky Fellows.** A Book for Boys. With 6 Illustrations. Fifth Edition. Crown 8vo, 3*s*. 6*d*.

MALET, Lucas.—**Little Peter.** A Christmas Morality for Children of any Age. With numerous Illustrations. 5*s*.

REANEY, Mrs. G. S.—**Waking and Working;** or, From Girlhood to Womanhood. New and Cheaper Edition. With a Frontispiece. Crown 8vo, 3*s*. 6*d*.

    Blessing and Blessed: a Sketch of Girl Life. New and Cheaper Edition. Crown 8vo, 3*s*. 6*d*.

    Rose Gurney's Discovery. A Story for Girls. Dedicated to their Mothers. Crown 8vo, 3*s*. 6*d*.

    English Girls: Their Place and Power. With Preface by the Rev. R. W. Dale. Fifth Edition. Fcap. 8vo, 2*s*. 6*d*.

    Just Anyone, and other Stories. Three Illustrations. Royal 16mo, 1*s*. 6*d*.

    Sunbeam Willie, and other Stories. Three Illustrations. Royal 16mo, 1*s*. 6*d*.

    Sunshine Jenny, and other Stories. Three Illustrations. Royal 16mo, 1*s*. 6*d*.

STORR, Francis, and TURNER, Hawes.—**Canterbury Chimes;** or, Chaucer Tales re-told to Children. With 6 Illustrations from the Ellesmere Manuscript. Third Edition. Fcap. 8vo, 3*s*. 6*d*.

STRETTON, Hesba.—**David Lloyd's Last Will.** With 4 Illustrations. New Edition. Royal 16mo, 2*s*. 6*d*.

WHITAKER, Florence.—**Christy's Inheritance.** A London Story. Illustrated. Royal 16mo, 1*s*. 6*d*.

PRINTED BY WILLIAM CLOWES AND SONS, LIMITED,
LONDON AND BECCLES.

[P. T. O.

SHAKSPERE'S WORKS.

THE AVON EDITION.

Printed on thin opaque paper, and forming 12 handy volumes, cloth, 18*s.*, or bound in 6 volumes, 15*s.*

The set of 12 volumes may also be had in a cloth box, price 21*s.*, or bound in Roan, Persian, Crushed Persian Levant, Calf, or Morocco, and enclosed in an attractive leather box at prices from 31*s.* 6*d.* upwards.

SOME PRESS NOTICES.

" This edition will be useful to those who want a good text, well and clearly printed, in convenient little volumes that will slip easily into an overcoat pocket or a travelling-bag."—*St. James's Gazette.*

" We know no prettier edition of Shakspere for the price."—*Academy.*

" It is refreshing to meet with an edition of Shakspere of convenient size and low price, without either notes or introductions of any sort to distract the attention of the reader."—*Saturday Review.*

" It is exquisite.   Each volume is handy, is beautifully printed, and in every way lends itself to the taste of the cultivated student of Shak- spere."—*Scotsman.*

LONDON: KEGAN PAUL, TRENCH & CO., 1, PATERNOSTER SQUARE,

SHAKSPERE'S WORKS.

THE PARCHMENT LIBRARY EDITION.

In 12 volumes Elzevir 8vo., choicely printed on hand-made paper, and bound in parchment or cloth, price £3 12s., or in vellum, price £4 10s.

The set of 12 volumes may also be had in a strong cloth box, price £3 17s., or with an oak hanging shelf, £3 18s.

SOME PRESS NOTICES.

". . . There is, perhaps, no edition in which the works of Shakspere can be read in such luxury of type and quiet distinction of form as this, and we warmly recommend it."—*Pall Mall Gazette.*

"For elegance of form and beauty of typography, no edition of Shakspere hitherto published has excelled the 'Parchment Library Edition.' . . . They are in the strictest sense pocket volumes, yet the type is bold, and, being on fine white hand-made paper, can hardly tax the weakest of sight. The print is judiciously confined to the text, notes being more appropriate to library editions. The whole will be comprised in the cream-coloured parchment which gives the name to the series."—*Daily News.*

"The Parchment Library Edition of Shakspere needs no further praise."—*Saturday Review.*

Just published.   Price 5s.

AN INDEX TO THE WORKS OF SHAKSPERE.

Applicable to all editions of Shakspere, and giving reference, by topics, to notable passages and significant expressions; brief histories of the plays; geographical names and historic incidents; mention of all characters and sketches of important ones; together with explanations of allusions and obscure and obsolete words and phrases.

By EVANGELINE M. O'CONNOR.

London : Kegan Paul, Trench & Co., 1, Paternoster Square.

SHAKSPERE'S WORKS.

SPECIMEN OF TYPE.

    Salar.   My wind, cooling my broth,
Would blow me to an ague, when I thought
What harm a wind too great might do at sea.
I should not see the sandy hour-glass run
But I should think of shallows and of flats,
And see my wealthy Andrew, dock'd in sand,
Vailing her high-top lower than her ribs
To kiss her burial.   Should I go to church
And see the holy edifice of stone,
And not bethink me straight of dangerous rocks,
Which touching but my gentle vessel's side,
Would scatter all her spices on the stream,
Enrobe the roaring waters with my silks,
And, in a word, but even now worth this,
And now worth nothing? Shall I have the thought
To think on this, and shall I lack the thought
That such a thing bechanc'd would make me sad?
But tell not me: I know Antonio
Is sad to think upon his merchandise.

    Ant. Believe me, no: I thank my fortune for it,
My ventures are not in one bottom trusted,
Nor to one place; nor is my whole estate
Upon the fortune of this present year:
Therefore my merchandise makes me not sad.

    Salar. Why, then you are in love.

    Ant.   Fie, fie!

    Salar. Not in love neither? Then let us say you
          are sad,
Because you are not merry; and 'twere as easy
For you to laugh, and leap, and say you are merry,
Because you are not sad. Now, by two-headed
          Janus,
Nature hath fram'd strange fellows in her time:
Some that will evermore peep through their eyes
And laugh like parrots at a bag-piper;
And other of such vinegar aspect